TIDES *of* TRIUMPH:

The Maratha Navy Saga

TIDES *of* TRIUMPH:

The Maratha Navy Saga

EDITED BY

AMARENDRA KUMAR

HARPER VANTAGE

An imprint of HarperCollins *Publishers*

First published in India by HarperVantage 2025
An imprint of HarperCollins *Publishers*
HarperCollins *Publishers* India, Cyber City, Building 10-A,
Gurugram, Haryana-122002, India
www.harpercollins.co.in

2 4 6 8 10 9 7 5 3 1

P-ISBN: 978-93-6569-094-1
E-ISBN: 978-93-6569-767-4

Typeset in_12/17 Berling LT Std
by HarperCollins *Publishers* India Pvt. Ltd

Printed and bound at
Thomson Press (India) Ltd

MIX
Paper | Supporting responsible forestry
FSC® C010615

This book is produced from independently certified FSC® paper
to ensure responsible forest management.

*

HarperCollins *Publishers*, Macken House, 39/40 Mayor Street Upper,
Dublin 1, D01 C9W8, Ireland

Contents

List of Abbreviations

- EEIC: English East India Company
- HRA: High Risk Area
- INS: Indian Naval Ship
- IOR: Indian Ocean Region
- LND: Local Naval Defence
- MAC: Marine Archaeology Centre
- MARCOS: Marine Commandos
- SAGAR: Security And Growth for All in the Region
- SLOCs: Sea Lines of Communications
- VOC: Dutch East India Company (Dutch: Vereenigde Oostindische Compagnie)

List of Contributors

⚓⚓⚓

Dr Amarendra Kumar is an Associate Professor at Visva-Bharati, a central university and an Institute of National Importance (INI), in Santiniketan, West Bengal. He also taught at the National Defence Academy in Khadakwasla, Pune, for a decade, from 2000 to 2011. He completed his Masters and MPhil from Jawaharlal Nehru University (JNU), and in 2010, he was awarded PhD from University of Pune for his thesis titled 'Maratha Navy: An Enquiry into its Limitations and Contemporary Challenges.' His goal is to connect Maratha naval history with the broader field of Indian Ocean studies. More recently, his research on the Maratha Navy has been published in the *Routledge Handbook of the Global History of Warfare* and the *Oxford Handbook of Warfare in Asia*.

Vaibhav Purandare is a historian and author of *Shivaji: India's Great Warrior King*. His other books are *Tilak: The Empire's Biggest Enemy; Hitler and India: The Untold Story of His Hatred for the Country and Its People; Savarkar: The True Story of the Father of Hindutva; Sachin Tendulkar: The Definitive Biography* and *Bal Thackeray and the Rise of the Shiv Sena*. He works as a senior editor with a leading media organization.

Prof Lakshmi Subramanian is a former Research Professor and Dean (Academic Studies) from the Centre for Studies in Social Sciences Calcutta (CSSSC), Kolkata, and Department of Humanities and Social Sciences, BITS Pilani, Goa. She has also been a Visiting Professor at several universities including the University of Glasgow, Jawaharlal Nehru University, Flinders University in Adelaide, University of Göttingen, Indian Institute of Science and University of Singapore. She is also an Associate Member at the Institute of Advanced Studies, Nantes, France. Prof Lakshmi has authored over ten books on the economic and cultural history of India. Her areas of interest are trade and social networks in the Indian Ocean and the social history of music in modern south India. Some of her major works are *The Sovereign and the Pirate Ordering Maritime Subjects in India's Western Littoral, Three Merchants of Bombay, A History of India 1707-1857* and *Medieval Seafarers of India.*

Dr Radhika Seshan is a former Professor and Head, Department of History, Savitribai Phule Pune University, and is now a Visiting Faculty at the Symbiosis School for Liberal Arts, Pune. Within the broad area of medieval Indian history, her research focuses on trade, especially textiles and maritime networks. She has numerous research papers to her credit in national and international journals. Her most recent publications include *Empires of the Sea: A Brief Human History of the Indian Ocean World; The Constructions of the East in Western Travel Narratives, 1300-1800; Archives and Archiving in the 21st century* (edited);

Connecting the Indian Ocean World: Across Sea and Land; *Merchants and Ports in the Indian Ocean World: Across Sea and Land*, jointly edited with Ryuto Shimada; and *Wage Earners in India 1500-1900: Regional Approaches in an International Context*, jointly edited with Jan Lucassen.

Anirudh Deshpande is Professor of Modern History, Department of History, Faculty of Social Sciences, University of Delhi. He has authored the following books: *The British Raj and Its Indian Armed Forces, 1857–1939* (2002); *British Military Policy in India 1900-1945: Colonial Constraints and Declining Power* (2005); *Class, Power and Consciousness in Indian Cinema and Television* (2009); *The First Line of Defence: Glorious 50 Years of the Border Security Force* (2015); *Hope and Despair: Mutiny, Rebellion and Death in India, 1946* (2016); *Dreamt Lives: A Novel* (2018); *The Practice of History: Essays in Search of a New Past* (2020); *The Rise and Fall of a Brown Water Navy: Sarkhel Kanhoji Angre and Maratha Seapower on the Arabian Sea in the 17th and 18th Centuries* (2021); *Social Science Perspectives and Indian Cinema* (2023); *Corona Fieldwork and Other Stories* (2023); *King, Country and War: Ideology and the Writing of Indian History* (2024) along with *Aitihasik Nausainik Vidroh 1946 Aur Bharatiya Jan Andolan* (Hindi, 2022) and *Bisween Sadi Mein Vishwa Itihaas Ke Pramukh Mudde: Badalte Ayam Aur Dishayen* (edited, Hindi, 2021).

Pushkar Sohoni received his doctorate from the University of Pennsylvania for his work on the medieval Deccan, after training as a conservation architect. He has written several essays and books on the material history of South Asia, including architecture and numismatics. He also has an interest in languages and scripts. He currently teaches at the Indian Institute of Science Education and Research, Pune.

Commodore Ajay Agarwal (Retd) commenced his naval career with Operation Pawan as a part of Indian Peace Keeping Force (IPKF), specializing in Navigation and Direction. He has served onboard ten Indian Navy ships, including the commissioning crew of INS Kirpan. He has commanded three warships, including a guided missile frigate and a flotilla. He has served as an instructor at the National Defence Academy, Defence Services Staff College and the Higher Command Course (HCC) Wing of Army War College. His avid interest in matters maritime, cultivated over three decades, led to him opting for a PhD programme of University of Mumbai through the Naval War College, Goa. He has submitted his thesis on Indian Country Craft (Dhows). His academic interests include coastal security, maritime history and net assessment.

Commander Ankush Banerjee was commissioned on 1 January 2008. The officer is an alumnus of the erstwhile Naval Academy and has served at the Centre of Excellence in Ethics, Leadership and Behavioural Studies (CELABS), Indian Naval Academy, Naval History Division, and the National Defence College, New Delhi. Three time recipient of the United Services Institution Gold Medal Essay Prize (2015, 2017, 2021) and the erstwhile Commodore Nott Essay Prize (2018), 2019 All India Poetry Prize, and the 2023 National Poetry Competition (organized by NDA), his work appears in *The Indian Express*, *Journal of Defence Studies*, Scroll, *Best Asian Poetry 2021*, *Converse: Contemporary English Poetry by Indians*, and *Defence & Diplomacy*, among others. He is pursuing his PhD in Gender Studies from BITS Pilani and has authored a book of poems, *An Essence of Eternity*.

Janhavi Lokegaonkar is a Senior Research Associate at the Maritime History Society (MHS), Mumbai, an academic initiative of the Western Naval Command, Indian Navy. Alongside her role at MHS, she is currently pursuing a PhD on maritime history at the Department of History, University of Mumbai, where she is further refining her expertise in this domain. Maritime and naval history, urban history, migration and diaspora studies are her primary areas of interest. Lokegaonkar has been actively presenting papers at various national and international conferences, and has published extensively in the domain of maritime history.

Admiral Dinesh K Tripathi
PVSM, AVSM, NM
Chief of the Naval Staff

Ministry of Defence
Naval Headquarters
New Delhi – 110011

Foreword

⚓ ⚓ ⚓

India's long and illustrious maritime history is one of the lesser-explored dimensions of its rich cultural heritage. Stretching back over millennia, the nation's epochal maritime traditions reflect a deep connection with the sea, not only for commerce and cultural exchange of ideas and faith but also for defence and sovereignty.

India's maritime story begins in ancient times, with the Sindhu – Saraswati civilisation, known for its robust trading networks extending across the Arabian Sea, reaching as far as Mesopotamia (present day Iraq). From the ancient texts like the *Periplus of the Erythraean Sea* to the maritime activities of the Cholas, India's coastlines were active participants in the thriving global exchanges of goods, ideas, and culture. India's strategic location between the East and the West made its ports and maritime presence central to ancient and medieval trade networks, as well as to the development of local naval power.

Traditionally, Indian history has been overshadowed by land-based narratives, particularly during the colonial and post-colonial periods. However, the importance of maritime power in shaping the Indian subcontinent's political, cultural, and economic landscape cannot be overstated. The rise of European colonialism in India was as much a naval conquest as it was a territorial one, and the engagements of the Maratha Navy to protect India's coastline represent one of the earliest organised resistances to this incursion.

The naval and maritime legacy of the Maratha Empire under the leadership of Chhatrapati Shivaji Maharaj still remains one of the underexplored areas in Indian history. Despite the far-reaching consequences of Chhatrapati Shivaji's naval strategy on the Indian subcontinent's defence and trade dynamics, academic literature has continued to overlook the significance of the Maratha Navy.

It may be recalled that in the early years of his career, Chhatrapati Shivaji Maharaj was engaged in contests against land-based powers, such as the Mughals and the Deccan Sultanates. However, he realised that establishing a powerful navy was integral to securing the western coast of India against European and regional threats, ensuring the protection of vital sea routes, and supporting the sovereignty of the Maratha

Empire. The Maratha Navy successfully defended against the Siddis, Portuguese, British, and Dutch encroachments, setting a precedent for indigenous maritime defence.

A comprehensive academic study analysing the Maratha *Armaar*—its composition, tactics, shipbuilding, and operations—offers valuable contributions not only to military history but also to the study of Indian maritime trade and diplomacy in the 17th century. The intricacies of shipbuilding under Chhatrapati Shivaji's reign, his cooperation with foreign naval architects, and the fleet's effectiveness in both warfare and protecting economic interests, which were further enhanced during Sarkhel Kanhoji Angre's times, merit a dedicated examination.

Hence, this edited volume titled 'Tides of Triumph: The Maratha Navy Saga', dedicated to the Maratha Navy, serves as a crucial contribution to reclaiming this significant aspect of Indian history. By examining a range of primary and secondary sources, this book, through carefully curated essays, presents a nuanced and in-depth account of a naval heritage that has shaped the destiny of the subcontinent in many profound ways. The Maratha Navy's legacy not only offers lessons in leadership, strategy, indigenous self-reliance and innovation but also serves as an enduring symbol of Indian resilience, sovereignty, and self-determination which is taken forward by the Indian Navy today.

'Tides of Triumph: The Maratha Navy Saga', therefore, is not just a historical reflection, but a celebration of India's long-standing engagement with the oceans, reminding us that the maritime domain has been, and remains, a vital element in the nation's defence, economy, and identity. By delving into the achievements of the Maratha Navy, this book seeks to instil pride in our heritage, one of the five *Panch Pran* enunciated by the Hon'ble Prime Minister of India Shri Narendra Modi at the Red Fort on 15 August 2022.

Sam Noh Varunah! Jai Hind!

(Dinesh K Tripathi)
Admiral

Introduction

Amarendra Kumar

⚓⚓⚓

> '*In warfare*, the consideration of Power, Place and Time are Mutually Beneficial.'
>
> —Kautilya, Book IX, Chapter 1, Verse 33
>
> [Emphasis mine]

The year 2024 marks the 350th anniversary of a defining moment in Indian history: the coronation of Chhatrapati Shivaji Maharaj, the founder of the Maratha Swarajya. This event signifies the emergence of the Marathas as a regional power in the era of Mughal imperialism. The coronation not only legitimized the sovereign rule of Shivaji, but also epitomized the spirit of liberation against tyranny. The legacy of the Maratha Swarajya and its leaders continues to resonate in many aspects of our country's social and cultural life. There could not have been a better occasion to publish this volume, which honours the achievements of the Maratha Navy and celebrates its legacy.

The present volume was conceived when the Director of the Maritime History Society, Mumbai, shared his plans with me to produce a volume on the Maratha Navy. After several discussions over the phone and online meetings, we decided to pay a fitting tribute to Chhatrapati Shivaji, the great Maratha visionary, by compiling this volume. It was agreed that the volume would consist of a collection of essays exploring the diverse aspects of the Maratha Navy. The ten essays in this volume explore various themes related to the maritime achievements of the Marathas following the establishment of the Maratha Navy by Chhatrapati Shivaji in 1659. Authored by leading scholars in their fields, the ten essays trace the rise and consolidation of the Maratha Navy, highlighting its significant accomplishments.

I

The discovery of sea routes to Asia from Europe and the prospects of colonization of the New World, made naval warfare an important and specialized affair at sea. The Treaty of Tordesillas signed in 1494 by the monarchs of Spain and Portugal, further propelled naval developments by dividing the globe into two 'spheres of European influence', facilitating exploration of the unknown world via sea routes.[1] Consequently, specialized sail-propelled warships emerged in the sixteenth-century Europe. In particular, their capacity to carry guns on high decks and the typical line formation during naval combat characterized this era of sailing warfare.

In contrast, the non-European world, with a few significant exceptions, did not witness such advancements in ship design or armaments. One such exception were the naval expeditions of the Cholas that occurred over half a millennium before the European overseas explorations. The year 2025 marks the culmination of a thousand years since the Cholas launched their naval campaigns, which extended Indian maritime influence over Southeast Asia. To celebrate this significant achievement, an edited volume commemorating the naval feats of the Cholas, was published nearly a decade ago.[2]

The second exception relates to a series of oceanic voyages fitted out by the Ming rulers of China early in the fifteenth century. The Ming rulers commissioned 'great overseas expeditions' that were undertaken by the most illustrious Chinese admiral of the time—Zheng He. While the very purpose and incentives behind such a grand show of Ming naval strength are still debatable, independent scholar Geoff Wade argues that Zheng He's maritime expeditions were in the nature of a 'tribute mission' involving the use of military force in, 'an attempt to impose a *pax Ming* on what we now know as Southeast Asia and the Indian Ocean'.[3] Whatever the case may be, the fact remains that the Ming naval experimentations halted entirely by the second half of the sixteenth century.

Meanwhile, by the seventeenth century, the nature of sea engagements in Europe had undergone a gradual transformation—from a confusing melee to the more organized fleet, comprising ships of the line. The European maritime nations worked on blueprints to expand and strengthen their naval capabilities. As the sea was the new medium of warfare, treatises on naval warfare were also composed. The first such work was authored by a Portuguese, Fernando Oliveira.[4] By the late eighteenth century, it had become known that the 'new world' was mainly dominated and colonized by the maritime powers of Europe, most of whom exercised sea power and claimed sovereignty over sea or sea lanes. This trend continued until the beginning of the First World War, the origins of which can be traced to the obdurate stance adopted by European maritime powers to protect their overseas colonial interests from being taken by a few 'newly-emerging' colonial powers.

The concept and theory of sea power—largely understood in terms of a state's capacity to deploy military power at the sea, or through the sea—was first brought under deeper focus by the great military theorist Captain Alfred Thayer Mahan in the nineteenth century. Through his seminal work, he identified six parameters influencing the choice of a nation, upon which sea power could be exerted.[5] Subsequently, Sir Julian Corbett, Admiral Philip Howard Colomb and Richmond Herbert—contemporaries of Capt. Mahan—also contributed significantly to the understanding of sea power and maritime strategy from the British perspective.

In recent years, scholarship has made significant progress in writing naval histories.[6] Most of these works deal with the historical evolution of navies, their role in state-building, and case studies of naval battles that highlight naval strategies and tactics. These studies underline the use of the navy as a means to accomplish overseas expansion by establishing control over sea lanes and lines of communication and crossing the seas. However, they have failed to adequately incorporate a vital aspect of maritime contestations, i.e., coastal warfare. This lacuna in historical scholarship was recently addressed by Trim and Fissel in their introduction to their edited volume on *Amphibious Warfare*.[7] The authors provide a refreshing insight into the nuances of coastal warfare as they take up its concept and context for critical analysis. The most significant takeaway points that emerge from their analysis of amphibious warfare in the pre-modern times may be summarized as follows: though a branch of sea warfare, the description of amphibious or coastal warfare is ambiguous mainly because of the lack of a clear distinction between pre-modern land warfare and naval operations. Moreover, amphibious warfare occurs on the coast, on island and on inland waterways, where the amphibious land-based and waterborne forces cooperate to fight an enemy that is solely land-based or waterborne.[8] This cooperation—which occurs in a multitude of forms between the waterborne and ground forces—is its most significant character.[9] During the pre-modern period, all European nations waged this 'most complex form of warfare'.[10]

Military units that function both on land and sea are rare. Still, cooperating for a single purpose involves an amalgamation of different elements at different levels, viz., strategic, operational, and tactical, etc.[11] For example, from the point of view of an island nation like Great Britain, this type of warfare would entail the projection of power 'from the sea' onto land, as it conceptualizes an aspect of maritime strategy that involves the movement of armies across the sea. This concept is akin to the naval strategy propagated by Julian Corbett, which lays emphasis upon securing sea lanes for such movements. On the other hand, at the tactical level, the conjunction or cooperation of ground forces and waterborne forces occurs during actual combat. What makes the characterization of amphibious warfare complex is the lack of a clear distinction between ship crew, i.e., between soldiers and mariners. In pre-modern times, the naval force looked more like a military force 'displaced to decks from soil'.[12]

From a perusal of salient features of amphibious warfare, it becomes relatively easy to identify striking similarities in Chola, Mughal and Maratha naval warfare. Whereas the Chola naval expeditions to Southeast Asia were strategically conceived to cross the high seas and land their troops to fight, the Mughal naval expeditions to Bengal and Assam during the reigns of Akbar and Aurangzeb respectively, consisted of concerted military actions at a tactical level, both on land and on water. The Marathas, too, excelled in coastal warfare as they used the waters in the vicinity of the coast to engage in naval contestations.

In the early eighteenth century, the Portuguese troops on land cooperated with the English East India Company (EEIC) forces on the sea to fight Maratha admiral, Kanhoji Angre. Incidentally, the Maratha Navy met its fate due to similar tactical 'cooperation' between the waterborne forces of the EEIC and the ground forces of the Maratha Peshwa (Prime Minister) at Vijaydurg in 1756. The Peshwa Balaji Bajirao had signed a treaty with the EEIC for help in attacking Vijaydurg, which belonged to his own admiral, Tulaji Angre (the son of Admiral Kanhoji Angre), so as to quell the growing power of the Angre dynasty.

II

Like many nations worldwide, India also has a rich maritime history that dates back to the fourth millennium BCE. The Harappan people exhibited sophistication and ingenuity by incorporating tidal movements into their navigation. The tidal dock excavated at Lothal on the mouth of Indus River indicates that the entry and exit of merchant ships to the port depended upon the occurrence of sea tides. Verses of the Rig Veda also mention shipwrecks, as well as ships having a hundred oars.[13] The Ramayana hints at familiarity with the hazards of sailing, as the crossing of the sea by Hanuman is likened to a ship tossed by the winds in the high seas.[14] Buddhist stories and paintings confirm the maritime skills of the people of that age.[15]

However, the first evidence of a state-owned naval organization comes from the Maurya period around 300 BCE. Kautilya mentions the state-owned flotilla under the command of the superintendent of the navy.[16] The boats were also probably used for ferrying the troops and ammunitions, as the term '*sena-bhand-pryagonam*' suggests. In second century CE, the Andhra rulers, Pulamayi and Yagnashri, issued coins portraying double-masted ships possibly to commemorate a naval victory.[17] During the Gupta period (fourth to sixth century CE), their navy was being used to transport troops through navigable rivers to fight wars.[18] Progress in the field of shipbuilding can be assessed through the eleventh-century text *Yukti-kalpataru*, authored by Bhojraj, King of Malwa. By 1000 CE, shipbuilding and navigation had advanced significantly, enabling the Chola rulers to dispatch great naval expeditions through the Bay of Bengal to suppress the piracy of Sumatran warlords. The Cholas subsequently controlled Burma, Malaya and Sumatra.[19] The Chola fleet must have facilitated the selection of a landing point across the sea.

By the eleventh century, depending upon geographical locations and geopolitical concerns, the local rulers in north India had also developed river-based fleets to control riverine transport and maintain their hold over distant areas. It is said that during one of his raids on India, Mahmud of Ghazni fought a naval battle with the Jats of Punjab, using purpose-built boats with iron spikes for ramming action. The fighting crew on both sides included archers, and tactics included causing fire by throwing incendiaries like naphtha on the enemy's ships.[20]

After the establishment of the Delhi Sultanate in 1206 its navy played a crucial role in state-building and consolidation. Contemporary accounts indicate that Sultan Balban (r. 1266-87) employed a fleet of ships to transport his troops to Bengal to suppress the revolt of Tughril Khan.[21] Later, Sultan Firoz Shah Tughlaq used his fleet on two occasions to transport troops and elephants to confront his enemies.[22]

During the fifteenth century, before the arrival of the Portuguese in India, the ruler of Calicut adopted the title of 'sovereign of the mountains and the sea'.[23] To protect the state's interests, the Zamorin of Calicut maintained a sizeable fleet which he used to confront the Portuguese. According to contemporary accounts, in 1504, his fleet consisted of 160 'paraos' (outrigger boats with sails), each equipped with two guns, and engines.[24] Later in the century, the Kunjali Marakkars, the hereditary admirals of the Zamorin, organized the naval defence against the Portuguese onslaughts by making effective use of the lightweight paraos.[25] During the sixteenth century, Mughal emperor Akbar created the Mughal Navy, which, in essence, was a green-water navy. The Mughal fleet, known as the Nawarra, was primarily stationed in deltaic Bengal. It is said that Aurangzeb wanted to expand Mughal naval strength, but instead of taking initiatives, he allied with the Sidi of Janjira by offering the Sidi chief the post of a Mughal Admiral.

During the second half of the seventeenth century, Chhatrapati Shivaji fought the Mughals simultaneously on land and sea along the Konkan coast. The Sidi and the Marathas vied for the control of the sea off the coast of Konkan, as both claimed sovereign rights over it. However, in the ensuing Maratha-Sidi naval contestations, the Maratha Chhatrapati could not overpower the Sidi of Janjira. Nonetheless, he ensured that the Maratha naval capabilities reached the threshold necessary to protect and promote the interests of the nascent Maratha Swarajya (self-rule). During the first half of the eighteenth century, however, we find that the Marathas, led by Admiral Kanhoji Angre and his descendants, engaged in intense naval rivalry with the Europeans, especially the EEIC, for the control of the Konkan waters, which came to an end with the downfall of the Maratha Navy in 1756.

A few scholars have dealt with the structure, function and the exploits of the Maratha Navy. The most prominent among them is B.K. Apte.[26] While renowned scholars like Jadunath Sarkar and Surendranath Sen took up the discussion of the Maratha Navy in their respective monographs, a nationalistic approach to understand the career of the Maratha Admiral Kanhoji Angre was made by Malgonkar.[27,28] As the Maratha Navy, under the leadership of Admiral Kanhoji Angre, made European fleets look insignificant in the Konkan waters, the exploits of the formidable Maratha admiral also found place in some European works, notably those of G.A. Ballard and John Bidulph.[29] The combined deployment of land and sea power by Angre and his descendants, has recently been briefly analysed, and attempts have been made to demystify the persona and character of Kanhoji Angre.[30] A comprehensive account of the Maratha Navy and its exploits is still unavailable.

III

The present volume begins with Vaibhav Purandare's essay, 'Shivaji: Pioneer King and Plucky Visionary'. This essay contextualizes the character of Chhatrapati Shivaji within the politico-military-cultural setting of the seventeenth century. Purandare emphasizes that Shivaji's achievements were nothing less than a revolution that seemed unlikely to take place, until he made it happen. This chapter highlights the intrinsic values and qualities he represented as a leader, and also speaks of the inspiration that countless people derived from him, as they selflessly pledged themselves to his mission of creating a Swarajya. Purandare, a biographer of Chhatrapati Shivaji himself, offers fresh insight into Shivaji's strategic understanding of the complex world around him.[31]

He argues that among all his contemporaries, Shivaji uniquely realized the significance of the sea for both defence and trade—especially at a time when the Maratha Swarajya was still in its infancy, being built brick by brick. This underscores Shivaji's sharp acumen and visionary genius. The indigenous navy that he created continues to be an enduring source of inspiration for the twenty-first century Indian Navy, as reflected in the Navy's 2022 dedication of its emblem to Shivaji's Royal Octagonal Seal. Purandare's essay sets the tone for this volume, as the succeeding chapters explore various aspects of the Maratha Navy.

The Maratha Navy emerged at a time when European seafaring nations had firmly entrenched themselves in the distant corners of the globe in search of bullion, trade, colony and slaves. Their navies not only served as vital links to connect the mother country with its remote settlements, but were also the mainstay of the military success of their nations in the non-European world. The concept of control and sovereignty of sea in the non-European world, was thus already deeply ingrained in the thoughts and practices of the European navies and seafarers, when they arrived in the Indian Ocean Region (IOR) during the late sixteenth century.

What is particularly interesting is their insistence on claiming sovereignty over the sea, even though this concept had no parallel in the European world. Beginning with the Portugese—who created a mechanism to control trade and navigation by instituting the cartaz, a system of navigational permits or 'passes'—most European nations issued their own passes. Rothermund describes this system as 'protection rent' system.[32] It was mandatory for native shipping to purchase the European navigational passes. Those who fell outside this system were deemed pirates.

These passes later became a perpetual source of conflict. According to Edward Alpers, an ironic consequence of this competition in the Indian Ocean was that every player regarded themselves the rightful claimant to domination, while viewing its rivals as pirates.[33] Against this backdrop, Lakshmi Subramanian has framed her essay, 'Imagining Sovereignty over Waters: Seafarers, Rulers and Detractors in India's West Coast, 1500-1800'. This essay serves as Chapter 2 of this volume. Subramanian closely examines how various players—including the Marathas, the Sidi of Janjira, Europeans and other coastal chiefs—engaged in political imagination and articulation over water, the high seas and the coastal regions of the Konkan. In this chapter, she addresses critical issues such as the ownership of the sea, the construct of legitimacy, and piracy.

Furthermore, she considers the Anglo-Angre confrontation as just one strand in the broader coastal politics of the Konkan in the eighteenth century, arguing that it was, in part, a fallout of the EEIC's resolve to exercise total maritime control over the littoral and the seas, eliminate all contenders, assert the inviolability and legitimacy of the English pass, and escalate the rhetoric of piracy. Subramanian's essay introduces readers to the maritime world of the Indian Ocean, with a particular focus on the Indian West Coast.

In Chapter 3 of this volume, titled 'The Naval Setup of the Marathas', the author, Amarendra Kumar, introduces the Maratha Navy, which was established by Chhatrapati Shivaji in 1659. At the beginning of his essay Kumar examines the considerations and compulsions behind the creation of the Maratha Navy, focusing on threat perception and politico-economic motives. By judiciously using contemporary vernacular and modern scholarship, he explores aspects such as shipbuilding and estimates the Maratha flotilla during the seventeenth and eighteenth centuries. Further, his essay outlines the aims and objectives of the Maratha Navy under Shivaji, as detailed in contemporary sources. The essay briefly discusses Maratha's naval administration and examines the significance of the ships, crew, armaments and forts as the essential components of the Maratha naval setup.

A navy performs multifarious functions related to state formation, including military, political, diplomatic and economic roles. To gain a clearer understanding of the Maratha Navy, we should evaluate its achievements against these very parameters. In Chapter 4 of this volume, titled 'Trade and Economy: The Marathas in Coastal Political Economy in the Early Modern Period', Radhika Seshan emphasizes the economic aspects. Her essay primarily focuses on the coastal political economy and how it intersects with the concerns of the emerging state system, as the formation of the Maratha state and the establishment of its navy progressed simultaneously. It examines the dynamics of the coastal economy and explores the implications of European attempts to dominate the trading world of the Indian Ocean through various means. Seshan also critically analyses the importance of ports, their connections to the hinterland, the commodities traded and the patterns of trading voyages, all within the context of the coastal political economy. The chapter concludes by highlighting the Maratha state's directive to ensure the protection of trade.

The economic implications can also be understood in term of the costs associated with the construction and maintenance of a naval setup. Protecting trade also meant managing navigation along trade routes. The Portuguese 'cafila system' serves as a case in point, as it aimed to control the trading voyages by providing armed protection against a nominal charge through their cartaz or navigational pass.[34] Issuing and enforcing navigational passes was a means of demonstrating naval power and sovereignty over the sea. The Europeans, the Sidi of Janjira and the Marathas under Shivaji and his successors issued their navigational passes for a fee. The Maratha passes, known as 'dastak' and 'caul', mandated strict compliance in the Konkan region.[35] Consequently, during the seventeenth and eighteenth centuries, maritime passes became a continuous source of conflict on the West Coast of India. This theme is central to Chapter 5 of this volume titled 'Dastak: Competing Sovereignties, and the Maratha Naval Prowess in the Konkan in the Eighteenth Century'. Anirudh Deshpande, the author of this essay, scrutinizes the economy surrounding the institution of navigational passes.

The essay discusses the naval achievements of the House of Angres, beginning with the appointment of Kanhoji Angre as the Maratha *Sarkhel* (Admiral). Maratha naval capabilities were significantly augmented under the Angres, bringing them into close competition with the EEIC for dominance over the West Coast of India. Deshpande, however, warns against discussing Kanhoji Angre and his successors strictly within a Eurocentric piratical framework as is reflected in Kanhoji Angre's historiography. While analysing the causes of the downfall of the Maratha Navy in less than three decades after the death of Kanhoji Angre, this essay highlights the differences that arose between the Maratha Peshwa and the Maratha admiral. According to Deshpande, these differences stemmed from the Peshwa's lack of awareness and understanding of the concept of maritime sovereignty. Consequently, the short-sightedness of the Peshwa in planning a 'joint-action' with the EEIC against the admiral's strongholds is regarded as a primary cause of the downfall of the Maratha Navy.

The Konkan region is defined by a coastal plain of variable altitude and width, bordered to the east by the escarpment of the Western Ghats, and to the west by the Arabian Sea which may or may not feature cliffs.[36] More precisely, the region is a distinct strip of lowland, interspersed with hills, rising in elevation from the sea level to 150 metres and, at places to more than 300 metres.[37] This Arabian Sea littoral of Maharashtra stretches from the Damanganga River in the north (north of Mumbai) to Terekhol River in the south. Throughout this stretch, on the whole, we find rugged and challenging terrain, intersected by numerous creeks and abounding in isolated peaks and detached range of hills.

Shivaji controlled a coast of approximately the same length—from Tarapur to Karwar—barring the coastal pockets held by the other powers, such as the English, Sidi and Portuguese, at Mumbai, Janjira and Goa respectively. On the ground, the narrow strip of the coast in the west, ranging from 12 to 20 kilometers in width, merges with the Arabian Sea. It has numerous creeks and inlets over which the influence of the sea is felt in the form of tides. These tides penetrate deep into the land, fostering the growth of several littoral and estuary ports such as Suppara (Sopara), Kallinea (Kalyan), Semylla (Chaul), Byzantium (Vijayadurg), among others during the ancient period.

Due to the economic significance of ports, globally coastal polities have endeavoured to facilitate trade by providing security through coastal fortifications. Excavations along the Indian Ocean coast have revealed that many commercial settlements and ports coexisted with military, political and fortified settlements even in ancient times.[38] Pushkar Sohoni's essay, 'Maritime Fortifications: Defending Land and Sea', which serves as Chapter 6 of this volume, takes note of the coastal and off-shore fortifications along the Konkan littoral. These fortifications provided significant strategic advantages to the coastal polities during the seventeenth and eighteenth centuries. Sohoni points out that the density of maritime forts—typically one or more at the mouth of every estuary, and several on islands not far away from the mainland—is notably absent from the rest of the Indian seaboard. Therefore, he considers it essential to study the seascape of the period to gain a proper understanding of the Maratha Navy.

Sohoni further argues that, since the Marathas did not possess large ships capable of broadside attacks, maritime forts were crucial for them, functioning like stationary ships armed with artillery. Additionally, these fortifications served multiple purposes—they safeguarded trading routes, provided bases for naval operations and acted as a deterrent against invasions from sea-based powers. This essay highlights salient features of fort architecture, which include elements specifically designed for maritime defence, such as high walls resistant to cannon fire, strategically placed artillery, intricate systems for storing fresh water and hidden underwater obstructions to damage enemy ships that ventured too close. Additionally, illustrations of a few significant forts, including those constructed by the European powers along the West Coast, enrich our understanding of the geopolitical landscape of the era.

The ships, crew and armaments are essential components of any navy. Maritime states project power at sea through purpose-built vessels that can be effectively utilized for operational, strategic and tactical roles. The strategic deployment of warships ensures freedom of navigation, which is crucial for both economic and military objectives. Additionally, the navy defends a nation from external aggression by policing its coastal waters. Ships are designed and equipped based on their operational, strategic or tactical roles. Consequently, shipbuilding has been a key factor in the success of nations seeking to project naval power.

We can trace the evolution of shipbuilding traditions in India from pre-modern to modern times primarily through ethnographic studies.[39] Traditional carpenters belonging to the Viswakarma or Sutar caste worked in shipyards. They had an experienced headman or master craftsman called 'mestri', a term likely derived from the Portuguese word 'mester', meaning master.[40] In his monograph *Shipbuilding, Navigation and the Portuguese in Pre-modern India*, Mathew details the stages of shipbuilding, the materials used, the treatment of the hull with special coating, caulking, tonnage, design, and vocabulary and nomenclature of ships, as well as aspects of navigation.[41]

The Western Coast of India is renowned for excellent varieties of timber used for shipbuilding, especially teak wood.

The southernmost part of the Western Coast, namely Malabar, is known for its network of lagoons and small rivers that connect the hinterland with ports like Quilon, Cochin, Cranganore, Calicut and Cannanore. Therefore, from time immemorial, vessels were built in Beypore near Calicut.[42] In the sixteenth century, Cochin excelled as a shipbuilding centre under Portuguese influence, on account of the availability of timber in the hinterland.[43] Apte's seminal work, *A History of Maratha Navy and Merchantships*, explores various aspects of Maratha shipbuilding during the eras of Shivaji and Kanhoji Angre.[44]

Chapter 7 of the present volume, titled 'Ships, Armaments and Manpower of Maratha Navy in the Seventeenth to Eighteenth Centuries: A Comparative Study', is authored by Ajay Agarwal, who made his career in the Indian Navy. His essay offers valuable insights from the perspective of an experienced naval professional in his examination of the subject. In the first section of the essay, Agarwal discusses aspects of Maratha shipbuilding, hinting at the diffusion of European technologies that enhanced the war effectiveness of the Maratha fleet. Sketches and pictures, primarily adapted from Apte's work, highlight the specific features of the maritime vessels used by the Marathas. To some extent, Maratha naval warfare resembles 'total war', as the Marathas utilized merchant vessels for naval purposes. Consequently, Agarwal allocates space in his essay to describe these merchant ships before examining the features of European shipbuilding. The description of European ships in this chapter, particularly those traversing the IOR, offer a comparative perspective on the diverse design, rigging and ratings of the ships from that period. The section on the shipbuilding technique highlights the various methods employed by the natives as well as the Europeans, providing a deeper insight into this aspect. The essay ends with a brief overview of the composition of Maratha crew and their armaments.

Shipbuilding and navigation are directly linked to external factors like the depth of the sea, sea currents, wind pattern, and navigational hazards associated with the character of the seabed. The next essay of this volume, titled 'Navigational Awareness: Appreciation of Geography', closely examines these factors. Its author, Ankush Banerjee, a serving officer in the Indian Navy, takes a closer look at the geographical settings of the Maratha Swarajya, and argues that one of the primary reasons for the Maratha dominance and repeated successes at sea, was their intuitive knowledge and understanding of the geography in which they operated. This understanding, both conscious and subconscious, guided the Maratha seamen in exploiting various navigational aspects, allowing them to capitalize on the surrounding geography and gain a decisive tactical advantage over their adversaries during operations.

According to Banerjee, the traditional wisdom about the coast and its many vagaries enabled the Maratha seamen, primarily chosen from the coastal communities, to exploit the local conditions to their advantage. A case in point is the erection of underwater coastal defences, which further amplifies this wisdom and has its roots in the Maratha seamen's critical appreciation of their geographical context. This essay examines some of the Maratha tactics illustrating how their in-depth knowledge of geographical features was crucial in formulating strategies and gaining a decisive advantage in coastal warfare.

Amarendra Kumar offers a comprehensive analysis of the naval conflicts among the Marathas, the Sidi of Janjira and various European powers along India's West Coast in Chapter 9 of this volume. His essay, titled 'Naval Contestations for the Control of the Sea', primarily examines the reasons behind the Maratha naval wars and the manner in which they were fought. The author has framed his arguments in the backdrop of evident limitations, including resource constraints, technological challenges and the geopolitical context surrounding the Maratha Swarajya. Central to Kumar's argument is the ingenuity of the Maratha leadership in compensating for their naval weaknesses, both in terms of the number of ships and the weaponry. The Marathas achieved this by employing effective battle tactics and optimizing their limited resources.

In addition to appraising the strategic and tactical understanding of the Marathas—carefully adapted to the geographical setup in their naval contests—Kumar aims to delineate the subtle differences in the nature and objectives of the Maratha–Sidi and the Euro-Maratha conflicts, particularly during the time of Shivaji. The naval battles for a barren stretch of insignificant rocky projection off the coast, along with Shivaji's use of his navy as a diplomatic tool in relation to the Europeans, are clearly explained in the context of the Marathas' strategic requirements. The chapter also discusses the power dynamics along the Konkan littoral during the first half of the eighteenth century and argues that the balance of power had not yet tilted in favour of the Europeans by that time.

The last essay of this volume titled 'From Sail to Stealth: A Comparative Study of the Maratha Navy and the Indian Navy', is authored by Janhavi Lokegaonkar and celebrates the achievements of the Maratha Navy. By examining Maratha operational strategies, battle tactics and lessons learned,

Lokegaonkar attempts to draw parallels with the modern Indian Navy. The conscious inclusion of geo-economics and maritime awareness in the national discourse, as noted by her, remains a crucial takeaway for our national policy planners in the current context. Additionally, regarding the principles of speed, surprise and guerrilla tactics used in Maratha naval operations, the essay draws a parallel with the Indo-Pak War of 1971. It notes that during this war, the Indian Navy effectively employed guerrilla-style tactics, exemplified by the daring bombardment of Karachi harbor using a 'shoot and scoot' approach. Indian missile boats launched surprise attacks that destroyed Pakistani naval assets and cut-off vital supply chains that crippled their war effort. Lokegaonkar humbly submits that given the complex global environment in which the Indian Navy operates, balancing power projection with diplomatic engagement—similar to the Maratha policy—remains central to the twenty-first century naval doctrines.

Further, the author emphasizes that adopting guerrilla tactics does not always reflect or imply resource limitations in the nation that employs such tactics; it also showcases the nation's ingenuity in conducting asymmetrical naval warfare. Such tactics were especially relevant for the Marathas during the seventeenth and eighteenth centuries, as their navy fought against the significantly superior European naval powers. The essay also explores the relevance of 'sea control' and 'sea denial' concepts in the modern context. In her concluding remarks, the author highlights the differences between the Maratha Navy and the Indian Navy regarding their infrastructure, economic roles and strategic approaches, and contends that the Maratha Navy, motivated by the goal of regional dominance and economic control, laid the foundations of India's naval tradition.

The essays in this volume thus effectively present a variety of evidence highlighting the glorious naval traditions of the Maratha Swarajya. The contributors of the essays have contextualized and clearly articulated the diverse aspects of the Maratha Navy, which dominated the brown waters of the Konkan littoral from the mid-seventeenth to mid-eighteenth centuries. The true value of this volume will be realized if its essays manage to excite the imagination of the reader, and of researchers and historians alike, inspiring them to seek further evidence to empirically strengthen and retell the remarkable success story of the Marathas in riding the waves by navigating challenges. The legacy of the Maratha Navy endures. The newly adopted design of the Indian Navy's ensign introduced in September 2022, reflects India's rich maritime heritage while symbolizing a strong, courageous, confident and proud naval force. Jai Hind!

Notes

1 Treaty of Tordesillas, https://www.britannica.com/event/Treaty-of-Tordesillas (accessed 4 October 2024).

2 Hermann Kulke, K. Kesavapany and Vijay Sakhuja, eds., *Nagapattinam to Suvarnadwipa: Reflections on the Chola Naval Expeditions to Southeast Asia*, Manohar Publishers, 2010.

3 Geoff Wade, 'Zheng He and Ming China's Voyages in the Early 15th Century', *Oxford Research Encyclopedias*, Asian History, 2020. https://doi.org/10.1093/acrefore/9780190277727.013.235 (accessed 16 September, 2023).

4 See pp. 94-107, in Luis Nuno Sardinha Monteiro, 'Fernando Oliveira's *Art of War at Sea* (1555): A Pioneering Treatise on Naval Strategy', *Naval War College Review*, Vol. 68, No. 4, 2015.

5 Alfred Thayer Mahan, *The Influence of Sea Power upon History 1660-1783*, Little Brown and Company, 1949.

6 Jan Glete, *Warfare at Sea, 1500-1650: Maritime Conflicts and the Transformation of Europe*, Routledge, [e-book], 2001; Richard Harding, *Amphibious Warfare in the Eighteenth Century, The British Expedition to the West Indies 1740–1742*, Royal Historical Society Studies in History 62, Royal Historical Society,1991; Susan Rose, *Medieval Naval Warfare: 1000-1500*, Routledge, 2001; N.A.M. Rodger, *The Command of the Ocean: A Naval History of Britain, 1649-1815*, W.W. Norton, 2005.

7 See pp. 1-50, in D.J.B. Trim, and Mark Charles Fissel, eds., *Amphibious Warfare 1000-1700: Commerce, State Formation and European Expansion*, Brill, 2006.

8 Ibid., p. 3.

9 Ibid., p. 13.

10 Ibid., p. 13.

11 Ibid., p. 27.

12 Ibid., p. 26.

13 See p. 27, in Indra, *Ideologies of War and Peace in Ancient India*, Vishveshwaranand Vedic Research Institute, 1957.

14 See p. 288, V.R. Ramachandra Dikshitar, *War in Ancient India*, Motilal Banarasidass, 1987.

15 See pp. 23, 28, in R.K. Mookerji, *Indian Shipping (A History of the Sea-Borne Trade and Maritime Activity of the Indians from the Earliest Times)*, Orient Longmans, reprint, 1957.

16 See pp. 82-84, in Vol. I, Chapter II, of R.P. Kangle, ed., *The Kautilya Arthashastra*, Vol. I-III, Motilal Banarasidass, 1997.

17 See pp. 288-89, 291, in Dikshitar, *War in Ancient India*,1987.

18 See p. 27, Indra, *Ideologies of War*,1957.

19 See pp. 547-66, in B. Arunachalam, 'Naval Expeditions of Rajendra Chola: A Nautical Enquiry', *Journal of Indian Ocean Studies*, Vol. 10, No. 3, 2002.

20 See pp. 477-78, in Vol. II, of H.M. Elliot, *The History of India as Told by Its Own Historians*, ed., John Dawson, Vol. I-VIII, D. K. Publishers, reprint, 1996.

21 Ibid., pp. 115-21.

22 Ibid., pp. 298, 330-31.

23 See p. 64., in K.M. Panikkar, *Geographical Factors in Indian History*, Bharatiya Vidya Bhavan, 1955.

24 See p. 162, in K.V.K. Ayyar, *The Zamorins of Calicut (From the Earliest Times down to A.D. 1806)*, University of Calicut, 1938; see alsopp. 143-47, in K.S. Mathew, 'Taxation in the Coastal Towns of Western India and the Portuguese in the Sixteenth Century,' in K.S. Mathew (ed.), *Mariners, Merchants and Oceans: Studies in Maritime History*, Manohar, 2015.

25 See pp. 29-38, in R.R.S. Chauhan, 'Kunjali's Naval Challenge to the Portuguese', in *Essays in Goan History*, ed., Teotino R. De Souza, Concept Publishing Company,1989.

26 B.K. Apte, *A History of Maratha Navy and Merchantships*, State Board for Literature and Culture, Bombay (Mumbai), 1973.

27 Jadunath Sarkar, *Shivaji and His Times*, Orient Longman, reprint, 1973; S.N. Sen, *The Military System of the Marathas*, K.P. Bagchi, reprint, 1979; S.N. Sen, *Early Career of Kanhoji Angria and Other Papers*, Calcutta University, 1941.

28 Manohar Malgonkar, *Kanhoji Angrey, Maratha Admiral: An Account of His Life and His Battles with the English*, Asia Publishing House, 1959.

29 G.A. Ballard, *Rulers of the Indian Ocean*, Neeraj Publishing House, reprint, 1984; John Biddulph, *The Pirates of Malabar: And an Englishwoman in India Two Hundred Years Ago*, Lancer International, reprint, 1992.

30 Derek L. Elliot, 'Pirates, Polities and Companies: Global Politics on the Konkan Littoral, c.1690-1756', Working Papers No. 136/10, Department of Economic History, London School of Economics, 2010.

31 Vaibhav Purandare, *Shivaji: India's Great Warrior King*, Juggernaut Publications, 2022.

32 See pp. 63-75, in Dietmar Rothermund, *Violent Traders: Europeans in Asia in the Age of Mercantilism*, Manohar, 2014.

33 See p. 86, in Edward A. Alpers, *The Indian Ocean in World History*, Oxford University Press, 2014.

34 For a better understanding of the cartaz and cafila system, refer to Chapter 3 in M.N. Pearson, *The New Cambridge History of India: The Portuguese in India*, Cambridge University Press, 1987.

35 See pp. 255–61, in B.K. Apte, 'Sovereignty of the Sea as Practiced in the Maratha Period', *Proceedings of the Indian History Congress*, Vol. 29, No. 1, 1967.

36 See p. 654, in O.H.K. Spate and A.T.A. Learmonth, *India and Pakistan: A General and Regional Geography*, third revised edition, Methuen & Co. Ltd., 1967.

37 See pp. 910-11, in R.L. Singh, *India: A Regional Geography*, The Geographical Society of India, 1971.

38 See p. 17, in H.P. Ray, 'Shipping in the Indian Ocean', in *Ships and Development in Maritime Technology on the Indian Ocean*, ed., David Parkin and Ruth Barnes, Routledge, 2002.

39 See, for example, pp. 90-91, in Kirti Jain, 'Boat Building and the Son Kolis of the Raigad District, Maharashtra', *Marine Archaeology*, Vol. 4, 1993.

40 See p. 34, in K.S. Mathew, *Shipbuilding, Navigation and the Portuguese in Pre-modern India*, Manohar, 2017.

41 Ibid., pp. 26-65 (Chapter 2, 'Shipbuilding and Navigation in India Prior to 1500').

42 Ibid., p. 104.

43 Ibid., p. 105.

44 For a few paintings and sketches of the Maratha vessels, see pp. 119-40, in Apte, *A History of Maratha Navy*, 1973.

1

Shivaji: Pioneer King, Plucky Visionary

Vaibhav Purandare

⚓⚓⚓

Shivaji Raje Bhosle is a singular figure in the history of India. In the seventeenth century, he launched and led a political and military revolution, which coursed through the Deccan and rattled the foundations of the Mughal empire, which was then at the height of its glory under Aurangzeb. Shivaji's attack created the conditions for its eventual fall and collapse. Shivaji built an independent, inclusive and forward-looking Maratha state, which still constitutes a model template for modern state-builders, and he built an indigenous navy, which is an enduring source of inspiration for the twenty-first century Indian Navy, a fact reflected in the Navy's 2022 dedication of its emblem to the Chhatrapati. Shivaji's story is importantly the story of a revolution that looked unlikely to happen, until he made it happen.

When he was born on 19 February 1630 in the fort of Shivneri in Junnar near Pune, the western Deccan (a corruption of the term 'dakshin' or south) had three Islamic states—the

Nizam Shahi of Ahmadnagar, the Adil Shahi of Bijapur and the Qutub Shahi of Golconda.[1] These states were three of five that had emerged from the splintering of the Bahamani sultanate, which had ruled the region from the fourteenth to the early sixteenth century, and which itself had come into being following the invasion of Alauddin Khilji into the Deccan in the last decade of the thirteenth century.[2] These three sultanates were perennially at war with each other and in the early seventeenth century the Mughals, dominant in the north, began to make a major push into the Deccan to destroy the sultanates and seize the region.

The near-nonstop warfare of these four powers created massive tumult in the Deccan and unsteadily moved the contour lines of its politics. Entire populations were unsettled from time to time and famines raged, but with military matters acquiring priority, civilian administration was neglected and whatever was left of it was largely unjust, exploitative and more or less unaccountable. An illuminating example was that of the kasba or village marketplace of Pune at the time of Shivaji's birth in 1630. The town had been laid to waste by the devastation caused by the constantly warring Nizam Shahi and Adil Shahi armies there, and the cultivation and human settlements that still remained were ruined by the Deccan famine of 1629-31.[3]

What were the Marathas of western Deccan, who formed the region's native population, doing during this period? In the sixteenth century, the Marathas had emerged as talented and extremely competent military personnel. They were, however, engaged completely in serving one or the other of the four military powers, either as chieftains who received and implemented directives or as foot soldiers. Into this realm of military turbulence and political instability stepped Shivaji. His father, Shahaji Raje Bhosle, was a military general of repute and had played a big role in keeping the Nizam Shahi state from imminent collapse in the early 1630s. He had also had notable stints with the Adil Shahi sultanate and a short one with the Mughals.[4]

Shivaji grew up in the fort of Shivneri with his mother Jijabai, while ShahajiRaje was in and out, fighting for this army or that. Jijabai herself came from a family of military notables: her father Lukhji Jadhav Rao was a distinguished military man in the Nizam Shahi state and had also served Bijapur and the Mughals.[5] Jijabai, though, was independent of mind and spirit and inculcated a sense of independence into the mind of her little son. When Shivaji turned twelve, Shahaji—who was by this time, in the area known as present-day Bengaluru, looking after the place given to him as a jagir by Adil Shah—appointed his son Shivaji as administrator of his own jagir of Punc, which comprised not only the utterly devastated market town but its surroundings as well, including the hilly Maval region to the west of Pune.[6,7]

Shivaji started out as a teenage rebel of tremendous precocity. He firstly resettled the town of Pune by providing incentives for cultivation and resettlement and also monetary rewards to villagers who would kill the wild animals that had taken over the kasba and were preventing displaced locals from returning. Lands were given at nominal rents and significant returns were assured for trees planted and crops grown; lands were measured, ownership or rental status established, canals and wells constructed and remuneration paid to those who worked on them. Similar land and revenue arrangements were made in the surrounding parts, and this became the microcosm for the civil and revenue administration that Shivaji would systematically set up across the lands he later conquered over time and ruled during his political and military career.[8]

When he was sixteen-years-old, Shivaji issued his royal seal in Sanskrit, marking an important departure from the established tradition of the Persianate Age of having such imprimaturs in the dominant and then-official Persian language. In doing so, Shivaji indicated that though he was not against any language or culture, he would not allow his land's own cultural traditions to be wiped out. More importantly, Shivaji applied the principle of accountability in a place not known for responsible governance, where local revenue, administrative and policing officials—such as the patils and kulkarnis at the village level, and deshmukhs, deshkulkarnis and deshpandes at the district level—collected taxes and imposed fines and punishments on local populations, without demonstrating any transparency for their actions and where military officials worked on the principle of seizure, plunder and destruction.[9] On receiving a complaint of sexual assault made by an ordinary village woman against a patil in Khede Bare near Pune, Shivaji pronounced a decisive verdict, ordering that the patil be 'immediately arrested' and 'his hands and legs cut off.' This verdict—which is part of Shivaji's first available letter with his Sanskrit imprint and is dated 28 January 1646—sent a powerful message to the well-entrenched officialdom and likewise a strong, positive message to the vulnerable and powerless ordinary folk of the region who suddenly began to see signs of justice in a land of forlorn hopes.[10]

Shivaji announced his political rebellion around the same time by taking possession of four Adil Shahi forts in the region. The teenager's rebellion angered Bijapur, and suspecting that the father was quietly inciting it, Adil Shah ordered the arrest of Shahaji, his own distinguished military general. Shivaji was forced to give up a key fort to secure his father's release, but he did not deviate from the path of self-assertion. On the contrary, he systematically built up his strength while outwardly professing allegiance to Bijapur and served a bigger notice to the Adil Shah by capturing the strategically located Jaawali valley (near Mahabaleshwar) in 1656, which provided the pathway to the Sahyadri ranges as well as the Konkan coastline. And it wasn't Bijapur alone that he was taking on: soon after capturing Jaawali, he launched twin assaults on the Mughal strongholds of Junnar and Ahmadnagar (which had become the principal base of the Mughals in the Deccan after the collapse of the Nizam Shahis), climbing the walls of Junnar fort 'with rope-ladders' and slaying the fort's guardians.[11]

It was at this point in time, when he was twenty-seven years old in the year 1657, that Shivaji began setting up his own naval fleet. He captured the ports of Kalyan, Bhiwandi and Prabalgad near Panvel and ordered the construction of twenty small armed ships in the creeks beneath these three towns. He commissioned Portuguese officers for this purpose, who knew the art and craft of ship-building better than the local inhabitants, but roped in some locals to assist them so they too got trained in the process. Portuguese officials recorded that nearly 400 people were involved in the process.[12]

In doing so, Shivaji was breaking new ground. How? While the Cholas' naval prowess is well-known, after the end of that dynasty of southern India in the mid-1250s and the Islamic invasions and their aftermath, the various powers on Indian soil paid little attention to the massive coastline. So when Shivaji was born, the Mughal Empire ruled all of the north, but neither the Mughals nor the Deccan powers in the south such as the Nizam

Shahi, Adil Shahi or Qutubshahi sultanates had built themselves up as a naval force. The result was that coastal power across India was entirely in the hands of foreigners—the British, the Portuguese, the Dutch, the French, and, in small parts, in the hands of the African-Abyssinian Sidis. These foreign powers had taken control of the seafront to the extent that even if the Mughal Emperor and his kin, or the Deccani sultans, wanted to visit the holy shrine of Mecca or trade in goods and commodities, they needed approvals and licenses from the foreigners.

Shivaji was alone among all his contemporaries in recognizing the significance of the sea for both defence and trade, that too at a time when his own state had still not fully come into being but was being built, brick by brick, in a series of well-planned rebellious actions. To have thought of having a navy was itself out of the ordinary, given the shortsightedness all around him; to have done so well before his own possessions on land were adequate or completely secure, made it even more so. Shivaji combined vision, strategy, and extraordinary risk-taking and daring. Worried by his widening rebellion, the Adil Shahi sultan of Bijapur sent in his much-feared Afghan-born general Afzal Khan to kill Shivaji in 1659. When Afzal Khan held Shivaji in a deadly embrace and sought to plunge a dagger into his side, Shivaji pulled out the tiger claws concealed in his hands and pulled out the rival's entrails. This sent alarm bells ringing through the Adil Shahi sultan and further awakened the Mughals to the threat they knew Shivaji presented to their dominance.[13]

Not losing any time, Aurangzeb, who had ascended the throne in the late 1650s, dispatched his maternal uncle and noted Mughal military captain Shaista Khan to destroy Shivaji. Shaista Khan devastated Shivaji's lands for three full years, burning entire villages and even taking over Lal Mahal, the house in which Shivaji had spent his teenage years in Pune with his mother.[14] Shivaji struck back in stunning fashion. In the dead of night on 5-6 April 1663, he quietly entered Shaista Khan's quarters in Lal Mahal with a band of select soldiers. Before Shaista Khan could flee, he cut off three fingers of Khan's righthand, forcing the Mughal general to flee. Shaista Khan jumped off the balcony of Lal Mahal in terror and fled screaming for life and safety.[15] This nocturnal strike sent shockwaves throughout the Mughal empire, and the situation was made worse for Aurangzeb the following year when Shivaji sacked the key Mughal trading centre of Surat.[16]

Aurangzeb then sent in a formidable Rajput general of his, Mirza Raja Jai Singh, to rein in Shivaji, with a force of nearly one lakh. This force well and truly closed in on the Marathas, and Shivaji was forced to give up twenty-three of the thirty five forts he had conquered. Shivaji agreed to retreat, believing that if he survived, he would live to fight another day. The crisis soon grew graver for him when he went to Aurangzeb's court in Agra in May 1666 after being part-persuaded and part-pressured by Jai Singh, who had the upper hand in the situation, to do so. There, Aurangzeb deliberately humiliated Shivaji by placing him in a lineup of not-so notable military chieftains and proceeded to ignore him.[17] Shivaji flew into a rage and vociferously protested against the way he had been treated. Aurangzeb promptly imprisoned him with the idea of killing him.

A first attempt was made by asking him to go on a campaign to Kabul in Afghanistan, so he could be killed on the way. The Marathas in the Deccan would be sent a message that their leader had been killed by the enemy. This would prevent them from rising angrily in revolt.[18] The end of the intrepid Maratha looked imminent even to many who wished Shivaji well. But Shivaji had plans up his sleeve. After more than three months passed in confinement he sent away all the officials and the 2,500-odd Mavale soldiers, who had accompanied him to Agra, asking them to return home.[19] He only kept his nine-year-old son Sambhaji with him, along with a handful of aides.[20] And then he effected one of the most audacious and thrilling escapes in Indian history.

He pretended he was extremely ill and bought different kinds of sweetmeats, directing that they be distributed to Mughal officials and to holy men of the Hindu and Muslim faiths. The baskets were huge, each hanging from a wooden pole shouldered by two porters. The guards outside his place of confinement initially diligently checked the baskets, but in a few days slacked off, asking only occasionally for one or two of them to be opened before they were sent in for Shivaji to eat.

On the evening of 17 August 1666, Shivaji and his son Sambhaji squeezed themselves into two separate baskets. Their lids were shut tight and the baskets were carried out of the prison camp, past the row of guards a little after sunset. They were placed on the ground only once they were outside the town, at a pre-decided spot, where some of the officials Shivaji had sent back were waiting. Once Shivaji and Sambhaji stepped out, the entire escape party rode home on horseback, a journey of over a 1,000 km. This miraculous escape was an acute embarrassment and a serious setback for Aurangzeb, who believed he had 'got' Shivaji.[21]

Shivaji's return re-energized the Maratha nation and for three years thereafter, he spent his time rebuilding his forces and introducing reforms which included diktats to watandars (hereditary chiefs) not to build palatial houses, but to live like ordinary people in regular homes. He also set down stringent rules for civilian and military administration. Finally in 1670 Shivaji once again attacked the Mughals, who were now sitting atop his lost forts and won all twenty-three back in a matter of months.[22] His shrewd strategies had brought about these astounding military successes. He knew that the mountains and hills in the Deccan were his greatest strengths, and he was smart enough not to engage in pitched battles with his enemies in locations where his troops might end up getting vastly outnumbered, by these bigger and long-established states.

He calibrated his stand and took the measure of his opponents before he made his responses. He also offered them concessions and made retreats in order to gain time to re-equip himself and his forces and to make further gains on the ground. One of his extraordinary merits as a military leader and statesman was that he was as superbly adept at holding back as he was at launching the most fearlessly daring and seemingly impossible of attacks. Shivaji's opponents were flummoxed too by the unbending loyalty of his lieutenants and followers, all people drawn from ordinary families in the Deccan. One of his close aides, Baji Prabhu Deshpande, had held off a major Bijapur onslaught in 1660 in a narrow pass in the mountains with a group of just 300 men, to enable Shivaji to reach a place of safety. In the process Baji Prabhu had laid down his life, becoming a legend in his own right; as did Tanaji Malusare, who laid down his life whilst successfully re-claiming the lost fort of Kondhana or Sinhagad in 1670 from a strong Mughal garrison.

In 1674, aged forty-four, Shivaji took the truly momentous decision to crown himself 'chhatrapati' or sovereign. This would be a declaration of the establishment of his own independent state, and in heraldic terms, the start of a new era. By giving his rule a legal and official status, he robbed Aurangzeb, Bijapur, Golconda and anybody else for that matter of the opportunity to accuse him of overstepping the line. From now on, he was their equal, a king in his own right. He had pulled off the impossible. Even in naval terms. As noted earlier, he had started constructing his navy in 1657. By the time of his coronation in 1674—that is, in a span of a little over fifteen years—as a new power, he had built more than fifty combat vessels, among them the big 'ghurabs', the steady-paced 'galbats' or gunboats, and the lightly-built and speedy 'shibads.' If trading vessels were to be counted, the size of his fleet would likely exceed 500 at the time of his coronation in 1674.[23] This created fear in the minds of all his rivals; if he replicated his land exploits on the waters, they would be under serious threat.

As a liberator of the people, Shivaji was inclusive in his navy just as much as in other areas of organization and public life. His ideas of kingship and his polity were essentially Hindu in nature and character, but two of his naval chiefs—Daulat Khan and Darya Sarang Ventjee—were Muslims. One of his bitterest critics, the official Mughal chronicler Khafi Khan, wrote of him:

> He [Shivaji] made it a rule that wherever his followers went plundering, they should do no harm to the mosques, the Book of God, or the women of anyone. Whenever a copy of the sacred Koran came into his hands, he treated it with respect, and gave it to some of his *Musulman* followers. Whenever the women of any Hindu or Muhammadan were taken prisoners by his men, he watched over them until their relations came with a suitable ransom to buy their liberty ... Shivaji had always striven to maintain the honour of the people in his territories. He persevered in a course of rebellion, in plundering caravans, and troubling mankind, but he entirely abstained from other

> disgraceful acts, and was careful to maintain the honour of women and children of Muhammadans when they fell into his hands. His injunctions upon this point were very strict, and anyone who disobeyed them received punishment.[24]

When Aurangzeb, after destroying iconic Hindu temples in the early 1670s, imposed the jaziya or discriminatory tax on Hindus on the basis of their faith, Shivaji wrote a scathing letter to the Mughal Emperor, stating firmly and unambiguously that:

> Your Majesty, in the Quran, God has been described as the *Rabbul Alameen*, the Lord of the entire universe, and not as *Rabbul Mussalmin*, the Lord of the *Mussalmans*. In fact, Islam and Hinduism are both beautiful manifestations of the Divine Spirit. The call for prayers is given in the mosques, bells ring to the Divine glory in temples. Anyone bearing fanaticism and religious hatred must be said to be acting against the commands of God. To presume to draw lines on these pictures is verily to lay blame on the Divine Artist [God]. To point out blemishes in any creation only means you are blaming the creator. Do not do so.[25]

Shivaji was a benevolent founder and head of state who cared for the people and empowered the common folk. He took away a lot of the powers of officials who were in the habit of misusing it. His assault on deeply entrenched vested interests was extraordinary, because it placed the political revolution he was bringing about at risk of disturbance and sabotage at all levels. Nevertheless, it endeared him to the people and demonstrated that he was a plucky pioneer. He strictly forbade his army from taking anything from the lands and fields of ordinary farmers. If any of his soldiers flouted these rules and troubled the peasants and local villagers, they were swiftly punished. Among his remarkable written directives was that not a blade of grass should be touched and not a grain or morsel of food taken by force. If the soldiers did that, he stated, the villagers would think of them as worse than the Mughals, which underlines the subjugation of the people under Mughal rule.[26]

The state that Shivaji formed was the 'Hindavi Swarajya', a title that underlined its indigenous nature owing to the word 'Hindavi', which came into use in the thirteenth and fourteenth centuries, as a language that 'moved away from Persian'.[27] It gradually became a term that indicated the indigenous people of India. The addition of 'Swarajya,' (self-rule) made Hindavi Swarajya, the first successfully established indigenous independent state. This state is more popularly known as the Maratha Swarajya.

Shivaji died at the age of just fifty in 1680, but left behind such a wealth of foresight and motivation that his successors eventually took the Maratha Raj across the length and breadth of the land, its frontiers at one time stretching from Attock (which is in present-day Pakistan) to Cuttack in the east. No wonder that the Indian Navy today sees in Chhatrapati Shivaji Maharaj, in the edifice of his naval fleet, and moreover in his sterling vision, one of its greatest sources of inspiration.

Notes

1 The primary sources which confirm Shivaji's birthdate and birth year are contemporary texts: *Shree Shivabharata*, an account by Kavindra Parmananda; the *Jedhe Shakavali*, another contemporary chronicle of a Maratha family of the period; an inscription in Thanjavur; and three horoscopes of Shivaji found in Rajasthan, prepared when he was on his way to Agra, to Aurangzeb's court, in the year 1666. See p. 31, in

Kavindra Paramananda Govind Newaskar, *Shri Shivabharata*, translated from Sanskrit to Marathi by S.M. Divekar, Bharat Itihas Sanshodhak Mandal, Pune, 1927. In subsequent notes I will refer to a recent English translation of the Sanskrit work. See also p. 16, in A.R. Kulkarni, ed., *Jedhe Shakavali-Kareena*, Diamond Publications, 2007; for the Rajasthan horoscopes see p. 125, in the *BISM Quarterly*, Vol. XX, No. III, Bharat Itihas Sanshodhak Mandal, n.d.

2 The other two sultanates that were formed were the ones in Bidar and Berar. They had vanished by the time of Shivaji's birth.

3 A general of the Adil Shahi sultanate called Murar Jagdev was particularly responsible for vandalizing Pune in the late 1620s and early 1630s during the war with the Nizam Shahis. See p. 34, in Purandare, *Shivaji*, 2022.

4 For details of Shahaji's military career see pp. 21, 26, 28, 40-42, 45, 49-52, in Soniya Khare and Dr Jayashree Sathe, transl., *Shivabharata: Shree Shivabharata by Kavi Parmananda, The Only Contemporary Biography of Chhatrapati Shivaji Maharaj*, Murukumbi Itihas Upakram, 2024.

5 For details of Lukhji Jadhav Rao's military career, see pp. 169 and 182, in Abdul Hamid Lahori, *Badshah Nama* (Persian), ed., Maulvi Kabiruddin Ahmad and Maulvi Abd-ur-Rahim, Vol. I, Part I, Asiatic Society, Bengal, 1867; also see pp. 312-13 in Vol. I, and p. 218 in Vol. 2, of H. Beveridge, ed., *Tuzuk-i-Jahangiri or the Memoir of Jahangir*, transl., A. Rogers, Oriental Translation Fund, 1909.

6 See p. 98, in Khare and Sathe, transl., *Shivabharata*, 2024.

7 Ibid., pp. 105,108-09.

8 G.S. Sardesai, *New History of the Marathas*, Vol. 1, Munshiram Manoharlal Publishers,1986.

9 The patils and deshmukhs had revenue and policing duties at the village and district level respectively, while the kulkarnis and the deshkulkarnis/deshpandes kept the account books at the village and district levels. Patils and deshmukhs were also called to offer military services when required, though they were not part of the full-time military forces. For a good account of the civil and revenue administrative systems during this period, see Vol 1. of Sardesai, *New History of The Marathas*,1986; and Stewart Gordon, *The Marathas: 1600-1818*, The New Cambridge History of India series, Cambridge University Press, 1993.

10 See pp. 641-42, in Gajanan Bhaskar Mehendale, *Shri Raja Shiv Chhatrapati*, (Marathi), Vol. 1, Diamond Publications, 2008; and pp. 41-42, in Purandare, *Shivaji*, 2022.

11 See pp. 281-82, in Jadunath Sarkar, *History of Aurangzib*, Vol. 1, M.C. Sarkar & Sons, 1912.

12 See pp. 35-36, in P.S. Pissurlencar, *Portuguese–Mahratta Relations*, transl., T.V. Parvate, Maharashtra State Board for Literature and Culture, 1983.

13 Details of the Shivaji–Afzal Khan encounter are from two contemporary accounts. Newaskar, Kavindra Paramananda Govind. *Shri Shivabharata*. Translated from Sanskrit to Marathi by S.M. Divekar. Bharat Itihas Sanshodhak Mandal. 1927; and see pp.18-24, in Surendra Nath Sen, *Life of Siva Chhatrapati: Being a Translation of the Sabhasad Bakhar, Extracts and Documents Relating to Maratha History*, Vol. 1, University of Calcutta, 1920.

14 An official Mughal document from Aurangzeb's rule provides details of the burning of whole villages. See p. 217, the letter is in N.C. Kelkar and D.V. Apte, eds, *Shivkalin Patra Saar Sangraha*, (Marathi), Vol. 1, Shiva Charitra Karyalaya, 1930. See p. 106 for a full English translation, in Purandare, Shivaji, 2022.

15 See p. 44, in Sen, *Life of Siva Chhatrapati*, 1920.

16 Details of the sack of Surat can be found in the English Factory Records, quoted in Purandare (2022), *Shivaji*, pp. 122-36.

17 See pp. 109, in Sarkar, *Shivaji*, 2010.

18 See p. 165, in Jadunath Sarkar, *House of Shivaji*, S.C. Sarkar & Sons, 1948.

19 The term Mavale means the Mavals, or those who hail from the Maval region, a hilly area to the west of Pune.

20 See p. 113, in Sarkar, *Shivaji*, 2010.

21 See pp. 67-71, for details of the escape, in Sen, *Life of Siva Chhatrapati*, 1920; see pp. 170-75, in Sarkar, *House of Shivaji*, 1948; and see pp. 115-18, in Sarkar, *Shivaji and His Times*, 2010.

22 See pp. 204-05, in Setumadhavrao Pagadi, *Chhatrapati Shivaji*, Continental Prakashan, 2017; see p. 72, in Sen, *Life of Siva Chhatrapati*, 1920; see p. 174, in Sarkar, *History of Aurangzib*, 1912.

23 See pp. 70-73, in Apte, *A History of The Maratha Navy*, 1973.

24 See pp. 48-49, 93, in Elliot, *The History of India*, Vol. VII, 1996.

25 See pp. 257, in Purandare, *Shivaji*, 2022.

26 Ibid., pp. 209-10.

27 See p. 98 in Pagadi, *Chhatrapati Shivaji*, 2017; also see p. 194, in Pavan K. Varma, *The Great Hindu Civilisation: Achievement, Neglect, Bias and the Way Forward*, Westland, 2021.

2

Imagining Sovereignty Over Waters: Seafarers, Rulers and Detractors in India's West Coast, 1500-1800

Lakshmi Subramanian

⚓⚓⚓

The discovery of the direct sea route to India by Vasco Da Gama was followed by a proclamation of King Manuel I of Portugal, who styled himself 'Lord of Conquests, Seafaring and Commerce of Ethiopia, Arabia, Persia and India'. The proclamation was not in vain; not an expression of rhetorical conceit, but a clear articulation of a claim to space and its maritime dimensions. The king was not claiming his triumph over land in any sense, he specified commerce and seafaring which he claimed were his royal prerogatives. Cut to a century later, we find Shivaji, the Maratha ruler, undertaking an ambitious programme to build a navy to exercise control over commerce and prevent any infringement of his rights by Europeans. In the words of the *Ajnapatra* (a royal edict stating the principles of Maratha polity written by Ramchandra Pant Amatya), the navy was an essential and independent limb of the state for the mastery of the state lay in the hands of 'him who possesses the navy'.[1] But what was the navy expected to accomplish for a Maratha kingdom, whose vitality in the seventeenth century lay in its ability to galvanize aspirants in a war fought on the rugged hills of the Sahyadri, other than confront the intrusions of irksome littoral neighbours like the Sidis of Janjira and the aggression of the English Company whose settlements could be targeted and attacked for petty gain? Or was the investment in the navy by Shivaji a marked shift in the political paradigm of the coast and representative of a new understanding of power and sovereignty over waters?

The question is not easy to answer for we depend on retrospective reflections of historians, some of whom see Shivaji as the great innovator to be credited with every conceivable achievement. On the other side, we have to contend with the weight of European bias that looked at Maratha coastal elements as pirates and predators who flouted conventions of fair trade on the high seas although, in fact, the writ of the coastal chiefs rarely ran beyond the immediate territorial waters of their small domain. Balancing the contrasting registers of representation, this essay intends to examine the nature of political imagination and articulation over water, the high seas and the littoral, exercised by a variety of coastal chiefs who could broadly be subsumed under the category of Maratha, in the sense that they bore loose allegiance to the Maratha power and were deployed by Shivaji and his successors to share power along the coast with other claimants, notably the Sidi and the Europeans.

⚓ ⚓ ⚓

Who Owned the Ocean?

We ask this question specifically in relation to the western Indian littoral which was a key maritime region, dotted with ports and harbours and by extension, overseen by local/regional political interests in collaboration with merchants who were predictably the most significant stakeholders of maintaining peace and stability in and around the ocean. However, the question of ownership, as it developed in Europe, did not seem to have the same resonance in India wherein, littoral states implicitly abided by the freedom of navigation for all in the sea. This was admittedly the case even in Roman law although in fact, it was not practiced; and in the context of Rome's decline, and the growth of commerce in the later Middle Ages, maritime powers exercised control over vast stretches of the sea.[2]

Control assumed the form of claims to sole navigation rights on the ocean, trade routes and to the exclusion of other states over newly discovered lands via the ocean. These claims were contested fiercely with the result that the sea became the site of bitter inter-European rivalries that by default, affected non-Europeans as well. Asian states did not articulate a similar set of claims to hegemony over the high seas but on the other hand were not disinvested in the sea or in its resources that could be taxed. Rulers like the Zamorin of Calicut patronized foreign trade and merchants in a big way. Further north, the Silharas in the Konkan made efforts to create a unified trading region and oversee naval efforts. In fact, historian Sebastian Prange argues that maritime violence was not Europe's contribution to the Indian Ocean, and that political competition was ubiquitous in the ocean leading to naval skirmishes and contestation of claims. He refers, in particular, to states such as the Cholas in peninsular India, to the kingdom of Srivijaya in Southeast Asia, the latter deploying maritime communities (Orang Laut) to coerce shipping to come to its ports and pay taxes, very much like the later (Portuguese overseas State of India) Estado-da-India.[3]

The difference of course lay in scale and also in the fact that Srivijaya did not set out to institute a protection mechanism like the Portuguese cartaz-cafila-armada system that assumed responsibility for protection and control over the high seas. According to Prange, limited editions of this experiment existed in the case of states like Makran in the Gulf of Oman. However, these did not approximate to the kind of political imagination and claim that Europeans assumed over waters; the abiding impression about Asian claims, especially along the Indian littoral, is that these remained localized and confined to designated territorial waters. These claims were contested in the wake of the steady extension of Portuguese maritime power as well as of the Mughal imperial project that experimented with a limited naval initiative as a supplement to their land ambitions.

With the steady expansion of Portuguese control on the western littoral through the cartaz-cafila-armada system, the workings of maritime power were in full display.[4] A series of spectacular naval demonstrations enabled the Portuguese to build a seaborne empire in the form of a string of forts on vital coastal points all along the Indian Ocean, stretching from Sofala and Mozambique in East Africa to Malacca in Southeast Asia, subsuming key ports in India. Backed by a strong naval force, they were able to attack local shipping in the Indian Ocean, to insist on them accepting the Portuguese pass and protection and obliging them to pay customs duties in designated ports and centres. Traders had to buy a cartaz that gave them the sanction to sail and obligated them to touch base at certain ports along the seaborne empire and pay customs duties. Thus, it was not only an insignia of maritime hegemony, but also a device to extract revenues to maintain the Portuguese Estado.

The efficacy of the system was guaranteed by the superior naval power of the Portuguese, who were able to blockade ports and hold them ransom and to provide effective protection against piracy on the high seas. On the other hand, the military violence and aggression resulted in the displacement of merchants, especially Arab merchants, involved in the carrying out trade of spices and of smaller coastal interests, who found their commercial and quasi-political ambitions thwarted. For most merchants, the system represented an additional operating cost, and they tried to bypass it when they could. In Malabar, the assault was especially violent and the consequence was the crystallization of strong maritime aspirations undertaken by merchants with political will.

The case of the Marakkars is an instance in point. They were premier Muslim merchants of Cochin but under pressure, shifted their loyalty to the Zamorin of Calicut and emerged as principal opponents to resist the cartaz system of the Portuguese and in the process establish their own hegemony over specific stretches—the Ceylon-Coromandel segment, the Gulf of Mannar, which was vital to their stakes in the pearl trade. What is noteworthy was how merchants soon doubled up as political agents and galvanized capital and access to fighting fleets, in resisting the Portuguese on their own terms. These ventures were not always effective but they definitely spoke to a conception of sea-power as a resource for commercial hegemony and even for state building, as was the case with the Mamales of Cannanore and their special zone of influence over the Maldives.[5]

According to Pius Malekandethil, the experiment of the Mamales of Cannanore was inspirational and persuaded Kunjali Marakkar, the naval chief of the Zamorin, to conceive of a similar experiment of state building that was predicated upon commercial wealth and control over trading posts in the rim of the ocean.[6] Maritime power was not a peripheral concern. Malekandathil quotes a German document of 1588 which attested to Kunjali Marakkar's influence from Diu to

Cape Comorin.[7] Without overreading this document, one may legitimately argue that the powers in Malabar were resisting Portuguese claims and by extension conceiving of sealanes as vital capillaries of power. Further down south, along the Konkan, the situation was different in that the decision to experiment with maritime power was taken up by the ruling states in the Deccan, which saw coastal hegemony as a valuable addition to their land-based dominance as a means to check the aspirations of Europeans and to extract from overseas commerce benefits, which were tangible.

The conquest of Goa (1511) resulted in the substitution of Bijapur's power along the Konkan by that of the Portuguese, whose cartaz-cafila-armada system we have already had occasion to comment on. The principal rulers of the region—Ahmednagar, Bijapur and subsequently the Mughals—did not immediately put forward a plan to resist the Portuguese and instead relied on local coastal expertise to oversee Haj traffic and to retain some degree of control over trade and commercial resources. The idea of a fleet to protect commercial and religious interests took hold as the rulers of Bijapur approached the Sidis of Janjira to function as admirals and guardians of the seas off the western and northwestern littoral. The Sidis eventually transferred their allegiance to the Mughal emperor.

⚓ ⚓ ⚓

The Mughals and Marathas on the Coast: Naval Experiments

The Mughals were a land empire with virtually no maritime ambitions to speak of. There was no question of imagining a seaborne empire and for the most part, the concerns were to utilize internal waterways optimally for war and trade and to safeguard the arrival of bullion fleets from West Asia and the Haj traffic to Mecca. Thus, the first salt-water navy was assembled by Akbar in the late sixteenth century, after his conquests in Gujarat and Bengal. It provided him with access to the sea; he saw the sea for the first time in 1572 from Cambay and one can only imagine his excitement and understanding of a strange space waiting to be overcome.

His naval programme was designed principally to maintain a fleet for combat in areas where land and water operations had to be combined, for protection of trade and ensuring customs revenues. For the most part, Akbar acknowledged the power of the Portuguese at sea and complied with their requirements as far as applying for cartazes to trade and navigate. The Portuguese Crown sanctioned one cartaz each year to the Mughal Emperor. There were occasional skirmishes caused by acts of petty interference in disputes with rival contenders and European trading companies, but these did not amount to a substantive engagement with naval control. According to K.M. Mathew, Portuguese maritime supremacy was never challenged by the Mughals even under Aurangzeb, who briefly toyed with the idea of maritime power but gave it up when he saw what was involved. Gossip had it that he abandoned the naval project saying that 'to sail over and fight in the ocean was not the thing for the people of Hindustan but only suited to European alertness and boldness.'[8]

By the middle and latter decades of the seventeenth century, however, two other issues had become pressing—the growing perils of piracy on the high seas occasioned by inter-European rivalries, and the growing contestation of claims along the littoral between the Mughals and the Marathas, who under

Shivaji had become a presence to be reckoned with. It was in this context that Aurangzeb entertained the idea of expanding the naval presence of the Mughals through the agency of the Sidis of Janjira who had already established their reputation as seasoned seafarers, offering their services to protect coastal trade and the interests of regional Islamic sultanates like Bijapur. Their base of operations was Janjira, and they held additional strongholds in Daman further north. Their operations involved protection to trade in designated stretches, carrying on their own trade and competing with Europeans on the coast. The Mughal state entered into an agreement with the Sidis giving them the charge of the imperial admiralty, a charge that gave them some benefits in relation to the European companies and that invited the sustained hostility of the Marathas who were interested in securing access to Janjira.[9]

The Maratha naval experiment was directly connected with Shivaji's project of securing comprehensive control over the coast (Konkan) and the desh, i.e. the core area of the Maratha kingdom in the Deccan, distinct from the coast. By 1653, when the first contours of the Maratha Swarajya were delineated, Shivaji had already toured the Konkan and appraised its importance, in terms of its commercial potential. Virtually every European trading company had their settlements in the region (Rajapur and Bombay under the English, Vengurla under the Dutch, and Chaul was already an old Portuguese settlement), while the presence of the Sidi in Janjira threatened Maratha aspirations. Shivaji lost no time in conquering key points and entering into a collaboration with chieftains like the Desai of Sawantwadi whose allegiance vacillated between the Bijapur state and the Maratha ruler and who tried to leverage with the Portuguese power as well. Coastal chiefs like the Desai (also called the Kudal) of Sawantwadi built up small fleets and embarked on coastal expansion and raids against the Portuguese, but whether these were informed by a new conception of maritime power is hard to say. The focus was territorial gain along the coast and extraction of revenues from trade.[10]

What was Shivaji's rationale in developing a naval agenda? What do the various encounters between the Sidi and Shivaji, between coastal chiefs like the ruler of Sawantwadi and the Portuguese tell us about actual conditions at sea, off the coast and about their ideas of sovereign control over the spaces? According to Philip MacDougall, the creation of a Maratha fleet was largely to support land-based operations and to enforce the right to issue passes to traders who navigated a designated stretch. In his view, the navy was used for the exclusive purpose of organizing power over the Konkan, a right that was also outsourced to local chiefs.[11] For the Europeans, the operations of the Maratha coastal elements were akin to acts of piracy and did not correspond to their idea of protection over what was 'a free sea'—free, of course, for them to oversee. Shivaji's naval agenda did not technically question this right and for all practical purposes, was limited to the protection of trade and merchants and to the safeguarding of his immediate kingdom, the security of which entailed a measure of control over the waters. This may well have been a response to the naval domination of the Europeans on the coast, which revealed to the local powers, including Shivaji, the inadequacy of their own naval strength.

Consequently Shivaji built up a fleet of ghurabs and galbats, that were small in comparison to the European ships but equipped with light canon and well suited to operations along narrow inlets and creeks. We also find decisive moments of action and as a brown-water coastal force, Shivaji's navy was significant in developing a clear statement of marking out specific zones of interest and turning them over to designated chiefs like the Angres, who as privateers engaged with naval action more forcefully. However, at no stage did Shivaji or his client, Kanhoji Angre or the Desai/Kudal of Sawantwadi ever conceptualize rights to a broader maritime realm, something that was in stark contrast to the agenda of the Europeans, especially the English East India Company (EEIC) that took over the business of policing the seas and of countering any competition in this domain. Consequently, the coastal ambitions of local chiefs were dismissed by the English as acts of predation and piracy and their politics was seen as inimical to the interests of free and trade. Such a characterization was not entirely accurate nor does it reflect the realities of transitional politics along the littoral, wherein local interests began to seriously consider limited maritime jurisdiction as an integral part of their customary rights that the British trampled upon—when they insisted for example, that no power barring them could maintain a navy.[12]

⚓⚓⚓

The Rise of Kanhoji Angre and the Newly Emerging Coastal Dispensation in the Konkan

Maratha presence in the Konkan in the eighteenth century was performed principally through Kanhoji Angre who was made Sarkhel (admiral) of the Maratha force in 1698. One of his first acts seems to have been to extend the jurisdiction of his pass or dastak to maritime merchants operating in the

Konkan.[13] The English were initially exempt from this, but by the first decade of the eighteenth century as Kanhoji expanded his influence, it was evident that he could not be ignored. In fact, Kanhoji was able to challenge the existing coastal balance and fought against the Portuguese, the English and stepped up the pressure to legitimize his position and passes. According to historians like Sen, Kanhoji Angre radically altered the balance and staked his claim to sovereignty over the seas, while modern scholars like Derek Elliott suggest that Kanhoji was really an ambitious privateer working for specific rulers who saw the littoral as an important sphere of influence that could not be ignored. It was also a case of sovereign rights, for Kanhoji insisted that dastaks or passes issued by him had to be accepted by private traders and that any exemption was only applicable to the EEIC, a position that was akin to that held by rulers like Mir Qasim in Bengal. S.N. Sen, for example, speaks of his influence in the Arabian Sea and how he insisted that country boats freighted by the English were obliged to take his passes. Sen quotes one of Kanhoji's messages that ran thus:

> The Savajees had done many services for the English that never kept their word with him; they had peace with the Portuguezc and every one of their portes free to them; was known they had hold out warr with the Mogull forty years, lived now by their sword and would seize what boates or other vessels belonging either to the Mogulls vessells from any of his forts or Mallabarr, excepting such as had Conjee Angras passports; the English being at liberty acting as they please.[14]

The first half of the eighteenth century witnessed an escalation of violence in the coast with the English in Bombay. The Angres in Kolaba and smaller powers like the Malvans and the ruler of

Sawantwadi engaged in constant skirmishes in the wake of raids on shipping and on jurisdiction issues. Most of the disputes were about who was provisioning whom, who was carrying goods to Bombay without heeding pass obligations, and involved local merchants who tried to reduce their own operating costs and bypassed existing restrictions. Occasionally we find an articulation of specific rights on the part of Kanhoji Angre that demonstrate a perceptible shift in what he saw as his sovereign claims which he phrased in a vocabulary of customary sanction. What is striking about this is how it set a template for others to follow; the later lives of coastal rulers and communities, dispossessed maritime groups in the latter decades of the century testify to this. Most of them worked for local bosses, who were part of a complex localized political economy involving small markets in captured and confiscated goods and who had specific commercial interests albeit small and dispersed.

Kanhoji, like many of his counterparts, was an autonomous coastal chief over a recognized territory. His own realm lay 'between the sea and the western ghats, extending from Bombay harbour to Vingorla, excluding the Seedee's territory, a tract, roughly speaking about two hundred and forty miles in length by forty miles in breadth.'[15] As the recognized chief of a population of hardy seamen, Kanhoji used his position to extend his ambit of protection along the littoral, by issuing passes to merchants, extracting protection money and carrying on his operations against the Sidi in the capacity of a privateer working for the Maratha power. All other chiefs and communities were part of an emerging structure of nested rights that crystallized during periods of conflict and saw jurisdiction over sealanes as a means of exercising their power. By the eighteenth century, the littoral was an important site of control and contestation resulting in the formation of complex rights and practices pursued by chiefs, their subjects and the dispossessed seafaring communities that faced the brunt of the aggression of the English East India Company and its force the Bombay Marine.

The Anglo–Angre confrontation was but one strand in the overall coastal politics of the Konkan in the eighteenth century. It was in part, a fallout of the English Company's resolve to exercise total maritime control over the littoral and the seas (there was no distinction), to eliminate all contenders and insist on the sacro-sanctity and legitimacy of the English pass and to step up the rhetoric of piracy. In fact, the altercations revealed the workings of a complex political economy along the littoral, wherein contested claims over passes and despatch of goods to certain markets indexed a dense web of linkages between local traders, rulers and coastal communities. In 1754, for example, the Bombay Council met to deliberate on the case of the *Vithal Pasha*, a shybar craft (derived from Shahibar, a Mughal term for a swift sailing ship) belonging to the Maratha Governor of Bassein, whose cargo of sandalwood purchased at Onore, was intercepted because of the pass it carried.[16] The pass was issued by the Malvan chief—considered to be an enemy of the English—on the suspicion that the cargo was in all probability stolen from a Bombay trader during a piratical attack.

This was indicative of a nexus between merchants, illicit markets and coastal chiefs (in this case Vithal Rao of Bassein) who organized attacks against shipping that did not carry the right pass and recruited seamen (tindals) in his service.[17] Tulaji Angre and the Desai of Sawantwadi were both chastized for attacking coastal trade and accused of perfidy for failing to abide by their commitments.[18] The anti-piracy discourse was stepped up by the EEIC, which claimed exclusive rights to issue passes and provide protection to ensure free and fair trade. This did not, in the long run, produce a benign and passive littoral. Piracy or resistance to the new dispensation continued to persist right through the eighteenth and the first quarter of the nineteenth century. What is also to be noted here is how—despite shifts in the company's official representation of pirates and predation, moving away from the Malabari and Maratha pirates of the Konkan to the Cooley rovers of the Cutch and Kathiawad littoral (referred to by the English Company as the northward)—there was an implicit acknowledgement of a residual Maratha presence along the entire stretch of the littoral, one facet of which was deployment of maritime violence as a resource for state building. The rajas of Porbandar and Bhavnagar and the Nawab of Junagadh are instances in point, where a specifically maritime policy, involving the use of coastal seafaring groups to safeguard designated littoral stretches by organizing raids, was systematically pursued. Also, Maratha presence on the coast was by no means vague or indecisive—British reports referred to the demands and pressures the Marathas kept up on coastal rulers of Kathiawad and how these gave the politics of piracy a distinct twist.

⚓ ⚓ ⚓

The Political Imagination of Piracy: The Case of the Northward

With successful campaigns by the English, against Angre, Sawantwadi and the Malvans, the southern segment of the western littoral was pacified, with merchants of the region accepting English passes and colours. What the impact was on ordinary seafarers, who had offered their services to coastal chiefs and resisted English controls, is difficult to gauge, and it is likely that some of them moved up the coast to serve the rulers of their chieftains, in Cutch and Kathiawad. One may in this connection speculate about the peopling of Piram Island that seemed to house Kolis and men of Indo-Portuguese extraction, who presumably constituted part of the dispossessed coastal society. This coincided with the formation of new states among the Kathiawad and Cutch littoral and mainland.

With the erosion of Mughal authority and the Mulkgiri campaigns for revenue by the Marathas, regional chiefs reimagined their politics to subsume rights over the coast enforced by small fleets and agreements with coastal groups. Thus, in the case of Junagadh, Porbandar and Navnagar, territorial expansion was supplemented with commercial aspirations, as a result of which the maritime factor was always present as a silent referent. Even if they did not explicitly articulate maritime claims, they took part in informal arrangements that ensured them a proportion of the profits that accrued from limited privateering, from organized voyages to attack ships that carried foreign colours.[19] The Raja of Porbandar was a merchant and privateer and was supposed to have investments in an infantry and in sea raids. We also hear of merchants sponsoring raids for debt collection.

The exception to this was the Okhamandal Confederacy that was identified in European documentation as a cluster of pirate states inhabited by coastal communities referred to as Kolis and Sangarians who serviced the three principal chieftains of Armara, Poisitra and Beyt Dwarka. The three chieftains were of Rajput extraction but maintained their authority by a complex interlocking system of relations with the Waghers, the original inhabitants of the region and with rulers in Cutch and Kathiawad. Located in the western-most extremity of the Kathiawadi peninsula, the Okhamandal Confederacy was formed by an inlet of the sea and assumed a distinct maritime space. With a rugged coast abounding in small creeks, it afforded refuge and access to small crafts operated by seafarers especially those on the run.

Historically, the region had undergone successive waves of Rajput settlement, which was predicated on accommodation with local groups. The ruling lineages were Rathod, who along with the local subgroups of Wadhela and Wagher, ruled over the principalities of Dwarka, Aramra and Positra. For the most part, the revenue base was that of taxes on pilgrimage, sponsoring short piratical cruises, harbouring those who were engaged in sea raiding, and extracting a limited amount of protection money. What is noteworthy is how the space afforded asylum for waves of dispossessed groups who were recruited as labour for seafaring trips engaged in trade or raids. The chiefs had a special relationship with the temple at Dwarka, which enjoyed a certain proportion of the revenues gained in trade and protection, leading Company officials to suggest that piracy in India had the sanction of religion, thus reinforcing the binary of barbaric Asian predation and rational European privateering and protection.

This is not to suggest that the Okhamandal chiefs entertained an expansive conception of rights at sea or of shipwrecks and borders but merely to make the point that raids and predation were part of a local political economy of claims, small markets and exchanges.[20] This was, as Moloo Manik of Dwarka put it, their 'employment', which the Honourable Company

(EEIC) did not want them to pursue.[21] In fact, in subsequent engagements with the Company representatives, the chiefs of the Okhamandal Confederacy pointed to piracy as their livelihood and custom, and even insisted on being allowed to issue passes or cauls over limited stretches that stood for a notion of their sovereign power at sea.

Virtually all stakeholders in the Okhamandal Confederacy were dependent on proceeds from petty trade, predatory attacks and pilgrimage—all of which was organized around the principle of 'bhayad' or brotherhood, wherein, every petty chief had specific rights. Some EEIC officials like Alexander Walker, Resident of Baroda, entrusted with the responsibility of contending with piracy, recognized that the phenomenon of predation was actually an integral part of nested rights in the region, where violence had become part of a commercialized economy, enabling merchant and mariner, pirate and coastal boss, to operate in tandem. The Confederacy drew on its traditional understanding of sanction and survival, custom and coercion. As it happened the resistance of the Okhamandal chiefs petered out after decades of resistance and by 1810, the EEIC pushed its operations further north against the state of Cutch and the pirates they harboured.

The case of Cutch, and the piratical attacks that the state supported from 1810 onwards, point to yet another moment in and aspect of maritime violence in the region that cannot be buttonholed as simply lawlessness, or privateering or calculated resistance against the Company's ideology of maritime domination. While it is generally true that conditions of competition occasioned by pass politics and the systematic use of maritime violence as a tool of state building, had brought the sea into a dynamic conversation with politics of the hinterland via the littoral, it would not be appropriate to see this new understanding of the sea as an arena of power and sovereignty.

The littoral was important for coastal states and for communities that used it as a mobile corridor for their operations. They formed networks of information and sociability and relied on social connections for protection of their families when they went away on sea operations. We also find individual acts of spontaneous resistance when someone took to the sea, flouting both the restrictions imposed by the EEIC (the law of the sea as they defined it), as well as by their immediate bosses who always took the loot and left the pirate to take the blame. For these actors, the sea was clearly a space they could feel free in and where their skills as navigators and seamen came to good use.

We are fortunate in having some of the pirate depositions on the basis of which we can decode the complex world of seafarers caught between the devil and the deep sea. On the one hand, there were local political chiefs—the Raja of Cutch and the senior official of the port centre Mandavie—who utilized their services to attack English and any shipping that the English protected; on the other hand, was the EEIC determined to clean up the littoral seas and eradicate piracy with its own military solution. Several pirates turned approvers and helped the EEIC's Marine officials to track down and round up their former colleagues in haunts and creeks.[22]

The pirate depositions make for interesting reading as they index the personal experiences of men who lived off the sea and reacted to economic and political strains. They were expert navigators and were known to offer their services as steersmen to Europeans and local merchants, and chafed at the restrictions that the pass system involved. They doubled up as small-time privateers and worked for men like Fateh Muhammad of Cutch. Their disappointment with the latter for not standing up for their interests led them to flout all conventions and strike out against shipping at sea. What was striking was their access to information on shipping schedules and their ability to muster up motley crew members and embark on spontaneous raids whose proceeds ended up in grey markets.

⚓ ⚓ ⚓

Concluding Impressions

What can we make of these instances as far as the political imagination of Indian rulers with regards to the sea and its waters along the littoral were concerned? We have tracked in course of this brief excursus, the responses of coastal society to European aggression that came from the sea and was oriented towards its control. That the Europeans entertained an expansive and expansionist understanding of maritime dominion—buttressed by a powerful navy that provided protection to merchant shipping and defined the law of the sea by taking on the lawless pirate—was certainly evident in the systematic way they set about organizing a pass and convoy system in the Indian Ocean, which technically was policed and patrolled by them exclusively. It was not as though the ocean was known to them intimately; as Anirudh Deshpande has observed, it was only in the nineteenth century that systematic surveys were carried out and that the marine force became effective thanks to steam power.[23] But at no stage was the EEIC that replaced the Portuguese, prepared to relinquish rights to police the sea, control and contain piratical attacks, and thereby exercise the authority to issue passes that indigenous merchants were obligated to accept.

As early as 1779, the Court of Directors in London issued instructions to systematize surveys and the issuing of passes to configure the right order in the ocean. It was not a piecemeal approach but an application of the larger right to police the ocean which lay in their claimed realm of sovereign right and responsibility. This was not the case with the coastal states of India—most of them were used to customary rights over shipwrecks off the coast, some extracted duties on cargo and ships if they happened to stray into their ports. However, it would not be correct to argue that their responses remained static and unchanging. In fact, they adjusted to changing situations, as a result of which coastal society found itself working amidst constraints and challenges, and engaging with the idea of rights to the sea and its resources.

Some among the coastal states took greater initiative than others, examples being Shivaji, Kunjali Marakkar and Kanhoji Angre. There were also seafaring communities that capitalized on the changing conditions to offer their services as labour to aspiring chieftains or to engage in seasonal raids. All this meant that the very designation of piracy was complex and ambiguous in the period of our study, when competing policies for passes, inadequate security and the competing politics of convoys and protection made maritime violence a recurrent feature of littoral society and subsequently, gave the necessary rationale for the formation and consolidation of the Indian Navy.

Notes

1 See pp. 81-105, 207-21 in Parts 1-3 of Vol. 8, in S.V. Puntambekar, 'The Ajnapatra or Royal Edict, Relating to the principles of Maratha State polity', *Journal of Indian History*, 1929.

2 See pp. 252-69, 253, in Edward Gordon, 'Grotius and the freedom of the seas in the seventeenth century', *Williamette Journal of International Law and Dispute Resolution*, Vol. 16, No. 2, 2008.

3 See pp. 9-33, in Sebastian Prange, 'The Contested Sea: Regimes of Violence in the Pre-Modern Indian Ocean', *Journal of Early Modern History*, Vol. 17, No. 1, 2013.

4 See pp. 30-31, 40-42, in M.N.Pearson, *Merchants and Rulers in Gujarat: The Response to the Portuguese in the Sixteenth Century*, University of California Press, 2020.

5 Genevieve Bouchoin, *Regent of the sea: Cannanore's response to Portuguese expansion, 1507-1528*, transl., Louise Shacklin, Oxford University Press, 1988.

6 See pp. 466-90, in Pius Malekandathil, 'From merchant capitalists to corsairs, the response of the Muslim merchants of Malabar to the Portuguese commercial expansion (1498-1600)', *Proceedings of the Indian History Congress*, Vol. 64, 2003.

7 Ibid., p. 478.

8 K.M. Mathew, *History of the Portuguese navigation in India 1497-1600*, Mittal Publications, 1988.

9 See pp.1-4, Dolly Purohit, 'Relation between Marathas and the Sidis of Janjira in the seventeenth century', *Journal of Research in Humanities and Social Sciences*, Vol. 9, No. 7, 2021.

10 S.K. Mhamai, *The Sawants of Wadi and the Portuguese*, Concept Publishing House, 2018.

11 Philip MacDougall, *Naval resistance to Britain's growing power in India, 1600-1800: The Saffron Banner and the Tiger of Mysore*, The Boydell Press, 2014.

12 See p. 440, in *Gazetteer of the Bombay Presidency: Ratnagiri and Savantvadi*, Vol. X, Government Central Press, 1880.

13 Elliott, 'Pirates, Polities and Companies', 2010.

14 See p. 9, in Sen, *Early Career of Kanhoji Angria*, 1941.

15 See p. 83, in Biddulph, *The Pirates of Malabar*, 1907.

16 See pp. 3, 299, in Apte, *A History of the Maratha Navy*, 1973.

17 See p. 44, in Lakshmi Subramanian, *The Sovereign and the Pirate: Ordering Maritime Subjects in India's Western Littoral*, Oxford University Press, 2016.

18 Ibid., p. 43.

19 With regard to their maritime claims, see: ibid. p. 56.

20 Ibid., pp. 49-50.

21 Ibid., p. 115.

22 Ibid., for details see pp. 161-83.

23 See pp. 284-85, 287, in Anirudh Deshpande, 'The Bombay Marine Aspects of Maritime history', in *Studies in History*, Vol. 11, No. 2, 1995.

3

The Naval Setup of the Marathas

Amarendra Kumar

Introduction

Navies are means of projecting power on and along navigable waterways, whether these be lakes, rivers, seas or oceans. States must, therefore, have outlets to seas and oceans, and access to navigable rivers and lakes, if they need to project sovereign power through the navy. States with coastal boundaries or inland waterways have used naval power in state-building or other commercial and economic enterprises since the ancient period. The nature and extent of their maritime apparatus has corresponded to the geographical milieu and declared objectives. The basics have stayed the same, even during the age of sail and geographical discoveries. These maritime explorations usually meant long-duration oceanic voyages and the rigours of such journeys were harsh.

These factors facilitated the advancement of ship design and construction. The compulsions of waging wars on the high seas also initiated significant advances in ship-rigging, which became more complex. The need to accommodate heavier guns onboard, led to further vital changes in ship design.[1] There is a consensus among naval historians that advantages, such as the weather gauge for instance, also facilitated the efforts of seafaring states such as the Portuguese in suppressing the challenges they faced in the Indian Ocean Region (IOR) from the likes of the Zamorin of Calicut, etc.[2]

The Zamorin of Calicut was primarily a ruler whose territorial possessions included a stretch of coast in the Malabar region of India, known for its thriving overseas trade. He maintained a naval fleet to fight against potential enemies, including pirates, and exercised his authority in the coastal vicinity. His fleet frequently challenged the Portuguese in the sixteenth century and kept them at bay. Before Zamorin, the Chola rulers had successfully projected their naval prowess. Crossing the Bay of Bengal region, they had established their politico-military authority over the Southeast Asian states in the eleventh century. They also encouraged maritime trade and commerce through trade missions.[3] The Mauryan rulers, who preceded the Chola kings, also maintained a state-owned navy.[4] Unlike the Chola and Zamorin navies that navigated the seas, the Mauryan Empire, being in a landlocked region, plied its vessels only in rivers and lakes.

India's naval and maritime traditions can be traced back to the pre-Vedic period. The excavation of a tidal dockyard at Lothal in Gujarat confirms the Indus Valley people's knowledge of navigation at sea. Further, the depiction of ships bearing two masts on the lead coins issued by the Satvahana rulers, also affirm their engagement in seafaring activities. The sculptures and paintings of the Buddha's era and the Jataka tales also acquaint us with the shipbuilding skills of the Gupta period.

Geographical factors exerted a decisive influence upon the temperament of maritime interactions in the past. At the same time, the disposition of any naval setup also depends upon the objectives the state wishes to achieve through its navy. As far as the Marathas are concerned, the prime aim of Shivaji behind the creation of the Maratha Swarajya, was to rid the country of the control of the Mughals by bringing together the people of the Maratha race. His reign is marked by continual land-based war against the Mughals, Bijapur, Golconda and a few recalcitrant Maratha chiefs affiliated with these powers. His warfare involved guerrilla tactics, encompassing the use of terrain to his advantage since his resources were fewer than those of his enemies. His military success over his adversaries enabled him to establish an independent rule sometime around 1657.[5] Incidentally, we also get a confirmative reference to the inauguration of the Maratha naval enterprise under his leadership in 1659.[6] As a result, the immediate query arising in our mind relates to Shivaji's urgency to commence building a maritime set-up, when he should have been striving hard to consolidate his land conquests.

⚓ ⚓ ⚓

Why Did Shivaji Want a Navy?

The question of 'why a navy' becomes pertinent for many reasons. For example, the rivers from Konkan that flowed through the Swarajya, were un-navigable owing to their steep gradients. This ruled out any economic or strategic usage of these rivers in the interest of the Swarajya, prima facie. Furthermore, only an insignificant stretch of the coastline was under his control when Shivaji was fighting wars to establish his Maratha Swarajya. Was the navy a prerequisite to achieving this goal? If not, why would he need a navy? Where would his navy operate? What would be its objective? Was it the Mughal experiment that he wanted to emulate, or did he anticipate a more significant challenge in European presence along the coast?

It ought to be noted that Akbar had already commissioned the Mughal flotilla and followed it up with the conquest of Gujarat and Bengal, allowing him to use the sea for economic and religious purposes. During the Mughal conquest of Bengal, the Mughal Navy played an integral role in transporting troops, provisions and munitions through navigable rivers on war boats.[7] Jahangir also used the Mughal flotilla, the 'nawwara', in the state-building exercise.[8] Aurangzeb tried to follow it up with his naval endeavour to conquer Kamrup (Assam), albeit with mixed results.

In his fight against Shivaji, Aurangzeb allied with the Sidi of Janjira. The Sidi, it may be recollected, were adventure seekers with a workable flotilla. The seat of Sidi power was an island off the Konkan coast on which the impregnable sea fortress called Janjira was located. In the past, the Sidi owed allegiance to the Nizam Shahis and to the Adil Shah of Bijapur. In return for these services—mostly related to convoying Muslim pilgrims to West Asia by sea route—the Sidi chief enjoyed control over the coastal territory opposite Janjira fort, as his fief. The so-called fief was crucial for the survival of the Sidi clan, as Janjira fort was simply a military base that could not be self-sufficient. Observing that Shivaji was a common enemy of the Mughals and the Sidi of Janjira, and in the Maratha-Sidi wars the Sidi chief had been making depredatory attacks on the Maratha coast in the Thal area, Aurangzeb offered him the post of Mughal admiral on the west coast, thus ensuring the presence of the 'Mughal fleet' in the Arabian Sea.

Aurangzeb's action, thus, was also driven by the Maratha Chhatrapati's naval endeavours. He wanted to simultaneously engage Shivaji on two war fronts of different natures and thus get the better of him in the Mughal-Maratha war. By then, the Maratha Navy had emphatically underlined its purpose in the Konkan waters. In 1665, with a fleet of over sixty assorted vessels, the Maratha Navy sailed unhindered through the sea lanes of Goa—the headquarters of the Portuguese Estado-da-India—in full view of its armada.[9] The Maratha troops descended from the fleet at Basrur, carried out an amphibious assault on the local Nayaka territory, and returned with booty. Indeed, this feat of the Maratha Navy was not ordinary. By registering a fearless presence in the Arabian Sea, it had conveyed a strong message to the Europeans. But the question is whether Shivaji really wanted to warn the Europeans to keep away from Maratha 'territorial waters'. Was the Maratha leader interested in creating a maritime empire like the Europeans, or did he want to use the navy for the defences of his Swarajya? Could it be possible that the Maratha flotilla was intended for state-building exercises like the Mughals? Let us understand Shivaji's motives from a critical discussion of the Maratha naval enterprise, its organization and its activities.

⚓ ⚓ ⚓

Inauguration and Consolidation

The Maratha naval beginnings under Shivaji were not sudden. Instead, they appear to be a well-considered project. The conquest of Kalyan and Bhiwandi from the Mughals in 1657, facilitated this project.[10] The tidal backwaters, away from the open sea, could be profitably utilized as a shipbuilding yard. A Portuguese document of 1659 refers to Maratha shipbuilding in Kalyan-Bhiwandi docks.[11] Maratha ships were launched from Durgadi creek, which was fortified by Shivaji. The initial phase of the Maratha naval project concurred with the period of Mughal political unrest, as north India was embroiled in the bloody war of succession initiated by Aurangzeb, the incumbent Mughal Viceroy of Deccan. Shivaji took advantage of the Mughal absence by forcing a war on Adil Shah of Bijapur. He subsequently conquered the Tal-Konkan or the southern part of the Konkan. As a result, the Konkan littoral was brought under the ambit of the Swarajya. This region gradually developed as the core area from where the Maratha Navy operated and exercised the state's power.

The contemporary Maratha policy document, the *Ajnapatra* of Ramchandra Pant Amatya, considered the navy an independent limb of the state, which must be nurtured by making all efforts.[12] The nineteenth-century EEIC administrator James Grant Duff, who penned down the first comprehensive history of the Marathas, appreciated Shivaji's occupation of strategic locations along the coast and headlands and his purposeful use of them for naval purposes.[13] Shivaji also planned marine island bases in the Arabian Sea, such as at Sindhudurg and Padmadurg.

Krishnaji Anant Sabhasad, the contemporary biographer of Chhatrapati Shivaji, highlights the importance of marine forts and war vessels for, 'saddling the sea'.[14] He further informs us that the Maratha naval ships controlled the sea as they successfully fought against the navies of twenty-seven nations and brought enormous wealth.[15] The accounts of Khafi Khan, a contemporary Mughal chronicler, also confirm that 'Shivaji had secured several islands ... he has also built many forts in those parts'.[16]

⚓ ⚓ ⚓

Shipbuilding and Naval Strength

Ships of various shapes and sizes were constructed at different shipbuilding centres. The Malvan coast was one such area that had a dockyard. The proximity of the area from the Goa, attracted Portuguese shipwrights, including renegades.[17] In the absence of conclusive evidence, however, it isn't easy to assess the extent of influence of European techniques on the design of the Maratha ships. Some interactions must have taken place. The documentary evidence and nomenclature of Maratha ships inform us about vessels varying in shape, size and functionality constituting the Maratha fleet. They ranged from the small, coastal fishing ships called the hodi, to the bigger sailing ships called the ghurab, which had two masts.

Dhabu, in his book on the history of the Angre family, gives a list of fifty-two types of Maratha ships of various sizes and displacement capacities.[18] The ghurab and pal were the biggest naval ships in the Maratha inventory. While the ghurab mostly had two masts, the pal had three, with a gun-port on the broadside. Robert Orme noted that the Maratha ghurabs were ships of 150-300 tonnage, fitted with two or three masts. The ghurabs displaced little water, and had prows projecting like that of Mediterranean galley, covered with a strong deck. On the main deck, under the forecastle, were mounted two pieces of cannon (nine or twelve-pounders), pointing forward through the portholes cut in the bulkhead, and fired over the prow; the cannon on the broadside ranged from six to nine-pounders.[19]

Khafi Khan puts it on record that Shivaji had built a new fleet through which he had secured coastal areas.[20] The gradual expansion of the naval establishment of the Marathas has been well-endorsed in contemporary European communications. In 1662, the Portuguese governor of Goa wrote that the Marathas had requested him to allow five warships ('sanguiceis') and one 'pataxo' interned in the Karanja creek to go out to the sea.[21] By 1670, the EEIC estimated that the Maratha admiral (the letter mentions one Ventaji Sarungee [perhaps Darya Sarang]) commanded an assorted fleet of 160 vessels.[22] Another correspondence of the EEIC informs that in 1672, six small boats, recently constructed at the Kalyan-Bhiwandi dockyard, were ready to be used by the Marathas.[23] By 1677, the Portuguese Captain of Chaul claimed to have spotted ten Maratha galbats and thirteen other ships at Nagaon.[24] Such Maratha shipbuilding activities on a large scale were possible because of the presence of teak forests in the vicinity of the coast. It seems probable that at its peak under Shivaji, the Maratha fleet must have consisted of over 400 ships. Elaborating upon the naval administration under Chattrapati Shivaji, the *Sabhasad Bakhar* informs us that the Maratha flotilla was organized under two naval subas (districts), each consisting of 200 ships.[25]

The only contemporary attempt to make a rough estimate of the Maratha fleet under Shivaji, was by an EEIC official, who noted that a Maratha Admiral, Ventji Sarungee, had 160 'small vessels' under his command.[26] Because the Maratha fleet was organized in two districts, each under the command of an admiral, the EEIC estimate comes to 320, which is quite close to the number projected by the *Sabhasad Bakhar*. That many of the vessels were of smaller, could be ascertained from the fact that the construction of bigger ships with two or three masts required time and quality timber. Shivaji was preoccupied with a terminal war with the Sidi of Janjira, so the Marathas needed a steady supply of fighting ships.

We may form a rough estimate of the ships required from the perusal of a contemporary EEIC document of 1672, which noted that Shivaji lost fifty war boats in his naval engagement against the Sidi of Janjira.[27] Therefore, as detailed in the *Shivrajniti*, the Maratha naval policy recommended that medium-sized rowing vessels be constructed for the fleet.[28] Unlike a sailing ship, the rowing vessel was easy to manoeuvre in the coastal vicinity, as it was independent of the vagaries of wind. Moreover, because of tides, the water depth also varied near the coast, exposing the bigger ships to navigational dangers posed by the shallow water and submerged rocks or sand bars. Above all, the logic of economics prevailed since the cost of construction and equipping of specialized war vessels like the galbats and ghurabs was enormous. In the case of these vessels during action, it severely compromised the strength of the flotilla as it was difficult to get an immediate replacement.

⚓ ⚓ ⚓

Naval Objectives and Administration

The *Shivrajniti* asserts that it should be a continuous endeavour of the Maratha King to develop and reinforce the navy as an independent component of the state apparatus. We have noted above that the Maratha Navy was organized under two naval districts, each under an admiral. It seems that for administrative convenience and operational efficacy, the fleet was grouped in separate (fighting) units, each containing five ghurabs and fifteen galbats. Each unit was placed under a governor or sar-subha.[29] During the reign of Shivaji, we come across the names of Darya Sarang, Mainak Bhandari and Daulat Khan as admirals of the fleet. Daulat Khan was instrumental in the Anglo–Maratha naval contestation, for the capture of the Khanderi rock.[30] He seems to have continued under Sambhaji. The name of Kanhoji Angre emerges after the demise of Sambhaji, when a large portion of the Konkan coast was overrun by the Mughals and its control transferred to the Sidi of Janjira.

The Marathas took great care to protect and maintain their fleet strength. A policy statement clearly states that during the monsoon season, when sea navigation could not be permitted owing to the ferocity of winds and tides, ships were to be overhauled at safer coastal locations that were inaccessible to enemies. Such a location could, for instance, be a creek that was well defended by a fort at its mouth. Dockyard facilities were duly made available in select Maratha marine forts like Vijaydurg, which were developed and expanded by Kanhoji Angre. Even here, the emphasis was on 'not keeping the vessels at one place' for overhauling.

At night, the troops were tasked with patrolling both creek and land.[31] It is important to remember that one commonly used strategy to harm the enemy fleet, without engaging in direct naval combat, was to covertly destroy it by setting it ablaze. The security measures put in place, could have ensured the safety of the vessels against fire. Moreover, underwater defensive structures have also come to light during marine archaeological explorations.[32]

The role of the Maratha Navy was carved out, particularly in military and economic terms.[33] It ranged from enhancing territorial integrity through coastal security, to projecting military power along the littoral. It was also intended to protect and foster economic prosperity by protecting sea trade. The Maratha Navy also aided in creating a distinct identity for the Maratha Swarajya, since it aimed to project maritime sovereignty by contesting the navigational claims of Europeans and other regional powers in the Arabian Sea, off the Konkan coast.

Shivaji had conquered some flourishing ports in the Konkan region.[34] Their port taxes contributed handsomely to the Maratha Swarajya's coffers. In addition, the state participated in overseas trade and established monopoly on certain commodities. Salt was one such item monopolized by the Maratha state. We find a reference to Shivaji's 'salt fleet' in EEIC records.[35] Some localities known for salt manufacture were Pen, Panvel, Uran and Karanja.[36] The Maratha state regularly participated in overseas trading ventures.[37] One particular piece of evidence regarding its participation in overseas trade comes from the correspondence of an EEIC official in 1662, who noted that at Jaitapur port, Shivaji had fitted out 'two vessels of considerable burden laden with rice' which he intended to trade with Mocha.[38] The Maratha Swarajya was also aware of the rules of jetsam as it could competently negotiate with the other parties on this.[39] It isn't improbable that the Maratha Navy may have also thought of, or even provided, security by organizing convoys for ships that bought Maratha navigational passes. For this, the state needed specialized, well-equipped vessels with armed men on board.

To further control and regulate shipping in the Konkan waters, Shivaji thus inaugurated two types of Maratha navigational passes—dastak and caul.[40] Merchant ships operating in Maratha waters were required to obtain these navigational passes, which were inspected by the Maratha coastal police. If a vessel of any nationality was found without a valid Maratha pass during inspection, it was not permitted to proceed. Maratha vessels escorted it to the nearest port.[41] There, the seized vessel was made to pay a fine for its release. It should be noted that the Maratha navigational passes continuously caused frustration for European and Mughal shipping. The Marathas' insistence on enforcing their passes was primarily driven by their desire to assert sovereign authority in the Konkan waters.

It may be recalled that following the example of Portuguese cartaz, every European company in the seventeenth century issued its own navigational pass. The company ships, therefore, refused to accept Maratha passes, leading to naval confrontations between the Europeans and the Marathas along the Konkan coast. Shivaji prudently chose to avoid unnecessary conflicts in maritime affairs, recognizing that the Europeans could significantly contribute towards strengthening his naval capabilities. While the Portuguese assisted him in constructing and equipping his early ships, nearly all European powers regularly supplied the Marathas with small guns for maritime usage. Contemporary documents are replete with evidence of sale of European firearms to the Marathas.[42] Shivaji used his navy as a diplomatic and bargaining tool vis-à-vis the Europeans, to further the interests of the Maratha Swarajya. Consequently, his naval actions against the Europeans were neither colossal nor prolonged, as such actions would have adversely impacted the economic and military prospects of the Swarajya. This policy sharply contrasted with the approach taken by the Marathas against the Sidi of Janjira, which was ultimately destructive.

⚓⚓⚓

Manning and Maintaining the Navy

It was recommended that the navy be well-equipped with brave and efficient fighters, as well as guns, short guns, matchlocks, ammunition, grenades and other materials for naval use.[43] Was there any specific policy of crew recruitment followed by Shivaji? From the perusal of available documents, it is likely that Shivaji preferred to recruit men belonging to coastal communities who explored and made use of sea resources for their livelihood. Among the Hindu castes, were the Bhandari, Son-Koli, Bhoi and Gabit. Among the Muslims, there were the Daldi, the Kharvi, the Bhadela and Wagher.[44] Most of them ventured or made use of the sea for livelihood, etc. For example, the Koli, or the community of fishermen, had for generations known the sea, the seabed, and the sea's behaviour under any given circumstances. They would prove better navigators and sailors because their knowledge of the sea winds and currents could be utilized to adjust the sails of Maratha ships and steer them away from any danger. They were part of the Maratha expeditionary force, which attempted to capture Ghodbandar, a coastal foothold near Bombay.[45]

Men of the Bhandari caste, traditionally engaged in toddy tapping, could also be gainfully employed on board Maratha vessels. Adept climbers of palm trees, they were best suited to keeping watch over the naval battlefield by positioning themselves atop the ship's mast. Similarly, the Son-Koli community had traditionally engaged in boat-building activities. They could help fix leakages and carry out immediate repairs in ships during military actions.

We do not have enough documents to shed light on aspects of Maratha naval recruitment, training, crew wages, etc. We have noted above that constraints of time, technology and resources prompted Shivaji to apply the simplest logic by preferring the ablest talent from the coastal community to be the crew members. This way, he could utilize valuable traditional knowledge and expertise, in his nascent naval setup.

Further, we need to remember how the Maratha Navy fought its wars during its formative years. Aspects of Maratha naval combat have been discussed in a separate chapter later in this volume. However, a brief idea will help us understand the nature and function of the crew members.

In the initial period, the small, flat-bottomed Maratha rowing vessels mostly had armed soldiers onboard. Their main task was to board the enemy vessel by climbing ladders they carried with them and then undertake hand-to-hand combat on its deck. Men of the Bhandari community must have formed the core of this fighting group. This can be guessed from the contemporary EEIC document, which mentions that the Bhandari were a 'courageous people' belonging to a 'military caste'.[46] While there were a couple of experts to operate the gun—if there were any guns along the prow—there were a few men whose task was to steer and man the vessel. Just as on land, in their naval engagements too the Marathas followed guerrilla tactics. This not only gave them freedom to choose the point and time of contact (attack), but also kept open the option of a quick escape under duress.

While deciding the point of disengagement, the Marathas ensured that the enemy was thrust into conditions for which the enemy was not adequately prepared. For example, the Marathas often lured the bigger ships of their opponents to the vicinity of the coast, thereby exposing them to conditions such as low wind velocity, shallow waters (preferably with rocks close to the surface), an area or time of known adverse tidal occurrences, etc.—all of which adversely affected manoeuvrability. After disengaging, the Koli men would be put to use as they had the capacity to easily steer the Maratha vessels into the safety of numerous creeks and coves.

Unfortunately, however, we have no information about the different categories of the crew or even their payment under the Marathas. This contrasts sharply with the Mughals, who organized their navy under an official called Mir Bahr. In the *Ain-i-Akbari*, the Mughal court chronicler Abul Fazl provides a detailed list of various categories of crew members, their duties as well as their allowances.[47] Similar practices must have prevailed under the Marathas, but so far precise documented evidence has eluded us. The *Sabhasad Bakhar* glorifies the activities of the Maratha Navy by pointing out that it plundered the cities and ports of the enemies, fought naval combats, and brought grains and provisions to the Raje, after providing for its own needs.[48]

Does this indicate that the navy had become self-sufficient? And were crew members paid out of the loot? The answer to these is negative. This would undoubtedly have set a wrong precedent. Shivaji would never have allowed this to happen. The potential of announcing lucrative incentives for volunteering in risky war undertakings is well understood. This approach has been a time-tested policy among ambitious rulers. For example, Sambhaji, the son and successor of Shivaji, had announced rewards for direct action against the Sidi of Janjira. However, fighting and plundering for loot, can never be a recommended policy. A probable solution to this can be found in Amatya's policy handbook, which advises that the salary should be paid as per the rules.[49]

The section on the naval policy—particularly concerning the operation and security of naval vessels—advocates distributing the fleet's vessels among various coastal forts.[50] Therefore, it is highly likely that the payment was disbursed through the forts to which the vessels were attached. During the medieval and early modern periods, a dynamic market for military labour thrived in

India. The Marathas capitalized on the situation, to furnish and equip their navy. Portuguese records indicate that Portuguese renegades played a role in designing and constructing early Maratha warships. The involvement of Portuguese adventurers with the Maratha military was so evident that Mirza Raja Jai Singh had to instruct the Portuguese governor of Goa to stop assisting Shivaji, as it could hinder Mughal military operations against the Marathas.[51] Niccolao Manucci, a Venetian military adventurer, also served under Jai Singh. During Kanhoji Angre's time, Portuguese military personnel and mariners were also employed in the Maratha Navy.

⚓ ⚓ ⚓

Forts, Bases and Naval Paraphernalia

Ramchandra Pant Amatya asserts that 'the essence of the whole Kingdom is [the] fort'.[52] Shivaji lost no time in converting his conquests into strategically fortified settlements. Bal Krishna, one of the early biographers of Shivaji, appreciated the latter's selection of Raigad hill fort as his capital, describing it as 'the frowning fortress … secluded by encircling hills far away from the plains which the vast armies of Aurangzeb could easily desolate … was like a lion's den …', which no one could approach.[53] A similar appreciation can be found in the writings of Abbe Carre, who noted that the marine forts of Shivaji were 'easier to defend and more difficult to attack' due to their strategic location.[54] Naravane's recent study has concluded that more than eighty forts, roughly corresponding to one-fifth of the total number of forts in Maharashtra, can be termed coastal or marine forts.[55] James Grant Duff also attested to the construction of new forts and the refurbishing of older forts, which were attained through military conquest. Duff mentions that Shivaji built the Sindhudurg fort in Malvan, rebuilt and strengthened Kolaba, repaired Suvarnadurg and Vijaydurg, and constructed vessels at all these places.[56] The vision of Shivaji regarding navy and marine fortifications could be well comprehended from the fact that while Mirza Raja Jai Singh was advancing into the Deccan with a massive Mughal army to subdue Shivaji, the latter was laying the foundations of the island fort of Sindhudurg (1664). Additionally, in 1665, the Maratha fleet, with its visionary leader aboard, accomplished the Basrur mission in full view of the Portuguese at Goa.

Marine fortifications can be categorized into three groups based on their geographical surroundings: coastal, off-shore and promontories or fortified headlands. The Maratha marine forts were crucial in the projection of sovereignty in the coastal waters. Most of them were near the important ports, or guarded the tidal mouths of the various Konkan rivers, or provided security to the dockyards.[57] Because of their location, they played a crucial role in formulating the strategy for naval engagements. Moreover, since these forts were equipped with cannons and big guns, they could guard the coast against the amphibious landing of the enemy. Given that Maratha Navy was essentially a brown-water navy, the Maratha vessels found it convenient to operate and fight under the protection of the coastal forts/guns. This was the strategy which Admiral Mahan recommended for a 'weaker' navy exactly after a couple of centuries.

Hence, many such forts were built or refurbished with additional defensive measures. The most prominent marine forts are mentioned in the list provided by Krishnaji Anant Sabhasad, the contemporary biographer of Shivaji.[58] Some of these forts were also shipbuilding centres, while many extended overhaul and repair facilities. This is supported by Amatya, who advises against using the same forts for annual shelter due to the risk of sabotage. Consequently, the vessels were wisely distributed for wintering each year, and perhaps the fort's name was kept secret.[59] Vijaydurg fort, for example, had a well-planned dry dockyard and additional underwater security architecture. As per an estimate, this dockyard could accommodate ships of the ghurab type up to 109 meters in length, corresponding to a tonnage of up to 500 tons. The size of such vessel corresponded to a typical British twenty-gun, single deck warship of sixth rate of that period, which was ideal for coastal warfare.[60]

A detailed explanation of the role of the Maratha maritime forts can be found in Chapter 6 of this volume, while the following chapter deals with the Maratha navy's contribution in securing the economic foundations of the Swarajya.

Notes

1 See pp. 233-52, in Richard W. Unger, 'Warships and Cargo Ships in Medieval Europe', in *Technology and Culture*, Vol. 22, No. 2 1981.

2 See pp. 45-49, in Ballard, *Rulers of the Indian Ocean*, 1984.

3 See Kulke, Kesavapany and Sekhuja, *Nagapattinam to Suvarnadwipa*, 2010.

4 See pp. 82-84 in Vol. I, Chapter II, in Kangle, *The Kautilya Arthashastra*, 1997.

5 See pp. 44-46, in D.V. Apte, 'When Did Shivaji Start His Career of Independence?', in *The Indian Historical Records Commission* (Proceedings of Meeting), XVII Session, Baroda, 1940.

6 See pp. 41-42, in P.S. Pissurlencar, *Portuguese Marathe Sambandha*, (*arthat Portugezanchya Daftaratil Marathayancha Itihash*), (Marathi), Pune University Press, 1967.

7 See pp. 289-92, in Abul Fazl Allami, *Ain-i-Akbari*, ed., D.C. Phillot and transl., H. Blochmann, Vol. I-III, second edition, The Asiatic Society of Bengal, 1927.

8 See pp. 6-8, in Mirza Nathan, *Baharistan-i-Ghaybi: A History of Mughal Wars in Assam, Cooch Behar, Bengal, Bihar and Orissa during*

the reign of Jahangir and Shahjahan, transl., M.I. Borah, Vol. I-II, Government Press, Assam, 1936.

9 See pp. 135-46, in T.S. Shejwalker, 'Shivaji's Raid on Basrur', in *Bulletin of Deccan College Research Institute*, Vol. 4, No. 2, 1942; see p. 87, in Krishnaji Anant Sabhasad, *Sabhasad Virachit Chhatrapati Shivaji Raje Yanchi Bakhar*, (Marathi), ed., U.M. Pathan, Snehvardhan Publishing House, 2000; see pp. 231-33 in, Sarkar, *Shivaji and His Times*, 1973.

10 See pp. 53-58, in Sarkar, *Shivaji and His Times*, 1973.

11 See pp. 41-42, in Pissurlencar, *Portuguese Marathe Sambandha*, 1967.

12 See p. 48, in Ramchandra Pant Amatya, *Shivrajniti: A Royal Edict on the Principles of State Policy Organisation*, transl., S.V. Puntambekar, Diocesan Press, 1928.

13 Se ep. 137, Vol. 1, in James Grant Duff, *History of the Mahrattas*, Vol. I-III, Avishkar Publishers, reprint, 1986; also see pp. 73-74, in A.K. Nairne, *History of the Konkan*, Asian Education Services, reprint, 1988.

14 See pp. 89-90, in Sabhasad, *Sabhasad Bakhar*, 2000.

15 Ibid, p. 94.

16 See p. 258, in Khafi Khan, *Muntakhab-ul-Lubab*, in Elliot, *The History of India*, Vol. VII, 1996.

17 See p. 219 in Vol. I, in Sardesai, *New History of the Marathas, 1986.*

18 D.G. Dhabu, *Kulabkar Angre Sarkhel (Angre Gharanachya Itihas)*, Alibag, 1959, originally published in 1939; see also pp. 93-94, in Sabhasad, *Sabhasad Bakhar*, 2000.

19 See p. 159 in Sen, *Military System of the Marathas*, 1979.

20 See p. 258 in Khan, *Muntakhab-ul-Lubab* in Elliot, *The History of India*, Vol. III, 1996. Khafi Khan writes, 'Shivaji had secured several islands in the sea by means of a fleet which he had formed ... He had also built many forts in those parts ...'

21 See p.43, in Pissurlencar, *Portuguese Marathe Sambandha*, 1967.

22 See Vol. I, No. 238, in B.G. Paranjape, ed., *English Records on Shivaji (1659-1682)*, Vol. I-II, Shiv Charitra Karyalaya, 1931.

23 See Vol. 1, No. 333, in Paranjape, *English Records on Shivaji*, 1931.

24 See p. 48, in Pissurlencar, *Portuguese Marathe Sambandha*, 1967.

25 See p. 94, in Sabhasad, *Sabhasad Bakhar*, 2000.

26 See Vol 1, No. 238, in Paranjape, *English Records on Shivaji*, 1931.

27 Quoted on p. 13 by (and in) W.S. Desai, *Bombay and the Marathas up to 1774*, Munshiram Manoharlal, 1970.

28 See pp. 48–9, in Amatya, *Shivrajniti.*1928.

29 Ibid.

30 John Fryer, a contemporary traveller and a surgeon by profession, identified Khanderi as 'the great rock or barren islet of Henry-Kenry', and describes Bombay, Trombay, Elephanta, Karanja, with Rock of Henry-Kenry as 'so many mountains arising out of sea ...'. See pp. 159-60, in Vol. I, in John Fryer, *A New Account of East India and Persia: Being Nine Years' Travels, 1672-1681*, ed., with notes and an Introduction, by William Crooke, Vol. I-III, Kraus Reprint. 1967.

31 See pp. 50-51, in Amatya, *Shivrajniti*, 1928.

32 See pp. 51-63, in S. Tripathi et al., 'Marine archaeological exploration and excavation of Vijaydurg: a naval base of the Maratha Period, Maharashtra, on the west coast of India', in *The International Journal of Nautical Archaeology*, Vol. 21, No. 1, 1998.

33 See pp. 157-88, in Amarendra Kumar, 'The Idea of Navy and Naval Warfare under Shivaji', in *Warfare and Politics in South Asia from Ancient to Modern Times*, ed., Kaushik Roy, Manohar,2011.

34 See pp. 326-35, in B.G. Tamaskar, 'Ports and Harbours of Shivaji's Kingdom', in *Proceedings of the Indian History Congress*, Vol. 40, 1979.

35 See Vol. 1, No. 189, in Paranjape, *English Records on Shivaji*, 1931.

36 See p. 233, in A.R. Kulkarni, *Maharashtra in the Age of Shivaji (A Study in Economic History)*, Diamond Publications, reprint, 2008.

37 See Vol. 1, No. 106, in Paranjape, *English Records on Shivaji*, 1931.

38 Ibid., Vol. 1, No. 52.

39 Jetsam and Flotsam denote goods floating in the sea either from a shipwreck or deliberately discarded from a ship during a state of distress. Theoretically these items belonged to the original owner, however, once they washed up ashore, they were claimed by the ruler of the land.

40 See pp. 255-61 in Vol. 29, No. 1, in Apte, 'Sovereignty of the Sea',1967.

41 See pp. 49-50, in Amatya, *Shivrajniti*, 1928.

42 See, for example, letter numbers: 1389, 1399, 1431, 1592, 1675, etc., in Vol. III, of S.N. Joshi, ed., *Shiva Kalin Patra-Saar Samgraha*, Vol. I-III, Shiv Charitra Karyalaya, 1930-37. See also Vol. II, No. 279, etc., in Paranjape, *English Records on Shivaji*, 1931, for incidences of European sale of firearms to the Marathas.

43 See pp. 48-49, in Amatya, *Shivrajniti*, 1928.

44 See pp. 208-10, in N.G. Bhaware, 'Castes, Favours, Patronage and Privileges under Shivaji's Rule', in *Studies in Shivaji and His Times*, ed., B.R. Kamble, Shivaji University, 1982.

45 See Vol. 1, No. 309, in Paranjape, *English Records on Shivaji*, 1931.

46 See p. 65, Vol. II, in G.W. Forrest, ed., *Selections from the Letters, Dispatches and other State Papers preserved in the Bombay Secretariat*, (*Home Series*), Vol. I-II, Bombay Central Press, 1887.

47 See pp. 202-03, Vol. II, of Allami, *Ain-i-Akbari*, 1927; also see pp. 148-49, in Mookerji, *Indian Shipping*, 1957.

48 See p. 94, in Sabhasad, *Sabhasad Bakhar*, 2000.

49 See pp. 19-20, in Amatya, *Shivrajniti*, 1928.

50 Ibid, p. 51.

51 See pp. 184-94, in Jagadish Narayan Sarkar, 'New Light on Mughal-Portuguese Relations, 1665-67 (Based on Portuguese Sources)', in *Proceedings of the Indian History Congress*, Vol. 31, 1969.

52 See pp. 38-39, in Amatya, *Shivrajniti*, 1928.

53 See p. 2, in Part 1, Vol. II, of Bal Krishna, *Shivaji The Great*, Vol. I-IV, D.B. Taraporewala Sons & Co., 1938.

54 See 'Abbe Carre' in pp. 154-55, in S.N. Sen, *Foreign Biographies of Shivaji*, K.P. Bagchi, 1977.

55 See p. 270, in M.S. Naravane, *Forts of Maharashtra*, APH Publishing Corporation, 1995.

56 See p. 137, Vol. 1, in Duff, *History of the Mahrattas*, 1986.

57 See p. 270, in Naravane, *Forts of Maharashtra*, 1995.

58 See pp. 114-18, in Sabhasad, *Sabhasad Bakhar*, 2000.

59 See pp. 49, 51, Amatya, *Shivrajniti*, 1928.

60 See p. 111, in MacDougall, *Naval Resistance to Britain's Growing Power in India*, 2014. The British Royal Navy categorized and rated its ships based on their capacity, crew size, and the number and types of guns they carried.

4

Trade and Economy: The Marathas in Coastal Political Economy in the Early Modern Period

Radhika Seshan

⚓ ⚓ ⚓

This chapter talks of the economy, of contested territory, and of the many factors that necessitated a navy. It begins by describing the specific conditions on the Konkan coast in the seventeenth and eighteenth centuries, to try and understand whether these conditions necessitated a navy. The founding of a navy by Chhatrapati Shivaji has to be understood against the background of many things—the concerns of the newly emerging kingdom, the areas of contested territory, the role of the land-based empires and the Sidis on the coast, and of course the European presence. The focus is primarily the coastal political economy, and the ways in which this intersected with the concerns of the emerging state system.

⚓ ⚓ ⚓

Background and Historiography

How does one define a coastal political economy? Very often and very unfortunately, the study of the coast begins with the sixteenth century and the arrival of the Portuguese, as though to say that there was no engagement with the seas prior to this, particularly on the west coast of India. On the east coast, we have of course the great Chola expedition of the eleventh century, but this is treated as the exception that proves the rule, rather than as a more vigorous manifestation of the links to the seas and to the worlds beyond. Perhaps one of the earliest examples of this engagement comes from the royal title of 'Samudradipati', or sometimes 'Trisamudradipati', meaning 'lords of the ocean' or 'lords of the three oceans'. And in the seventh century we have the record of Chalukya King Pulakesin's attack and his subsequent conquest of 'Puri', the island of Elephanta.

In his work, *A History of the Maratha Navy and Merchantships*, B.K. Apte has given a fairly comprehensive account of the engagement of the medieval rulers with the west coast of India.[1] Beginning with the Bahmanis, the links of the interior to the coast began to expand with the conquest of Mahim and Salsette from the Gujarat rulers in 1429. In response, Ahmed Shah dispatched a fleet of seventeen ships from Diu, Gogha and Cambay to attack the Bahmani forces, and regained the ports.[2]

But what of the coast and its economy, as well as its links to the hinterland and the foreland in later times? The tendency has been to see this through the lens of what Sardar Pannikar called the 'Vasco da Gama epoch'—in other words, only through European eyes. The impact was undoubtedly great, but again needs to be situated within the time and the context to include the Indian polities and their reactions to the arrival of the European nations. Two of these reactions have deservedly received considerable attention—those of the Marathas and the Travancore state. The eighteenth century has also been a subject of considerable debate in the history of India. The debate itself is nothing new, for the idea of the eighteenth century being a 'Dark Age,' has a very long history.

Slightly more recently, the debate revolved around questions of continuity and change, prosperity and decline, and evolution and revolution.[3] However, the concern has often been with the internal dynamics of the country, and so—while economic prosperity and decline is an issue—the focus has been on the economic bases of the kingdoms that emerged in the first half of the eighteenth century, or with the struggle between the English and the French, or with the impact of the beginnings of colonialism. As has often been the case, trade and other relations along the coast remain under-researched areas, with much research focusing on Surat and on the kingdom of Travancore.[4,5] This itself has often taken off from Ashin Das Gupta's works.

The entry of the Portuguese into Asian trading waters has long been understood to have marked a dramatic change from past methods of trade in the region. One of the major concerns of historians is about the actual extent of the impact of the Portuguese—C.R. Boxer called it the Portuguese seaborne empire; A.J.R. Russel-Wood called it a world on the move.[6] The Portuguese did dominate the trading networks of the Indian Ocean world for a century and when their dominance was challenged it was primarily by the Dutch. Historians such as K.M. Pannikar have pointed to this entry as marking the beginning of Western dominance, for with the Portuguese came methods of war at sea that had until then been unknown in Asian waters. While it is necessary to reiterate that such thinking had its roots in the colonial world and its legacy, it is also perhaps necessary to study the impact of the Portuguese and the Dutch in their own time as well, and to examine the ways in which the European entry was perceived.

> Historians have long debated the reasons for these voyages. Why was almost a century spent on thrusting down the West African coast, and why was it the Portuguese rather than some other European power who undertook these voyages? The much-quoted answer tells us that a member of da Gama's crew, when asked in Calicut 'What brought you here?' replied 'We seek Christians and Spices.' Such a reply was actually a cliché even in the fifteenth century; Portuguese kings in their letters explained not only the discoveries but almost everything else they did as being designed to 'serve God and make a profit for ourselves'. Some later Portuguese explanations, flying even further in the face of both facts and probability, stress solely religious motives.[7]

Later historiography tended to stress the economic aspect—thus, Portuguese expansion into Asian waters was often portrayed as a conscious and carefully crafted attempt to expand into areas that would provide both grain and other kinds of produce, which could be either absorbed locally, or sold for a sizeable profit elsewhere in Europe. Pearson has also pointed to the 'political imperatives,' including the steadily declining seigneurial revenues from land, as being causes for the voyages of exploration.[8] Since the 1970s, yet another dimension of historiography has emerged—primarily that of Asian scholars. They emphasize the continued Asian participation in Asian trade, as well as the methods used by these trades to subvert European monopolies. For example, the Portuguese domination through Melaka was subverted by the emergence of Aceh as a hub for Asian traders.

It is to be remembered that the Asian trading world, contrary to traditional European notions was not 'created' by the Europeans. As is now well known, the Asian trading networks were dominated by spices, cotton cloth, horses and silk cloth. The Europeans interposed themselves into these networks and while they did change some aspects, they probably did not succeed in transforming them totally until the establishment of colonialism.

> From the beginning, Indians did not just tolerate the Europeans; they employed them, rewarded them with revenue rights, and sought their protection in trade, in the process teaching them how to exploit the immense talents of the Indian peoples for production, commerce, and warfare. Thus European participation in Indian politics and political economy, not just profits of trade, sustained the European presence in the Indian Ocean from the sixteenth century on. Until about 1750, the Europeans had demonstrated distinctive "statist" modes of cohesion in simply surviving in the Indian Ocean and in articulating unusually wide systems of commercial coordination.[9]

The history of the Deccan has, in common with much of peninsular India, suffered from a dearth of research for the medieval period. Much of the extant research has focused on the socio-economic aspects, especially of the medieval period, but has also tended to be very dynasty oriented. This is particularly well represented in the works of, for example, H.K. Sherwani or G.H. Yazdani. These have focused on the Bahmani, Adil Shahi and Qutb Shahi sultanates in particular but have tended to ignore the other Deccani sultanates. There is one extensive work on the sultanate of Ahmednagar, by Radhey Shyam, but none on Bidar and Berar. The works of M.A. Nayeem did initially study the diplomatic relations of the Bijapur sultanate, but his later works are more concerned with art and architecture.

There is also a considerable body of research on Maratha history, including that of the late Professor A.R. Kulkarni and many others who continue to work on aspects of Maratha history. However, it should be pointed out that this research is much more concerned with the seventeenth century and later, and tends to view the earlier dynasties, especially the Bahmani and Adil Shahi, as the backdrop against which Maratha history can be taken further forward. As said earlier, these tend to focus on the medieval period. For the study of the early Deccan, again Yazdani's work is of considerable importance. In more recent years, Himanshu Prabha Ray has focused on aspects of economic history of the Satvahanas, with particular reference to the nature of land grants and to maritime history. Ranabir Chakravarti has also studied economic history of the early medieval age, especially the trade networks of the region.

⚓ ⚓ ⚓

The Economy

From the time of Alauddin Khilji, the wealth of the Deccan was well known, for it has been argued that it was the wealth that he acquired through his raids on the Deccan that enabled him to get the throne of Delhi. It may perhaps be pointed out that this ultimately became standard practice, for in the middle of the seventeenth century, Aurangzeb too launched his bid for the throne of Delhi from his base in the Deccan. Even at the end of the century, following Saqi Mustaid Khan's account, when Aurangzeb finally conquered Golconda and transferred the treasure from there to the north, the caravan carrying the treasure stretched for miles. In the nineteenth and twentieth centuries, the nizams of Hyderabad similarly enjoyed the reputation of being immensely wealthy, at least personally.

Where did this wealth come from—did it come from land, mineral resources, artisanal production or trade? There were a great many people involved in trade belonging to different communities and located, not just in the ports, but at various places in the interior as well. Who were the locals and who were the foreigners? Were they identified in terms of community, religion, ethnicity, or sphere of action? What role did the state play in granting them status, or in underscoring their claims to legitimacy and identity? Were there conflicts among the different communities/groups? And were these conflicts over the actual control of resources, or were they geared more towards power and ideology? Did the different groups of merchants occupy any special position vis-à-vis the state in the ports? What were the networks of trade that existed across the peninsula, or the Arabian Sea or the Bay of Bengal, or along the coasts themselves? Were there specific connections between particular ports? What were the routes from the ports to the interior?

Crucial to peninsular economy as a whole, was of course the trade in textiles and in spices. While these two dominated, it is to be remembered that these were far from being the only items of trade. Basrur, on the Karnataka coast, was a major centre for the rice trade, as Sanjay Subrahmanyam has shown.[10] Involved in this trade were the Portuguese, including their private traders, and Asian merchants. It is important to remember that the port of Basrur was linked to a strong agrarian hinterland. The importance of rice to the economy of the states is clear from early times, with Rashtrakuta inscriptions mentioning taxes on a great many varieties of rice.[11]

In similar fashion, Rajapur on the Konkan coast was a very important port, mostly because it was connected to the markets at Rairi, an important market both for pepper and for rice. Further north, Thane had long been known as *the* port for the import of horses and for the export of rice, ginger, sugarcane and possibly sesame and/or cottonseed oil. Other exports—not just from Thane but also other ports of the Konkan coast—included wheat, coconuts, areca nuts and probably mangoes. Imports included ceramics from China, something that apparently came to other ports as well, as has been proved by the excavations at Chaul; and according to Apte, mirrors from Venice.[12]

An extensive network of roads connected the ports to the interior. Kos minar (or their remnants) can be seen on many of the roads leading from Chaul and Rajapur to the interior.[13] European records have many references to inns or serai, and to caravanserai, and again in Chaul, the remnants of a caravanserai and of a hammam (a public bath house) can be seen in the Indian part of the settlement (today called Rewadanda). In the eighteenth century, Marathi records in the Modi script describe coastal trading voyages from Chaul to Gujarat, possibly touching the ports of Sashti and Ashtami on the way. Outgoing cargo from Chaul seems to primarily have been stalks of the sugarcane plant after the harvest, used as fodder for cattle in Gujarat; and the incoming cargo on the return from Chaul, seems to have primarily been Gujarat cotton textiles. On the other side of the peninsula, between Hyderabad and Masulipatam/Machilipatnam, there are a number of kos minar that can still be seen.

Russian merchant Afanasy Nikitin has described in great detail his journey from Chaul to Bidar and Gulbarga via Junnar, and Abdur Razzaq has described the route from Mangalore to Hampi.[14] In the middle of the seventeenth century, the account of the Abbe Carre also gives us the routes that criss-crossed the Deccan as a whole.[15] All this indicates the constant movement between different parts of the peninsula, and points to the trade that was carried out—local, regional, and long-distance. This was the economic base, connecting coast, hinterland and foreland, that was a crucial source of revenue for the Deccan polities, which all sought to tax, encourage, or sometimes obstruct. The trade of the Europeans was also based on this widespread production, but in the seventeenth century they had very limited access to the interior, something that was possible only through their 'native brokers', and so, it is not surprising that they sought to use their naval superiority to control shipping rather than attempt to get access to internal markets.

Shivaji seems to have understood the importance of seaborne trade as well, for the *Sabhasad Bakhar* mentions the trade in salt, and the three-masted ships used in the trade with Mocha.[16] The need to maintain and protect trade is underlined in the eighteenth-century work of Ramachandra Pant Amatya, the *Ajnapatra*.[17]

⚓⚓⚓

The Maratha Navy

What of the Marathas? While there are a number of studies on the Marathas, some of which have been listed in my discussion above, these have tended to focus more on the desh—the word used to describe the plateau region east of the Ghats—and ignored the concerns of the coast. Traditionally, it has been assumed that trade consistently formed a smaller part of the revenue collected by any empire, and this automatically led to the conclusion that the Europeans succeeded precisely because they controlled the trade and the sea. Can this be accepted? It is to be remembered that among the earliest expeditions undertaken by Chhatrapati Shivaji was one to the Ghat region, south of Pune, and that in 1656 he captured the fort of Javali; and in the process, got control of eight important passes between the desh region and the Konkan.[18] In the same year (1656), he also attacked and captured the towns of Kalyan and Bhiwandi (both now part of the metropolitan region of Mumbai). Not surprisingly, these raids and conquests drew the attention of the Europeans on the coast—the Portuguese in particular, but also the English and the Dutch, and later the French.

The Sidis of Janjira were perhaps the 'strongest actual power on the coast', as Gordon has said.[19] The Sidis shifted allegiance from Ahmednagar to Bijapur to the Mughals, and particularly for the last two, were seen as crucial in the strategies against the Marathas. It is probable that a navy was felt to be necessary, because of the need to challenge and contain the Sidis (something that was never actually done by Shivaji). So also, the sea forts—the construction of the sea fort of Vijaydurg, later the stronghold of Kanhoji Angre, was begun in 1653.

The Portuguese were the next set of players on the coast. With their forts at Daman, Diu, Vasai (Bassein), Thane and Chaul, and their fairly effective use of the cartaz (pass) mechanism, they were able, if not to totally redirect trade, then at least tax it fairly effectively. This last was of course due to their naval strength, something that the Indian powers, coastal or land-based, were unable to match. This power had begun to decline by the end of the sixteenth century itself, and in the seventeenth, was vigorously challenged by the Dutch. However, the Dutch had only one not very prominent settlement on the west coast at Vengurla, for their concern was much more with Southeast Asia and the Coromandel region. The British were, throughout most of this century, far weaker vis-à-vis the Dutch, as can be seen from the constant complaints about the Dutch in the factory records of the English East India Company. Their main base on the west coast was at Surat. However, as the English crown sanctioned other trading ventures such as Courteen's Association, other settlements were established at Rajapur and Karwar, and later at Dabhol.[20] The Association soon got the East India Company into trouble, by attacking Asian shipping, for which the English were penalized. According to a book published in 1907:

> The greatest sufferers [from pirates] among European traders in India were the English; for not only were the greater number of pirates of English blood, but pirate captains of other nationalities often sailed under English colours. The native officials, unable to distinguish the rogues from the honest traders, held the East India Company's servants responsible for the misdeeds of the piccaroons, from whom they suffered so grievously.[21]

It is against all these aspects that we need to place the founding of the Maratha Navy by Shivaji. As Biddulph says, 'The growth of the Mahratta power under Sivajee had been accompanied by the formation of a formidable fleet which harried the coast of the Concan, and against which the Seedee chief, the Emperor's representative afloat, could hardly maintain himself.'[22]

In January 1660, Shivaji attacked and captured Rajapur, and shortly after, problems between Shivaji and the English began.

Two Indian merchants, who had dealings with the English, were seized by Shivaji's forces, as was one of the Company factors. The Surat factors reporting this to the Company in London not, 'whom they cann but keepe prisoners so long as we cann have a letter carryed to there master Sevagy.'[23] The English factor, a merchant named Gyfford, was freed; but a year later, when two factors were sent to negotiate with Shivaji, they were imprisoned and kept prisoner for two years. The condition for their release was aid to Shivaji in his actions against the Sidis, something which never materialized. But problems continued, and in 1664, the English were made to pay £112 to Shivaji, to prevent him from plundering their factory at Hubli.[24]

Shivaji's actions on the coast continued, with his attack on Basrur with a fleet of seventy ships in 1665, after which he attempted his first attack on the Sidis of Janjira. While he succeeded in occupying Danda-Rajpuri, as said above, he never managed to get Janjira. In 1679, he attacked the island of Khanderi, which commanded the entrance to Bombay harbour, and immediately after, began fortifications on the island. The action at Khanderi can perhaps be seen to have laid the basis of later actions by the Maratha Navy, for here, the speed and manoeuvrability of the smaller and faster Maratha ships proved to be much more effective in the shallow waters around the coast.

It is to be noted that the Maratha Navy, for all its strength, was finally a coastal navy, for it patrolled the coast. The Europeans were not attacked at sea; rather, the old idea of control of the sea by preventing access to land was much more firmly and rigorously enforced. The continuity of coast and hinterland connections began to break down in the eighteenth century, and as the British got greater control over both land

and sea, the economy of both these regions began gradually to be subsumed into the politics and economics of colonialism.

The next chapter continues with the theme of the economic basis of power, focusing on the need for a state to exercise military power so as to retain its sovereignty.

Notes

1 Apte, *A History of the Maratha Navy*. 1973.

2 Ibid., p. 52-53.

3 See Seema Alavi, *The Eighteenth Century in India*, Oxford University Press, 2000; and P.J. Marshall, *The Eighteenth Century in India: Evolution or Revolution?* Oxford University Press, 2002.

4 Ashin Das Gupta, *Indian Merchants and the Decline of Surat c. 1700-1750*, reprint with a new Preface, Manohar,1994.

5 Ashin Das Gupta, *Malabar in Asian Trade, 1740-1800*, Cambridge University Press, Cambridge South Asian Studies,1967.

6 C.R. Boxer, *The Portuguese Sea-Borne Empire 1415-1825*, Alfred A. Knopf, 1969; A.J.R. Russel-Wood, *A World on the Move: The Portuguese in Africa, Asia and America 1415-1808*, Palgrave MacMillan, 1993.

7 See Chapter I, p. 5, in Pearson, *The Portuguese in India*, 2008.

8 Ibid., p. 5.

9 See p. 86, in John E. Wills Jr., 'Maritime Asia 1500-1800: The Interactive Emergence of European Domination', Review Article, in *The American Historical Review*, Vol. 98, No. 1,1993; accessed through JSTOR, 31 July 2014.

10 See pp. 433-64, in Sanjay Subrahmanyam, 'The Portuguese, the port of Basrur, and the rice trade, 1600-50', in *The Indian Economic and Social History Review*, Vol. 21, No. 4,1984.

11 In modern times, there are still about twenty-five varieties of rice that are popular in the regions on either side of the Western Ghats, the most widely available being 'indrayani', a variety of sticky rice.

12 See p. 54, in Apte, *A History of the Maratha Navy*.1973.

13 The term 'kos minar' denotes 'mile pillars', which were placed along royal and other important routes during the medieval period to serve as markers of distance.

14 Afanasy Nikitin, *Afanasy Nikitin's Voyage Beyond the Three Seas, 1466-1472*, Raduga Publishers,1995; also see Abdul Razzak,'Narrative of the Voyage of Abd-Er-Razzak, Ambassador from Shah Rukh – a.h. 845, 1442 a.d', in *India in the Fifteenth Century: Being a Collection of Narratives of Voyages to India, in the Century Preceding the Portugese Discovery of the Cape of Good Hope; From Latin, Persian, Russian and Italian Sources*, transl. and ed., R.H. Major, The Hakluyt Society,1857; available at: https://archive.org/details/indiainfifteenth00majo/page/n11/mode/1up?view=theater

15 Abbe Carre, *The Travels of the Abbe Carre in India and the Near East 1672 to 1674*, Asian Educational Services; reprint, 1990.

16 See p. 73 citing the *Sabhasad Bakhar*, in Apte, *A History of the Maratha Navy*, 1973.

17 Puntambekar, 'The Ajnapatra or Royal Edict', 1929.

18 See p. 63 citing the *Sabhasad Bakhar* and the *91-Kalami Bakhar*, in Gordon, *The Marathas: 1600-1818*. 2008.

19 Ibid., p. 64.

20 Courteen's Association was established in 1636 by Sir William Courteen, along with two former employees of the English East India Company. The Association was supposed to trade only in those areas where the East India Company did not operate, but that principle was soon violated. See especially Vol. 5 and 6, of William Foster, ed., *The English Factories in India, 1618-1621: A Calendar of Documents in the India Office, British Museum and Public Record Office*, Clarendon Press, 1906.

21 See p. x, in Biddulph, *The Pirates of* Malabar, 1907.

22 Ibid., p. 76.

23 See p. 357 in Vol. 10, and *passim*, Vol. 11, in *The English Factories in India:1618-1621*. 1906.

24 See p. 61, in Apte, *A History of Maratha Navy*,1973.

5

Dastak, Competing Sovereignties and Maratha Naval Prowess on the Konkan in the Eighteenth Century

Anirudh Deshpande

⚓ ⚓ ⚓

'Our readers would not thank us for a history of Kanhoji Angria's exploits. Each of the three great European nations in Indian waters had a shy at him and his family, and each came off second best.'[1]

—James Douglas

'An ironic consequence of European competition in the Indian Ocean during the early modern period is that every player regarded itself as the rightful claimant to domination and its rivals as pirates.'[2]

—Edward A. Alpers

⚓ ⚓ ⚓

Economic Surplus, State Power and Sovereignty

The production of economic surplus, the development of trade and the evolution of the state were simultaneous processes in history. It is a truism that having a monopoly in the areas of taxation and the exercise of military power, has always been integral to the sovereignty of a state because economic surplus and force are the two most important motors of history and historical change. From this it follows that if a state loses the monopoly of its armed forces and its taxation powers, both on land and sea, it no longer remains sovereign. The decline of the Mughal empire in the eighteenth century and the subsequent demise of Indian polities—at the hands of the English East India Company, in the same period—are cases in point and prove that economic independence and political sovereignty are inseparable for any state that seeks to speak in a sovereign voice.

Land-based medieval kingdoms used tolls to collect taxes which were remitted to the royal treasury by state officers in charge of these tolls. These tolls were collected on all minor and major trade routes and close to forts. In addition to the trade toll, medieval states also coerced other taxes from the populace. Well-organized groups of warrior elites ran this system. Superior military force was a prerequisite, as the tax collecting intermediaries tended to become refractory. Thus, all states faced centrifugal tendencies encouraged by local elites. At the same time, maritime taxes were collected in the form of customs and other duties paid by foreign ships at ports controlled by the state. Ships that evaded these duties were liable to heavy penalties, including seizure of goods and personnel.

This state of affairs was widely prevalent in the Indian Ocean world during the age of mercantilism, with seafaring at its centre. In the Arabian Sea, the major trading and naval powers, like the Portuguese and the English, exercised maritime sovereignty by resorting to the cart and pass systems in the seventeenth and eighteenth centuries. While the Portuguese, under the jurisdiction of the Portuguese crown, had colonized parts of the west coast of the Indian peninsula, during the sixteenth century; the English arrived in the seventeenth century and were permitted by the Mughal state to establish themselves in Surat and some other places. Since the English East India Company (EEIC) traded in India as a beneficiary of the Mughal state, it had no right to issue passes in imitation of the Portuguese in and around their colony, Estado da India. Further, the EEIC was a joint-stock corporation governed by its London directors, responsible to the influential company shareholders. In this context, the importance of the farman (diktat) issued by the indolent emperor Farukhsiyar in 1717 to the EEIC for duty-free internal trade should be noted. This licence to illegality fetched the Mughal treasury a paltry sum.

When Kanhoji Angre's star rose on the Konkan, the EEIC had already established itself in Surat and Bombay but found itself struggling against the Portuguese and Dutch.[3] On the high seas, the European companies faced the threat of heavily armed pirate ships operating from bases in the Caribbean and the Indian Ocean islands. By the early eighteenth century, Bombay—connected to the passes in the Western Ghats by a large natural harbour—had developed as the main naval and commercial base of English operations in the Indian Ocean region. It was strategically located between the southern and northern ports on the Konkan coast. A strong navy based in Bombay could easily exert maritime influence in both directions.

From the last decade of the seventeenth century till 1756, the EEIC had to contend with Kanhoji and his successors in the same way as the Portuguese had to struggle against the Kunjali Marrakars on the Malabar Coast in the sixteenth century. The age of mercantilism was marked by fluid political boundaries and competing sovereignties between the self-appointed custodians of trade and politics. In this context, Kanhoji emerged as an astute diplomat and military commander. He controlled a large strip of the Konkan coast, bordering Bombay; his domain was sandwiched between the Maratha 'desh' area (under the Peshwa) and the Arabian Sea where the Europeans held sway, well beyond the range of Kanhoji's cannons.

This coast—interspersed with forests and hills, rivers, creeks and numerous harbours—was known for the heavy traffic of European and Indian merchant ships. These ships regularly sailed between Gujarat and the Malabar coasts and beyond, facilitating trade between the hinterland and the coast. The forests of the Western Ghats provided good timber for shipbuilding and construction of buildings. Merchantmen anchored for wood, fresh water, victuals and commodities—including spices, salt, rice, coconuts, hemp, assorted grains and cotton—at the numerous ports that were under the protection of the well-appointed forts that Kanhoji commanded.[4] To avail these port facilities, European and Arab captains paid various duties. Most of the merchandise was carried in native vessels. Unlike the big ocean-going ships, the native vessels needed to visit ports frequently for supplies, and sailed close to the littoral. The ports also offered repair facilities and new ships could be built wherever shipbuilding docks existed.

The Konkan region, in the seventeenth and eighteenth centuries, often came under the triple influence of the Sidis, Marathas and the English. This caused endemic political and military conflict on the Konkan coast and in the hinterland, which the Angres used to their military advantage. Kanhoji, being the admiral of a brown-water navy, could rely on piracy to augment his purse only partially. Outright piracy, per se, was counter-productive because it would drive away the merchantmen that used his ports. The revenue from customs and other duties depended upon the frequency of anchoring ships; and this frequency depended upon the needs and will of the captains, who were fearful of pirates. Unable to take greater recourse to piracy, Kanhoji's solution was to devise the dastak system, taking a cue from the Portuguese cartaz system. Dastaks allowed him to milk the trade, because if ship captains were ready to pay the Europeans, what would stop them from paying the Angre?

⚓ ⚓ ⚓

The Angre Dastak System and the Contest for Sovereignty on the Konkan

The dastak system was contingent upon Maratha military prowess and pivoted on strong forts garrisoned with seasoned Maratha fighters and foreign mercenaries and gunners. The forts sheltered the harbours and docks and projected power on the lands stretching away from the creeks and estuaries towards the Ghats. The remains of Vijayadurg, Suvarnadurg and Kolaba Fort are a testimony to this. The Marathas' brown-water navy, using pack tactics, cornered and captured ships forcing the terrorized merchant ships to fall in line with the dastak system. The coastal waters were ideal for brown water naval operations—the Konkan coast had not been properly surveyed well into the eighteenth century, thus numerous perils awaited an inexperienced captain who happened to sail these waters in the preceding centuries. In comparison, the Angre Ghurabs and galbats carried sailors recruited from the local seafaring communities who knew the coastal waters like the back of their hands. Even the Bombay Marine and English merchant ships were worked by lascars and their navigation of the Arabian Sea depended upon the knowledge possessed by these hardy sailors.[5] An experienced Arab captain (nakhoda) could have been the equal or better than an Angre captain, but being surrounded by a pack of Maratha galbats or Ghurabs rendered even large merchant ships helpless. For such a ship, the alternative to surrender was being sunk with its expensive cargo. Hence, the merchants on board, who feared for their lives, usually caved in.

By the 1720s the dastak system was firmly in place and fetched Kanhoji lakhs of rupees, which were spent on salaries, forts, ships, guns and supplies. In addition, Angre revenues comprised the land revenue and tolls collected inland and near the forts. The Viceroy of Goa informed the king of Portugal on 22 January 1721 that:

> Kanhoji Angre is a powerful pirate and a cause of terror on Indian seas. He was the sole reason of the destruction of trade … without purchasing his passport, it is impossible for any merchant or ship to sail on the northern seas. Every year Angre earns seven lakh rupees from (this) tax. If tax is paid (if passport was purchased) then only ships will be secure. He never allows any ship to sail without his passport.[6]

Thus the coast between Goa and Bombay passed into Angre's hands. The Portuguese themselves earned lakhs from the cartaz system, based on several precedents prevalent in the

Indian Ocean World before 1498.[7] Nonetheless, an expert opines, that 'there can be little doubt that the scale on which this restrictive measure was used by the Portuguese was unprecedented. The measure indeed represented an institutional constraint on the freedom of navigation on the high seas.'[8] The Portuguese considered themselves sovereigns of the sea and exercised their self-assumed right to tax ships by implementing the cartaz system from their earliest days in India. The word 'pirate' was reserved for non-European actors on the scene or European rovers, usually ship captains or rebels-turned-pirates, who operated on the high seas and oceans. In 1501, the Portugese ruler, Manuel I, assumed the grandiose sounding title of, 'Lord of Navigation, Conquest, and Trade with Ethiopia, Arabia, Persia and India'.[9] Barrows defines the Portuguese position thus:

> It is true that there does exist a common right to all to navigate the seas and in Europe we acknowledge the right which others hold against us; but this right does not extend beyond Europe; and therefore the Portuguese as Lords of the Seas are justified in confiscating the goods of all those who navigate the seas without their permission.[10]

The imperialist, racist and Eurocentric nature of this position can hardly be missed. Asians were pirates, Europeans were not. The Portuguese wanted to ensure that no other power practiced the passport system. Their monopolist attitude was best expressed in the viceroy's letter to the Jesuit priest, Manueal da Figeredu. The viceroy instructed him to report about the Sidis of Janjira to the Mughal emperor. 'Nowadays,' the viceroy wrote, 'the Sidis have started issuing passports to the merchant ships. He is using this authority which is more than his status as *Nawab*. Only the Portuguese possess this authority and all the ships must purchase Portuguese passports.'[11] The cartaz system underlined the pompous Portuguese claim to maritime sovereignty. The English and Dutch, no less self-righteous than the Portuguese, tried their best to assert trade monopolies themselves. The EEIC often allied with the Portuguese against the Marathas during the first fifty years of the eighteenth century, but even as a team were usually unsuccessful.

Angre's dastak system was not simply a copy of the Portuguese. He cited the example of Mughal ships, which purchased his dastak and sailed safely along the coast to the English authorities in Bombay. Since the sovereign Mughals abided by his dastaks, the English, as dependents of the Mughals, could hardly refuse them. His correspondence with the English defined his notion of sea sovereignty which he derived from being an admiral of the house of Shivaji, whose descendants were at that time the sovereign of the Deccan. His letters in response to English complaints clearly stated that he did not attack any merchant ship which traded according to the *laws of his country*. Kanhoji also derived sovereignty from divinity, much as Shivaji himself had claimed in the seventeenth century. This was like the European powers, whose sovereignty derived from a crown which, in turn, was based on the divine right of Christian kings. The reference to the Mughals in his correspondence suggests that Kanhoji was aware of the political situation in India. He knew that the English and Dutch had obtained Mughal farmans and therefore their claim to sovereignty was suspect. If they could claim indirect sovereignty nothing could stop Kanhoji from doing the same as the naval representative of the Maratha Kings Raja Ram and Shahu.

⚓ ⚓ ⚓

Descriptions of Kanhoji Angre in Historiography

Kanhoji was called a pirate by the Europeans because he resisted them on the Arabian Sea. Clement Downing, an EEIC employee, wrote an eyewitness account of the war with Kanhoji glorifying the EEIC's activities as the suppression of piracy.[12] Abraham Anselm, captain of the *Derby*, captured by Sambhaji Angre in 1735, wrote *A Faithful Narrative of the Capture of the Ship DERBY*.[13] This narrative, published in London in 1738, is similar to the famous work of Robert Orme, *History of The Military Transactions of the British Nation in Indostan*, Vol. I, in 1745. Both describe Kanhoji as a pirate.[14] News praising victory over Tulaji Angre was printed in *The London Gazette* in its issue of 5-6 November 1756.[15] *The Scots* magazine published an anonymous account titled, 'An Authentick and Faithful History of That Arch-Pyrate Tulagee Angria', in 1756 and celebrated the EEIC's 'honourable' actions against Angre.[16] The influence of such writings on the British public can be imagined.

Later, colonialist historiography perpetuated the myth of Kanhoji the pirate. James Grant Duff's three-volume magnum opus, *A History of the Mahrattas* was first published in England in1826.[17] It labels Kanhoji a pirate. In 1877, Charles Rathbone Low wrote the *History of Indian Navy (1613-1863)* from the perspective of a former officer of the EEIC's Bombay

Marine.[18] Low denounced indigenous Indian sea power as piracy. Frederick Charles Danvers, in his work, *The Portuguese in India being a History of the Rise and Decline of Their Eastern Empire*, asserted that Angre's 'fleets crept out to plunder indiscriminately the vessels both of native traders and of European merchants, and for half a century the Angria pirates were a terror in the Bombay Seas.'[19] George W. Forrest, editor of *Selections from the Letters*, describes Kanhoji Angre as the 'founder of a piratical empire, which extended from Goa to Bombay'.[20] The colonial and colonized story of the Angre house continued in the twentieth century. John Biddulph's *The Pirates of Malabar and An English Woman in India Two Hundred Years Ago*, provides an account of the piratical activity of the Angres and celebrates the English victory over them.[21] Admiral G.A. Ballard's *Rulers of the Indian Ocean* is a meta-narrative of the establishment of the British paramountcy in the Indian Ocean. In his view Kanhoji:

> ... was devoted to sea plunder as a methodical industry, with such success that the adventurer of humble birth not only amassed sufficient wealth to found and maintain a realm repudiating any allegiance to a higher lord for half a century, which was passed on to his sons, but actually left a more conspicuous name in the saltwater annals of the east than any of the great dynastic rulers in the history of Asia excepting Kublai Khan.[22]

The Indian nationalist historians reacted to the colonialist historiography. The colonialist assertion that any 'non state' actor who resisted the rise of British power in India was a pirate or brigand was anathema to the nationalists who began the trend of identifying and glorifying the victims of British descriptions as national heroes. For instance, Radhakumud Mookerji, S.N. Sen, V.G. Dighe and D.G. Dhabbu have provided us the nationalist interpretations of the career of Kanhoji. Mookerji published, *Indian Shipping: A History of The Sea-Borne Trade and Maritime Activity of The Indians From The Earliest Times*, in 1912.[23] This book was possibly a reaction to the work of C.R. Low. It valorizes indigenous Indian maritime, including naval, activities across the ages. It presents Kanhoji as master of the Konkan coast from Bombay to Vengurla in the name of the Satara Chief.[24] *The Military System of The Marathas* by S.N. Sen, mentioned earlier, contains a detailed discussion on *piracy* and *sovereignty* on the Arabian Sea.[25] According to Sen:

> Kanhoji Angria may be regarded as the second founder of the Maratha navy, just as Baji Rao I has been styled the second founder of the Maratha empire. He was inspired, as he wrote in his letter to Governor Phipps, by Shivaji's example, and whatever may be said of his naval practices, he undoubtedly re-established Maratha prestige at sea.[26]

So impressed was S.N. Sen by Kanhoji that he wrote another book in 1941, especially about the house of the Angres—*Early Career of Kanhoji Angria and Other Papers*. Sen glorifies Kanhoji as a, 'daring sailor' whose 'prowess brought him eternal fame and untold wealth. Master of the Konkan littoral, lord of the neighbouring waters, he defied the country powers and challenged the might of the merchant nations of the west.'[27] He believed that it was important for Indians to get 'a most illuminating history of the Maratha navy'. Without that the Indians, as colonial subjects with low self-esteem, would not be in a 'position to estimate properly Kanhoji Angre's services to his King and Country'. It was necessary also to arrive at a thorough assessment of European sea power around India.[28] Sen suggested this as a reference to acts of piracy by the English, Portuguese, Dutch and French men-o'-war in the Indian Ocean till as late as the nineteenth century. In the pre-modern times everyone was a pirate as and when the occasion arose; Francis Drake and Walter Raleigh, the great heroes of English naval history, gained fame by preying on Spanish galleons carrying silver on the Atlantic. In fact, the ill-fated Spanish Armada was Spain's response to Tudor piracy on the high seas, which was bleeding the Spanish monarchy dry.

'Kanhoji Angria' by V.G. Dighe, published in the *Sardesai Commemoration Volume* in 1938 argued that, 'To get a right perspective of Kanhoji's maritime activities they must be viewed as part of the general struggle of the Maratha nation against the Mughal conquest of their homeland.'[29] By the 1930s the 'Maratha Nation' had become an established fact of medieval Indian history. While perceiving the Angres in a nationalist frame, it must be remembered that Kanhoji and his sons, especially Tulaji, fought several opponents simultaneously and the Sidis, with whom Kanhoji negotiated the dual control of the Konkan, were only one among them. The diplomatic acumen of Kanhoji befitted his stature as a great admiral. He knew when to fight and when to negotiate treaties in an era when enmity between rival powers was impermanent. The fact that the Sidis and English negotiated with him, lends credence to his claims of being a sovereign on the Konkan coast. His career was more than three decades long and exceptional by eighteenth-century standards. He left behind a family in control of strong forts and a well-organized navy. This enabled his successors to ward-off the Europeans and the land powers in the hinterland for almost twenty-seven years, till 1756.

There is reason to believe that had Manaji Angre not gone over to the Anglo–Peshwa alliance in 1755, the house of the Angres would have survived in good form for a longer time. The first complete Marathi history of the Angre family—*Kulabakar Angre Sarkhel (Angre Gharanyacha Itihas)*—written by D.G. Dhabu, was published in 1939.[30] This work exposes the differences between the characteristics of pirates and the Angres.[31] Further, since all the political actors in the Arabian Sea, in the seventeenth and eighteenth centuries, resorted to piracy, Kanhoji's acts of piracy were justified by contemporary standards.[32] Moreover, Kanhoji was an admiral appointed by the Maratha ruler.[33]

This view persists in postcolonial history writings on Kanhoji Angre. A number of historical biographies and novels on him have been published since 1947. These include Manohar Malgonkar's *Kanhoji Angre, Maratha Admiral: An Account of His Life and his Battles with the English* (1959) and *Sea Hawk*, another work by Malgonkar on Kanhoji, which was translated by the famous public intellectual, humourist and artist, P.L. Deshpande, as *Kanhoji Angre* (1986)—these works made Sarkhel Kanhoji Angre immensely popular in Maharashtra.[34] *Swami Daryache* (1997) by B.V. Athavale, D.R. Ketkar's *Sarkhel Kanhoji Angre* (1997), and Sadashiv Shivde's *Daryaraj Kanhoji Angre* (2006), are more recent biographies.[35] All the biographies and novels mentioned here promote the view popularized by the nationalist historians earlier. An illustrated and informative book written by B.K. Apte, *A History of the Maratha Navy and Merchantships*, was published in 1973 and remains an important source of

Maratha maritime history.[36] His chapter on 'Sovereignty of the Sea' offers the following:

> ... it can be safely concluded that the Angres ... followed the practice that was current in respect of their maritime rights. In their own waters, they had every right to establish their equality along with the Europeans. The attribute 'pirate' applied by the Europeans to the Angres in particular was simply abusive. As representatives of their sovereign power, the Angres were fully justified in exercising their maritime rights which in no way could be questioned at least by the Europeans who came from beyond the seven seas, and did not belong to this country.[37]

⚓ ⚓ ⚓

Defining the Concept of Maritime

What does 'maritime' connote in naval history? In general, it means something to do with the seas or oceans. Thus, historians write of maritime routes, trade and histories. In a naval context the word maritime refers to the capability to project power on the high seas.[38] Two factors are necessary to do so: a blue-water navy like the Indian Navy today, for example; and, far flung well-provisioned maritime bases, which may be founded on islands or coasts of obliging or conquered countries. *In this sense, no Indian medieval power was a maritime power*. All notable medieval Indian gunpowder kingdoms were primarily land-based. They did not, and in fact *could not*, visualize the open seas in the same way as the futuristic Europeans did. Indians sailed the high seas as merchants and pilgrims, but in their consciousness the ocean was not a battlefield on which the histories of countries would be decided. This was unlike the European consciousness, informed by naval wars in the Mediterranean and the Atlantic Ocean during the fifteenth and sixteenth centuries.

Indian political and military actors on the Malabar and Konkan coasts were essentially coastal powers in command of brown-water navies comprising native ships not designed to fight on the high seas. Further, these navies were dependent on support from the land powers. Many of the ships these navies fielded, were galleys which wasted a lot of human energy in an age dominated by the ocean-going men-o'-war. By the end of the eighteenth century, the age of sail had entered its last decades and steam ships were round the corner.

It is surmised that, Tipu Sultan was the only Indian ruler who understood the limitations of a brown-water navy and tried to make amends by planning the construction of a blue-water navy capable of fighting the English on the high seas. Before his plan could be put into practice, he was defeated and killed by the British in 1799. In a magisterial treatise on the Royal Navy called *The Navy*, Oliver Warner offers the following enlightening words to us:

> The facts upon which the Navy acted required it to ensure the sea-borne traffic of a world empire. It must deny the seas to the enemy; sustain allies; transport armies wherever strategy may decide; and supply them when landed. It must safeguard the country against invasion, and defeat the enemy in battle.[39]

Warner traces the evolution of the Royal Navy from the birth of an idea of navy during the Tudor times to its gradual emergence as an instrument of national policy in the modern age. This is also a history of port barons and admirals being brought into line by the emerging nation-state in Britain. Another well-known scholar of naval affairs was A.T. Mahan whose persuasive work, *The Influence of Sea Power Upon History, 1660-1783* (1890), influenced naval shipbuilding in many countries and especially Germany. The only country in Asia which could have followed the European route to naval greatness was China whose respected junks—larger and more solid than the European galleons of the sixteenth century—once sailed without fear on the high seas and, it is claimed, circumnavigated the world before Magellan. In India's case, the transition to a blue-water navy was pre-empted by the establishment of British colonialism quickly after 1757. Whether India's 'port barons' or autonomous admirals in possession of jagirs and lands would have been integrated into navies functioning in accordance with a national policy, remains a matter of speculation and counter history. Though, in the period from 1550 to 1750, some could have been identified on the western coast of India.

All local Asian navies in the early modern or late medieval centuries were brown-water navies. They performed admirably in the shallows, but without support from a major land power, which possessed the money for technological improvement, their fate was sealed. Meticulous documentation on their nature and modus operandi by European sources has come down to us, making possible research such as this.[40] The galley had its time and place in history but in the ultimate analysis lacked the 'powers to injure an enemy from a great distance, to manoeuvre for an unlimited length of time without wearing out the men, to devote the greater part of the crew to the offensive weapons instead of to the oar.'[41] Even the Bombay

Marine, the naval arm of the EEIC on the west coast of India, deployed galbats, Ghurabs and other native craft manned by Indian lascars but it enjoyed the support of the Royal Navy to which the Indian powers had no answer.

⚓⚓⚓

The Angre Naval Power Post-Kanhoji:1729-1756

Upon Kanhoji's death in 1729, his eldest son Sekhoji Angre, also known as Jaysing Angre, was appointed the Maratha Sarkhel by the Peshwa. Sekhoji continued the war against the EEIC and its allies the Sawants of Wadi and Sidis of Janjira. Emboldened by Kanhoji's death, the EEIC lost no time in launching new offensives against Sekhoji. By 1733, Sekhoji was also at loggerheads with the Portuguese, who accused him of breaking the truce treaty they had signed with his father in 1722. In 1733, Sekhoji enthusiastically supported Baji Rao I against the Sidis who were finally forced to surrender several important forts to the Marathas. With the Mughal empire in rapid decline, the reduction of Sidi power on the Konkan was a foregone conclusion.

Even as the Marathas were victorious against their old adversaries, internecine conflict arose between Sekhoji's brothers, Sambhaji and Manaji, after Sekhoji's premature death in 1734. Manaji solicited English support against his brother, which the EEIC gladly gave. The Portuguese first favoured Sambhaji, based closer to Goa, but later switched sides to Manaji. Consequently, in February 1735, the Peshwa negotiated peace between the warring brothers and the Konkan coast was divided between the two. Manaji was powerful in Kolaba, and Sambhaji in Suvarnadurg. Sambhaji retained the title of Sarkhel and Manaji was given a new title 'Vizaarat-mab' to keep him in good humour. However, the truce soon failed and Sambhaji invaded his brother's territory. Manaji managed to survive with help from the Peshwa and the EEIC. In the meantime, Sambhaji continued to follow the naval tradition established by his late father and between 1735 and 1742, when this intrepid naval commander died, numerous ships and fleets belonging to the Europeans were attacked relentlessly.[42] In 1758, Manaji too died, but not before antagonizing the EEIC and the Peshwa over the possession of the island of Karanja.

Tulaji Angre succeeded his brother Sambhaji as the Sarkhel in 1742, and quickly developed a reputation as the 'most dreaded buccaneer on the west coast'.[43] According to Apte he broke all Angre records 'in making prize of foreign ships'.[44] In the 1740s and 1750s, when the financially strained Peshwa and the adventurous Maratha Sardars were busy with their campaigns in Malwa, Gujarat and Hindustan, Tulaji emerged as a political challenger in the Peshwa's backyard. Simultaneously, Tulaji's audacity and capability left the EEIC hapless and the Arabian Sea trade vulnerable to his relentless attacks. Sea traffic between Madras, Bombay and Calcutta, the major EEIC centres of trade and commerce, was thrown out of gear. Even as the English fought the French on the Carnatic, Gujarati and Arab trading ships were seized regularly by Tulaji for huge ransoms.

According to Apte, the Peshwa invited the English to join in an alliance against Tulaji.[45] This invitation was based on the naval strength the EEIC commanded in comparison with the Peshwa. In early 1755 the Peshwa sent three letters to Governor Bourchier of Bombay in this regard. The letters led to a treaty that spelled out six important points, which no student of colonialism should miss. First, in the campaign against Tulaji the joint naval expedition would be led by the English. Two, Tulaji's ships taken prize would be divided equally between the allies. Three, after victory the Peshwa would cede to the English Bankot, Himmatgarh and five tax-exempt villages. Four, the English were tasked with launching a full-scale naval expedition against the Angre Navy. Five, treasure, munitions, guns and all material found in Tulaji's forts would be shared equally between the Peshwa and the English. Six, in the event of war against Manaji, the island of Khanderi would be ceded to the English.

In 1755, the Peshwa and the EEIC Bombay authorities duly signed the treaty and their combined forces inflicted a serious defeat on Tulaji at Suvarnadurg, the island fortress where his father, Kanhoji Angre, had started his military career. After the fall of Suvarnadurg in April 1755, the allies gathered their forces and allowed the monsoon to pass. They launched the next phase of the campaign against a weakened Tulaji in February 1756 in calmer weather. The English under Clive and Admiral Watson, who commanded the heavily armed Royal Navy men-o'-war, sailed from Bombay on 7 February 1756. This formidable armed force was joined by the Peshwa's brown-water ships closer to Vijaydurg. By then, a large Maratha army had blockaded Vijaydurg from the inland side. However, as was usual for them, the Marathas were disunited because one faction favoured a deal with Tulaji and appeared half-hearted in battle.

On 11 February 1756, the English armada anchored at Vijaydurg and sealed the creek to immobilize Tulaji's Navy. Admiral Watson, as *de jure* commander of the expedition, sent Tulaji a letter seeking surrender without bloodshed. The answer he received is worth quoting:

> ... the garrison were well apprised of the force he (Admiral) brought with him but if agreeable to the summons he sent he was resolved to be master of the fort he must take it by force for they (beleaguered) were resolved to defend themselves to the last extremity.

The next day the Angre ships, bottled in the creek with no chance of escaping into the open sea, opened fire on the English ships and the battle began. Soon a fire began on one of the Angre ships and spread rapidly across Tulaji's entire fleet, consuming it quickly. The dry dock was gutted. At the same time, either due to the fire spreading from the ships or as hell fired from an English ship, the gunpowder magazine in the fort blew up causing mayhem among the besieged. The fire raged through the night of 12 February, and finally forced Tulaji and his garrison to surrender on 13 February 1756.

Clive had militarily outsmarted the Marathas by easily positioning himself between the besieging Marathas on land and the fort, because he arrived from the mouth of the creek and landed on a beach close to the fort. The English had made haste because they suspected some Marathas of treachery. On 14 February 1756, following Tulaji's surrender, Clive led the EEIC units into the fort and hoisted the English flag. The English plundered the fort with piratical thoroughness—Rs 10,00,000 in cash and valuables to the tune of £4,000 were looted by them, while the Marathas stood outside the fort twiddling their thumbs.

No matter what the terms of the Anglo-Maratha Treaty of 1755 were, the English had been determined right from the beginning not to adhere to them. Clive, who hated India and Indians and had returned from England determined to make a large fortune, was not a man to be trifled with. Events proved that the politically short-sighted Peshwa, Balaji Baji Rao (Nana Saheb) had been taken for a ride by the EEIC. Except for the custody of Tulaji, the Peshwa got nothing from the fall of Vijaydurg. The mighty Peshwa *did not receive a single paisa*.

Tulaji was taken prisoner and spent the next thirty years of his life in various Maratha jails away from the coast. The EEIC retained Vijaydurg for five months till the humbled Peshwa fulfilled the promises *he* had made to the Company in 1755. Thus the meaning of sovereignty had obviously changed on the Konkan much before the Anglo–Maratha Wars (1775-82 and 1803-05) which put paid to Maratha ambitions in India. Fighting as commander of the EEIC forces during the Battle of Vijaydurg provided Clive valuable experience, which helped him defeat the nawab of Bengal in 1757.

The fall of Vijaydurg 'proved to be disastrous' for Maratha power on the Konkan and Apte places this fall at the door of the 'feudal system of the Marathas'.[46] After Tulaji, Maratha naval power declined rapidly. In north Konkan, Manaji was succeeded by Raghoji Angre who became the Peshwa's ally. Later, his descendants became minor players in the English Subsidiary Alliance Treaty System.

Notes

1 See p. 115, in James Douglas, *Bombay and Western India*, Vol. I, K.K. Book Distributors, 1985.

2 See p. 86, in Alpers, *The Indian Ocean in World History*, 2014.

3 For a full account of the rise and fall of the house of the Angre admirals, see Anirudh Deshpande and Muphid Mujawar, *The Rise and*

Fall of a Brown Water Navy: Sarkhel Kanhoji Angre and the Maratha Seapower on the Arabian Sea in the 17th and 18th Centuries, Aakar Books, 2021.

4 For details of navigation in the pre-modern Konkan area see the relevant chapters in, Shefali Balsari-Shah and Sunita Nair, eds, *Gateways to the Sea: Historic Ports and Docks of Mumbai Region*, Publications Division, Ministry of Information and Broadcasting, Government of India, 2024.

5 This point is underlined, *passim*, in Clements R. Markham, *A Memoir on the Indian Surveys*, W.H. Allen and Company, 1871; and by Charles Rathbone Low, *History of The Indian Navy (1613-1863)*, Vol. I, Manas Publication, reprint, 1985.

6 See pp.153,154, in *Marathyanchya Itihasachi Sadhane: Portuguese Dafter Khand 3: Asia Vibhag (Bhag 1-5) (1663-1739)*, translated into Marathi by S.S. Desai, Maharashtra Rajya Sahitya va Sanskruti Mandal, 1968. The original work was in Portuguese and was edited by A.B. de Bargança Pereira.

7 See pp. 65-85, in Luis Filipe F.R. Thomaz, 'Precedents and Parallels of the Portuguese Cartaz System', in *The Portuguese, Indian Ocean and European Bridgeheads, 1500-1800: Festschrift in Honour of Prof. K.S. Mathew*, ed. Pius Malekandathil and Jamal Mohammed, Institute for Research in Social Sciences and Humanities, MESHAR. 2001.

8 See p. 44, in Om Prakash, *European Commercial Enterprise in Pre-Colonial India*. The New Cambridge History of India series, Cambridge University Press,1998.

9 See p. 277, in K.S. Matthew, 'Portuguese Trade with India and Theory of Royal Monopoly in the Sixteenth Century', in *Essays in Medieval Indian Economic History*, ed., Satish Chandra, Indian History Congress, Golden Jubilee Year Publication, Vol. III, Munshiram Manoharlal Publishers, 1987.

10 See p. 200, in Apte, *The Maratha Navy*,1973.

11 See p. 288, in *Marathyanchya Itihasachi Sadhane*, 1968; see pp. 214-30, in Sen, *The Military System of the Marathas*, 1979; and see pp. 276-83 in Matthew, 'Portuguese Trade with India', 1987.

12 See p. 196, in Clement Downing, *A History of Indian Wars*, Oxford University Press, reprint, 1924, originally published in 1737.

13 Abraham Anselm, *A Faithful Narrative of the Capture of the Ship DERBY by Angria the Pirate, on the Coast of Malabar, December 26, 1735*, S. Osborn,1738.

14 See p. 408, in Vol. 1, of Robert Orme, *History of The Military Transactions of the British Nation in Indostan From the Year MDCCXLV: to which is prefixed a dissertation on the establishments made by Mohomedan conquerors in Indostan,* Vol. I. Printed for John Nourse, bookseller in ordinary to His Majesty. 1803.

15 *The London Gazette,* 5-6 November 1756.

16 See pp. 21-25, in Anonymous, 'An Authentick and *Faithful History* of That Arch-Pyrate Tulagee *Angria', The Scots magazine, 1756.*

17 James Grant Duff. *A History of the Marrattas,* Vol. I, R. Cambray & Co., 1918.

18 Low, *History of the Indian Navy,* 1985.

19 See p. 383, in Frederick Charles Danvers. The *Portuguese in India being a History of the Rise and Decline of Their Eastern Empire,* W.H. Allen & Co. Ltd., 1894.

20 See 'Introduction', in *Selections from the Letters, Despatches, and other State Papers,* Vol. I, Part I, 1885.

21 Biddulph, *The Pirates of Malabar,*1907.

22 See p. 234, in Ballard, *Rulers of the Indian Ocean,*1998.

23 Radhakumud Mookerji, *Indian Shipping: A History of the Sea-Borne Trade and Maritime Activity of the Indians from the Earliest Times,* re-published by Munshiram Manoharlal Publishers, 1999.

24 Ibid., pp. 239-40.

25 Sen, *The Military System of the Marathas,* 1979.

26 Ibid., p. 189.

27 Ibid., p. 190.

28 Ibid. pp. 10-11.

29 Ibid. p. 102.

30 Dhabu, D.G. *Kulabakar Angre Sarkhel (Angre Gharanyacha Itihas).* Alibag, 1939.

31 Ibid. pp. 416-17.

32 Ibid. p. 417.

33 Ibid.

34 Malgonkar, *Kanhoji Angre, Maratha Admiral, 1959.*

35 Manohar Malgonkar, *The Sea Hawk: Life and Battles of Kanhoji Angrey,* Mehta Publishing House, 1984. This book was translated into Marathi: P.L. Deshpande, transl., *Kanhoji Angre,* Mehta Publishing House, 1986.

36 Apte, A History of the Maratha Navy, 1973.

37 Ibid., p. 204.

38 For the distinctions between maritime and coastal forts see M.S. Naravane, *The Maritime and Coastal Forts of India*, APH Publishing Corporation, 2002.

39 See p. 84, in Oliver Warner, *The Navy*, Penguin Books Ltd., 1968.

40 Relevant details of the Southeast Asian brown-water navies are present in the Portuguese sources. See, *Portuguese Documents on Malacca*, collected, translated and annotated by M.J. Pintado, Vol. I, 1509-1511, National Archives of Malaysia, 1993. See p. 65 (ibid.) for the description of a naval engagement between the Portuguese and the warships of the Sultan of Malacca given by Diogo Lopez De Squeira in his account of a journey he made to Malacca and return to Portugal in the early sixteenth century. Also, p. 147 (ibid.) for the description of a naval battle between a native junk and the Portuguese, given by Afonso De Albuquerque (1511) on the route he took from Cochin to the island of Sumatra. This junk was used so skilfully by the Muslim naval sailors that the Portuguese called it the 'brave junk'. The natives used it as a fire ship against Afonso's galleon and managed to set its forecastle on fire after being damaged 'badly' by Portuguese artillery. The Admiral's galleon, *Flor de la Mar*, 'ungrappled' in time 'for the flames were already licking the forecastle of his galleon.' Later the Muslims doused the fire, started by the use of naptha, on the junk. Indian brown-water navies, in contrast, were unaware of naptha or other such substances which could be used to create fire ships.

41 See p. 66 in Mahan, *The Influence of Sea Power Upon History*, 2007.

42 See pp. 79-83, in Apte, *A History of the Maratha Navy*, 1973.

43 Ibid, p. 82.

44 Ibid.

45 Apte, *A History of the Maratha Navy*, 1973.

46 Ibid., pp. 82-83.

6

Maritime Fortifications: Defending Land and Sea

Pushkar Sohoni

⚓ ⚓ ⚓

The competition for naval prowess on the west coast was accompanied by intense building activity. Cartazes, dastaks, and other permits issued by competing sovereign sea-powers were enforced by manned sea-crafts, and a network of fortified strongholds that served a variety of military and strategic functions. The forts built by the Marathas became iconic of their navy, and serve as reminders of the visionary thinking of the founder of the Maratha kingdom, Chhatrapati Shivaji Maharaj.

The west coast of peninsular India has a long maritime history with evidence of at least two millennia of trade.[1] On this coast today, the coastline of the state of Maharashtra is about 720 kilometres along the Arabian Sea. The state of Maharashtra was founded only in 1960, but the Maratha Navy founded in 1659 by Chhatrapati Shivaji Maharaj controlled a coast of approximately the same length: from Tarapur to Karwar—barring the strongholds of other powers such as the English in Bombay, the Sidi in Janjira, and the Portuguese in Goa. Since its establishment in 1659, the Maratha Navy remained a vital and important force for over a hundred years, resisting the established sea-powers on the west coast.[2]

The navy comprised not only sea-craft and personnel, but a series of coastal strongholds that provided important logistical and military support. These locations had maritime forts and were often supplemented by smaller military bases. This density of maritime forts—one or more predictably at the mouth of every estuary, and several on islands at a short distance from the mainland—is absent from the rest of the Indian seaboard. Therefore, understanding them as part of the seascape of the period is important for a study of the Maratha Navy.

⚓ ⚓ ⚓

Early Naval Activity

From the sixteenth century onwards, there were several military entities on the west coast of India, including the Portuguese and the regional sultanates. The Deccan sultanates of Ahmadnagar and Bijapur were land-based kingdoms, but the coast was their frontier for trade. Their maritime networks ensured that they received a steady supply of goods and people from West Asia; warhorses and men of letters being particularly important.[3] These sultanates built forts such as Janjira (Ahmadnagar) and Gheria or Vijaydurg (Bijapur), mostly to protect their trading interests and their entrepôt settlements. The Portuguese, and generally European, attitude of preventing free trade and issuing permits for trading, disrupted the open seas.[4] Therefore, it is no surprise that as early as 1507 a joint force of the sultans of the Deccan and Gujarat along with the Mamluks of Egypt, fought and defeated a Portuguese naval force in the Battle of Chaul.[5]

From the early seventeenth century onwards, the English and the Sidi became significant maritime powers on the Konkan coast. The Sidi had been set up as naval commanders at Janjira by the Nizam Shahs of Ahmadnagar, and immediately after the regency of Malik Ambar in the early seventeenth century, they became nominal vassals of the Adil Shahs of Bijapur.[6] The EEIC came to the west coast seeking concessions for trading, but to protect its trading interests it quickly raised a military and naval establishment. All these powers, the English, Portuguese, and Sidi, made fickle alliances when it suited them. The Maratha Navy, raised in 1659 under Chhatrapati Shivaji Maharaj, rapidly grew in strength over the next hundred years. The Maratha naval enterprise was initially directed against the Sidi, who joined in any alliance against the Marathas, first with the Portuguese, then the English, and eventually the Mughals.[7] In 1670, the Sidi, who had for several decades operated on behalf of Bijapur, were appointed commanders of the Mughal Navy with the title of Yaqut Khan.[8]

All naval powers required support from the land, and through the seventeenth and eighteenth centuries, forts were acquired, built and captured, by the Portuguese, English, Sidi and the Marathas. The Marathas had a lot at stake, since they also had a deep territory to protect, not just an extensive shoreline. Therefore, a system of maritime fortifications was developed over time. There are broadly three types of maritime forts: those on the mainland, a second type on islands in the sea in close proximity to the land, and the third are on promontories sometimes connected by a narrow isthmus. The last have characteristics of both mainland and island forts. All these forts represent one end of the network of fortifications that commanded land and river routes over the Western Ghats up to the Deccan. Along the coast, they also formed a line of protection posts for coastal cruising, and for launching quick attacks against enemy ships. Almost all the estuaries had fortifications, to prevent enemy vessels from entering rivers which had harbours for the small craft of the Maratha Navy.

The forts also featured unique signalling systems, to communicate with other nearby forts and outposts, thus creating an early warning network along the coast. Such communication systems had already been devised for use on the hill forts of the Marathas. Thus the Maratha Navy, which started from scratch, primarily against the Sidi, but also the English and the Portuguese, did not possess any historic expertise in fighting at sea. It also had inherent weaknesses in not possessing the latest gunpowder technology, and often had to source artillery from the English.[9] Similarly, Chhatrapati Shivaji Maharaj's sea crafts were also all derived from Portuguese designs; he commissioned the first boats to be built in 1659 at Vasai by Portuguese shipbuilders Roe Leitao Viegas and his brother Fernao Leitao Viegas, with 300 to 400 people working for them.[10] But just within a few years, Shivaji had people building ships for his navy at several places, such as Chaul, Bhiwandi and Kalyan.

It is amply clear that the success of the naval enterprise was possible only because of the support of maritime fortifications, as is evidenced in the letter sent by the Viceroy at Goa, Conde de San Vicente, to the king of Portugal in 1667: 'I am afraid of Shivaji's naval ships. We did not take sufficient preventive steps and so he has built many a fort on the Konkan coast.'[11]

⚓⚓⚓

Maratha Naval Fortification

The Marathas acquired and inherited a number of forts built by the Adil Shahs of Bijapur and the Nizam Shahs of Ahmadnagar. But some of the most notable maritime forts in Maharashtra were built during the reign of Chhatrapati Shivaji Maharaj in the seventeenth century. While the Marathas understood the importance of naval power, they were essentially a territorial power; their navy was a green-water navy, capable only of movement in coastal waters, ports, and harbours, as opposed to a true blue-water navy which could sail out to high seas.[12] Given that they did not possess large ships with broadside attacks, maritime forts were important for them, as they functioned like stationary ships with artillery. These fortifications served multiple purposes: they safeguarded trading routes, provided bases for naval operations, and acted as a deterrent against invasions from sea-based powers.

The architecture of these forts incorporated elements specifically suited to maritime defences. High walls resistant to cannon fire, strategic placement of artillery and intricate systems for storing fresh water were common features. Many forts also included hidden underwater obstructions to damage enemy ships that ventured too close. Gunpowder was a very important element of coastal and naval warfare, particularly since it was easier to transport artillery by water than over land.[13] Besides, the large and open distances were conducive to fighting with large guns. Therefore, coastal forts had to defend against artillery from the sea, and also from land. The natural defensibility of a fort, being surrounded by water, or having a single access point from the mainland, also meant that the fort was very easily blockaded for supplies. Therefore, most important maritime forts had to be the centre of a cluster for forts from which diversionary parties could be sent to facilitate restocking of the fort.

Some of finest examples of coastal and maritime forts on the Maharashtra coast are Sindhudurg, Vijaydurg, Janjira, Kolaba and Vasai. They are a representative sample of five important maritime forts on the coast of Maharashtra; each one of them was supported by a group of smaller forts in the vicinity. These fortifications were designed to take advantage of their natural surroundings, often built on rocky outcrops or small islands. Their strategic locations allowed for control over shipping lanes and provided early warning systems against approaching enemy fleets. While all the fort sites have older histories, all of them were constructed in their present configuration between the sixteenth and eighteenth centuries: three of them by the Marathas, one by the Sidi, and one by the Portuguese. Construction technology, particularly of a specialized nature as in the building of forts, was not limited by ethnicity or statehood. The embrace of new forms of military architecture with an understanding of its utility against new war technologies, was the reason for the construction of these forts. The Marathas therefore did not shy away from using Portuguese or Sidi experts in the construction of their sea forts, or indeed for ship-building.[14]

⚓ ⚓ ⚓

Sindhudurg

Figure 1. West wall of Sindhudurg fort following the curves of the island.
Source: *Wikimedia Commons*, https://commons.wikimedia.org/wiki/File:Sindhudurg_Fort_West_wall.jpg

The fort was constructed by Chhatrapati Shivaji Maharaj between 1664 and 1667 as part of his naval stratagem. He had been unsuccessful at capturing Janjira, and to keep an eye on the Sidi, he built the fort as his coastal headquarters. Located on a low island just off the coast of Malvan, it had an irregular perimeter of just over 3 kilometres, and enclosed 48 acres. The many projections and indentations in the plan ensured gun coverage of all areas of the sea. The walls and ramparts were around 8 to 10 metres tall with thirty-two round towers, adequate to keep out any attackers by sea, and also to withstand cannon fire. Lead is said to have been used in its construction.[15] Portuguese engineers were employed in the construction.[16] This is likely given that the towers have fine embrasures for guns, a European feature.

Hiroji Indolkar, famous for building Raigad, is thought to have been responsible for designing the fort. The entrance to the fort faces the mainland, but is not easy to find, being cleverly concealed. In 1713, the fort was transferred to the Kolhapur branch of the Bhonsales, from where it was used to harass English ships.[17] It was captured by the English in 1765, and they renamed it Fort Augustus; however, they found it difficult to maintain or even dismantle it and returned it to Kolhapur with an assurance that it would not be used against them.[18] Around the fort, towards the mainland on a smaller island is the outpost known as Padmagad, part reef, part sand and only an acre. This was the site used to manufacture boats under Chhatrapati Shivaji Maharaj.[19] Just to the north, the cove that contains the Kolamb estuary is protected by two small fortified positions called Rajkot and Sarjekot.

⚓ ⚓ ⚓

Vijaydurg

Figure 2. Vijaydurg fort showing multiple lines of defensive walls.
Source: *Wikimedia Commons* https://upload.wikimedia.org/wikipedia/commons/0/03/Vijaydurg_fort_N-MH-M87.jpg

Built on a promontory at the estuary of the Vaghotan river, this fort is said to have pre-existed the Adil Shahs of Bijapur, who are credited with building it; they called it Gheria.[20] Chhatrapati Shivaji Maharaj captured it in 1653, renamed it Vijaydurg, and made several improvements, particularly the triple line of defensive walls with twenty-seven towers. This fort became the base for Kanhoji Angre, appointed as the Sarkhel (Admiral) of the Marathas in 1698. Angre harassed merchant ships incessantly, and despite several efforts of the English, Dutch and Portuguese to conquer the fort, individually and jointly, they could not capture it.

The harbour of the fort had shallow waters, and large vessels could not chase Angre's small craft when they sought protection in the estuary. Under Chhatrapati Shahu, Kanhoji

Angre became a loyalist of the Satara seat of the Marathas. After Kanhoji's death in 1729, his sons Sekhoji, Sambhaji and Tulaji, in turn kept the Maratha flag flying high in the Arabian Sea off the coast of Konkan. However, due to an internal feud between the Peshwa and Tulaji Angre, a joint force of the English and the Peshwas (representing the Chhatrapati at Satara) eventually reduced Tulaji to submission in 1756.

The English wanted to keep the fort, offering Bankot in exchange, but the Peshwa refused.[21] Ironically, the fort was then used as a base by the Peshwa's Admiral, Anandrao Dhulap, to raid English ships. Just 3 kilometres up the Vaghotan river is a Maratha dry dock. A Martello tower, a couple of kilometres further upstream and built in 1862, was reported in the *Gazetteer* less than a couple of decades later.[22] The fort of Ambolgad, just short of 10 kilometres north along the coast, guarded the estuary that leads to Rajapur. The large creek about 20 kilometres south was controlled by the fort of Devgad.

⚓ ⚓ ⚓

Janjira

Truly an impregnable fort that could not be conquered, despite constant attempts by the Marathas and the English, Janjira became synonymous with the Sidi, who occupied the fort from the early sixteenth century to the mid-twentieth.[23] The fort's walls are congruent with the perimeter of the island, and the waters that separate the mainland are shallow, thus allowing only punted boats at low tide. The walls are over 15 metres high when the sea is at its highest and are punctuated by seventeen towers that are somewhat evenly spaced at every 30 metres. The walls appear to be three-storied from the outside, with the uppermost storey for artillery. The middle storey has small square openings that would prevent scaling attacks but can be used for defences.

Figure 3. The impregnable island fort of Janjira.

Source: *Wikimedia Commons*, https://upload.wikimedia.org/wikipedia/commons/5/52/Janjira_fort_-_panoramio.jpg

Janjira has several large artillery pieces from different periods and places. Inside the fort were a number of administrative, military and residential buildings, since the island fort was the complete capital and residence of the Sidi. Many of these buildings were burnt in a fire in 1860.[24] The entrance was on the landward side, not easily discernible. Towards the sea was only a small postern. Across on the mainland was the fort of Rajpuri, built by the Marathas to check the Sidi, who conquered it in an attack in 1671.[25] The nearby island of Padmadurg was fortified in 1693, commanding the bay 3 kilometres north of Janjira.[26] Janjira was upgraded in at least three major building campaigns, the last one in the mid-eighteenth century. With its natural location and the liminal space that it occupied, neither land nor sea, it is a fort that resisted every territorial and naval power that tried to capture it.

⚓ ⚓ ⚓

Kolaba

Figure 4. Ramparts of Kolaba fort

Source: *Pushkar Sohoni*

Just off the coast of Alibag, built on a rocky outcrop that becomes an island at high-tide, lie the remains of the fort of Kolaba. The fort used tidal patterns as part of its defences.

During low-tide, the exposed shore was defended by a series of small cannons. Believed to have been built by Chhatrapati Shivaji Maharaj, it gained importance in the early eighteenth century when it became a stronghold of Kanhoji Angre.[27] It has defensive walls with seventeen towers and fortified outer work on the north. The land route to the north is controlled by a fortified outpost known as Sarjekot. It was said to have been built against artillery fire from Hirakot, which was built to the north-west of old Alibag town.

Water tanks, temples and some residential buildings are within the fort. Almost 10 kilometres north-west of the fort are the islands of Khanderi and Underi. The former was fortified under Chhatrapati Shivaji Maharaj in 1679, when he realized its advantage in controlling shipping lanes from Bombay to the south. While Khanderi was being built, it was repeatedly attacked by the English and the Sidi, but eventually the Sidi chief had to content himself with fortifying Underi instead. Kolaba fort was therefore extremely important for not only providing support to Khanderi, but also to blockade the sea-lanes—from the Portuguese Northern Provinces, from Bombay to Goa, and the southern ports.

⚓ ⚓ ⚓

Vasai

A formidable fort was built by the Portuguese in 1536 on an older fortified site that had been handed over to them a couple of years earlier by the Sultan of Gujarat as per a treaty, along with other islands in the region.[28] The fort was built over a period of half a century and had ten strong towers, but was lost to the Marathas in 1739. The architecture of the fort shows

European innovations, such as Vauban's 'trace Italienne' in its planning.[29] A ditch was also constructed around the fort, and filled with saltwater.[30] Much like the Portuguese fort at Revadanda, several churches and monasteries were built inside Vasai fort too.

Figure 5. Northern bastions of Vasai fort showing Vauban's 'trace Italienne'

Source: Google Earth

Guarding Vasai creek of the Ulhas river, the fort was an important location and controlled several land and sea routes. Agashi, Arnala (which has a Martello tower), Dharavi, were all fortified locations around the fort and provided support. The fort of Vasai itself was built in the form of an irregular decagon, approximately 2.5 kilometres in circumference. Each angle had a four-sided bastion, and the fort was mounted with ninety artillery pieces and seventy mortars.[31] Vasai was captured by the Marathas by using a two-pronged strategy: blockade from the sea by Angre's Navy, preventing reinforcements and supplies, and assaults from the land under Chimnaji Appa.

Maritime forts had some special requirements, including water-resistant construction that would prevent the extremely corrosive seawater from destroying material stored in the fort. Gunpowder magazines would have to be specially secured against humidity and saltwater. Apocryphally, such qualities of mortar are attributed to a variety of ingredients, including lead.[32] However, we also know of several fort walls with dry masonry, where no mortar was used, as in the walls at Kolaba fort.

Forts also required docking facilities, wherein ships could dock and be repaired. These docks had to be sheltered, so that they were not exposed to the enemy. Many of the docks were therefore on the landward side, where they were not in the line of sight of large craft. These docks were sometimes concealed, as in the case of Sindhudurg. Most importantly, all these forts integrated natural factors within their system of defences. For example, at several forts, the movement of tides added another layer of protection, as they would prevent large ships from approaching close. The timing of assaults and sieges was therefore synchronized with the knowledge of tidal movements. Kolaba fort, for instance, becomes an island at high tide and has an exposed causeway at low tide, and these changes were effectively used for logistical and naval movements.

All these forts had to have a secure supply of freshwater, usually stored in large cisterns. Sometimes, these cisterns were rain-fed, as in the case of Padmadurg, which would store rain-water for use through the entire year. In several other cases, such as Janjira, the large cisterns, tanks and wells, were reliant on fresh-water springs for their water supply. The ramparts of maritime forts had large guns with which enemy ships were kept at bay; this was particularly important because many of the European ships had powerful guns for effective broadside attacks. Allowing these ships close would have meant a bombardment of the fort walls. The guns therefore also had to be arranged in tiers, with the largest on the topmost ramparts of the fort, to give them the greatest range. Gun cavaliers and towers therefore played a very important role and had to be strong enough to withstand the vibrations from the firing of guns. Smaller guns were on the middle and lowest tiers. Kolaba fort is one such, where all three tiers of defence are seen. Artillery pieces, their mounts and the cavalier towers for them improved through the course of a century. Round towers were built in almost all the Maratha forts, and while they were better at deflecting shot than square towers, if a small boat was very close to the fort walls, it could result in a blind spot for those within the tower.

European tower designs, particularly after Vauban, were well-equipped to handle such contingencies. The Maratha Navy also evolved over time, and various kinds of craft are mentioned in different texts: the ghurab, tarande, taru, galbat, shibad, pagar, in the work of Krishnaji Anant Sabhasad; and machava, bathor, tirakati, pal, in the work of Malhar Ramrao Chitnis.[33] While the kinds of boats and craft kept changing, the broad patterns of naval warfare of the Marathas remained unchanged. Similarly, their fortifications did not evolve much through the seventeenth and eighteenth centuries. This was in keeping with a broader trend in the Deccan, wherein military architecture stopped directly responding to fast-evolving gunpowder technology after the sixteenth century.[34] Therefore, the changes occurred in all the mobile components of warfare such as artillery and infantry, and not so much in the static defences such as fortification, which remained quite conservative.

⚓⚓⚓

Conclusion

The Maharashtra Konkan was a rugged and hilly country, with dense forests, estuaries, streams and other impediments to the movement of large forces. Ruled by small chiefs and independent rulers, the interest for many of the states on the mainland was to secure passage to the many ports on the coast. With the arrival of European sea powers, maritime security took on a new dimension, as the Portuguese and later the English obtained concessions to build factories, which they used as a reason to possess forts and maintain troops. The sultans of Gujarat, the Nizam Shahs of Ahmadnagar, and the Adil Shahs of Bijapur too had several skirmishes between themselves in the Konkan. They had coerced several petty rulers in the Konkan into paying tribute and allowing mercantile movement. Forts were a means of keeping open trading passages and protecting mercantile interests. The Mughals nominally handed over the Konkan to the Adil Shahs in 1636 in return for annual tribute.[35] The Sidi shifted allegiance from the Nizam Shahs to the Adil Shahs and then to the Mughals, all in the course of the seventeenth century. They became a key power on the coast.

Chhatrapati Shivaji Maharaj started taking over the Konkan with his attack on Kalyan (1648), but despite many efforts, could not dislodge the Sidi from Janjira. He then set about building new inland forts like Birwadi and Lingana to keep the Sidi in check from land, and started strengthening his navy. The Maratha Navy was initially built to fend off the Sidi, and therefore it was no surprise that Shivaji 'fitted out a fleet in imitation of the Janjira Sidi'.[36] However, it is notable that European fort design barely affected Maratha fortification. In seventeenth-century Europe, military engineers and theorists were making revolutionary plans for defensive architecture, to keep pace with developments in guns and gunpowder manufacture. One of the most famous of these was Sébastien Le Prestre, Marquis of Vauban, known for devising principles of fort planning that eliminated blind spots for the defenders. These kinds of forts, using his famous 'trace Italienne' are popularly known as star forts, and the Portuguese forts in India show some of these principles, as can be seen in the bastions at Vasai and Revadanda. But Indian fortifications remained oblivious to these changes.

The reason for this was that Maratha war tactics could not keep pace with improvements in ships and their guns. While the defensive artillery on Maratha forts kept pace with changes in war, Maratha naval battle strategies remained essentially the same: guerrilla in their nature. Their major gambit was the swarming of large ships with light and nimble craft, making up for the lack of firepower with numbers and speed. Their attacking forces could quickly outmanoeuvre the English and Portuguese vessels, and also rapidly seek refuge in shallow estuarine waters, where large ships could not chase them. But the real advantage of the Marathas that all the other sea powers did not have, was the terrestrial support in terms of corresponding land-forts that could provide supply lines and reinforcements.

The English, Portuguese, and the Sidi, for the most part, were limited to their coastal enclaves, and used the forts to defend against land attacks. The Marathas, on the other hand, used their sea-forts as bases to control the sea through quick raiding movements. Forts were the nerve-centres from where dastaks and other permits could be enforced, taxes and tolls collected, and naval troops sustained and garrisoned. Eventually, none of these forts could withstand the firepower of the English by the end of the eighteenth century. Maratha prowess over the seas, which relied on able and energetic naval commanders, fast-moving and versatile crews, and guerrilla warfare, was not enough to withstand the onslaught of efficient rifled guns by the late eighteenth century.

Thus, Maratha maritime forts and naval tactics, which had been facing obsolescence since the inception of the navy, could not hold out against further technological advancements of war technology in the eighteenth century. And importantly, the formidable maritime forts certainly did not defend against political currents of the times, particularly after the Peshwa and the English collaborated to defeat Tulaji Angre as the rebel admiral of the Maratha Navy.

While Marathas made very innovative use of the coastal and the maritime forts to defend Konkan coast, they still needed floating forts - which were the mobile components supporting the maritime fortifications - to undertake offensive operations against their enemies. The details of Maratha Navy ships, it's crew and armament that helped establishing the Maratha Empire have been provided in the following chapter.

Notes

1 There is a rich body of scholarship on trade in the western Indian Ocean. See, for example, pp. 95-113, in Federico De Romanis, 'Patchworking the west coast of India: Notes on the Periplus of the Erythraean Sea', in *The Indian Ocean Trade in Antiquity*, Routledge, 2018.

2 To understand the Maratha Navy in a larger context, see MacDougall, *Naval Resistance to Britain's Growing Power in India*, 2014.

3 To get a sense of the trade in horses see pp. 123-38, in Ali Bahrani Pour, 'The Trade in Horses between Khorasan and India in the 13th – 17th centuries', in *The Silk Road*, Vol. 11, Silk Road Foundation. 2013, http://www.silkroadfoundation.org/newsletter/vol11/; to understand aspects of migration, see pp. 340-63, in Sanjay Subrahmanyam, 'Iranians Abroad: Intra-Asian Elite Migration and Early Modern State Formation', in *The Journal of Asian Studies*, Vol. 51, No. 2, May 1992.

4 For a change in attitudes, see Corey Tazzara, *Ports and free ports in the Old World: Political economy in the Mediterranean and the Indian Ocean (1500–1750)*, Routledge, 2024.

5 For a description of the battle of Chaul see pp. 92-93, in Shaykh Zaynuddin, *Tuḥfatu'l-Mujāhidīn*, transl. M.J. Rowlandson as *Tohfut-ul-Mujahideen*, 1833.

6 See pp. 174-82, esp. p. 175, in Pushkar Sohoni, 'Janjira Fort and Rajapuri Port: Connected Histories in a Coastal Complex', in *Gateways to the Sea*, ed., Balsari-Shah and Nair. 2024.

7 See pp. 320-24, esp. p. 320, in Amarendra Kumar, 'Keigwin's Bombay (1683-84) and The Maratha-Siddi Naval Conflict', in *Proceedings of the Indian History Congress*, Vol. 75, Platinum Jubilee, 2014.

8 See p. 303, in Sarkar, *Shivaji and His Times*, 1920.

9 See pp. 181-99, esp. p. 185, in Amarendra Kumar, 'The Politics of Military Control in the West Coast: Marathas, Mughals, and the Europeans, 1650-1730', in *Chinese and Indian Warfare: From the Classical Age to 1870*, ed., Kaushik Roy and Peter Lorge, Routledge, 2015.

10 See pp. 47-48, in Pissurlencar, *Portuguese–Mahratta Relations*, 1983.

11 Ibid., p. 49.

12 The Maratha Navy has also been called a brown-water navy, a term that would limit its operations to rivers and estuaries; see Aniruddh Deshpande and Muphid Mujawar, *The Rise and Fall of a Brown Water Navy: Sarkhel Kanhoji Angre and Maratha Sea Power on the Arabian Sea in the 17th and 18th Centuries*, Aakar Books, 2021.

13 See pp. 146-65, in Pratyay Nath, 'Battles, Boats, and Bridges, Mughal Amphibious Warfare, 1571-1612', in *Chinese and Indian Warfare: From the Classical Age to 1870*, ed. Kaushik Roy and Peter Lorge, Routledge, 2015.

14 See p. 51, in Apte, *A History of the Maratha Navy*, 1973.

15 See p. 25, in Naravane, *Forts of Maharashtra*, 1995.

16 Seep. 54, in Apte, A History of the Maratha Navy, 1973.

17 See p. 351, in *Gazetteer: Ratnagiri and Savantwadi*, Vol. X, 1880.

18 Ibid., p. 351.

19 See p. 50, in Apte, *A History of the Maratha Navy*, 1973.

20 See p. 380, in *Gazetteer: Ratnagiri and Savantwadi*, Vol. X, 1980.

21 Ibid., p. 383.

22 Ibid., p. 383. A Martello tower is a small, round independent fort-like defensive structure.

23 For a detailed description and history of the fort, see pp. 167-83, in Pushkar Sohoni, 'The Fort of Janjira', in *African Rulers and Generals in India*. Afro-South Asia in the Global African Diaspora, Vol. 1, University of North Carolina, Ethiopian and East African Studies Project; Ahmedabad Sidi Heritage and Educational Center, 2020.

24 See p. 463, *Gazetteer: Ratnagiri and Savantvadi*, Vol. X, 1880.

25 For the relationship between Janjira and Danda-Rajpuri, see pp. 174-82, in Pushkar Sohoni, 'Janjira Fort and Rajapuri Port: Connected Histories in a Coastal Complex', in *Gateways to the Sea*, ed., Balsari-Shah and Nair, 2024; also see p. 438, in the *Gazetteer: Kolaba and Janjira*, Vol XI, 1883.

26 See p. 466, *Gazetteer: Kolaba and Janjira*, Vol. XI, 1883.

27 See p. 260, in *Gazetteer: Kolaba and Janjira*, Vol. XI, 1883.

28 For a detailed history of Vasai fort and the region, see Joseph Gerson da Cunha, *Notes on the History and Antiquities of Chaul and Bassein*, Thacker, Vining & Co., 1876.

29 For the effectiveness of Vauban's designs, see pp. 297-330, in John A. Lynn, 'The Trace Italienne and the Growth of Armies: The French Case', in *The Journal of Military History*, Vol. 55, No. 3,1991.

30 See p. 29, in *Gazetteer: Thana – Places of Interest*, Vol. XIV, 1882.

31 Ibid., p. 30.

32 See p. 25, in Naravane, *Forts of Maharashtra*, 1995.

33 See p. 172, in Apte, *A History of the Maratha Navy*, 1973.

34 See pp. 111–26, in Pushkar Sohoni, 'From Defended Settlements to Fortified Strongholds: Responses to Gunpowder in the Early Modern Deccan' in *South Asian Studies*. British Association of South Asian Studies, Vol. 31, No. 1, January 2015.

35 See p. 143, *Gazetteer: Kolaba and Janjira*, Vol XI, 1883.

36 Ibid., p. 144.

7

Ships, Armament and Manpower of Maratha Navy from the Seventeenth to the Eighteenth Century: A Comparative Study

Ajay Agarwal

⚓ ⚓ ⚓

Introduction

In his seminal work, *The Influence of Sea Power upon History 1660-1783*, Alfred Thayer Mahan identified six constituents—geographical position, physical conformation, extent of territory, number of populations, character of the people and character of the government—that make any nation a great naval power. Thus, a country needs to ensure that these aspects are present in adequate measures and in harmony for it to be considered as a great maritime nation.[1] It seems that most of these factors fell in place in the sixteenth century in the Konkan region to give birth to an indigenous naval power, in the form of the Maratha Navy.

Till the end of the fifteenth century, prior to the arrival of the Europeans in the Indian Ocean, the concept of *mare liberum* existed at sea and the only interference in the maritime trade practiced by the merchants and ship's crew was from piracy.[2] However, the Portuguese changed it to *mare clausum* by introducing the 'cartaz system'.[3,4] When the Portuguese attempted to monopolize maritime trade, Indian sailors and merchants deeply resented these controls. In order to protect their source of revenue, the Marathas were also against any such restrictions imposed by foreign powers. This led to confrontations between the Marathas and the Portuguese, and later with the British too. These confrontations compelled Shivaji to invest in a navy, if only a modest one.

Marathas in the seventeenth century, under the dynamic great leadership of Chhatrapati Shivaji Maharaj, were attempting to establish 'Swarajya' (self-rule) while fighting with multiple enemies. On land it was the Mughals, the Sidis and some other minor neighbouring powers; on sea, there were equally formidable challenges from the Portuguese and the British. Hence the contestations on the land and sea had to be balanced with the limited resources held under the fledgling Maratha territories. It is here that the real genius and resourcefulness of the Marathas came into play as they delicately juggled existing resources to ensure that the enemy was kept off balance. They accomplished this by avoiding conventional military engagements on all war fronts, only using guerrilla-warfare tactics.

The Maratha armed forces were built on a very frugal scale and there was no high pomp and show involved. It is well known that most of the Maratha soldiers were relieved from active duty during the monsoon season so that they could engage in agricultural activities. The intensity of the monsoon also brought a halt to Maratha seafaring for a couple of months. Subsequently, when the sea became calm, the ships were again put out to sea. The creation of a naval establishment from scratch required significant expenditure which was not forthcoming, as Shivaji was clear that customs taxes and shipping revenue were not to be directly used for this purpose. While this may have resulted in a perpetual shortage of funds for the Maratha Navy, looking at the threat levels and the number of adversaries that the Maratha kings had to contend with, it appeared to be a prudent thought.

As is evident from the history of India, as compared to their land-based armies, kings and emperors have always shown lesser interest in naval matters. This is called 'sea-blindness' by some academic scholars. However, in the case of Shivaji, he understood the importance of the navy and ensured that a strong naval force was built and sustained. The weakness, in terms of number of ships and weapons, was compensated for by the use of highly effective battle tactics and the optimization of limited resources. By the early eighteenth century, the Maratha Navy had reached its zenith and held sway over the west coast of India under Kanhoji Angre, the sarkhel or admiral of the Maratha Navy. With a fleet of over 200 ships of various classes, Angre boldly confronted the enemies of the Maratha state, instilling fear in them.

This chapter presents an overview of Maratha ships, armaments and manpower that projected Maratha sovereign authority along the west coast of India. To enhance our understanding of the Maratha naval apparatus, a comparison with the Europeans forces has been included. This chapter is divided into two main sections. The first focuses upon shipbuilding and the armaments the ships were equipped with, and the second addresses the composition of the crew and manpower aboard the Maratha ships.

⚓ ⚓ ⚓

Shipbuilding and Naval Armaments

Indian-built ships and craft, propelled by sails and oars, have been sailing in the Indian Ocean since ancient times. These native ships were known by different names in the various regions where they were built—battelas, pattamars, kotias, manjis, batels (or baghlas), dinghis (or dhangis), manjis, odams, thonis, uru, etc.[5] India has an old and well-established boat-building industry spread along its west coast. The principal centres were Porbandar, Veraval, Kutch-Mandvi and Sikka-Bhavnagar on the Saurashtra and Kathiawar coast; Dabhol, Ratnagiri, Deogad and Malvanon the Konkan coast; Mangalore, Honnavar and Karwar in the Canara region; Calicut, Beypur and Kasaragod on the Malabar coast. On India's south-east coast were Tuticorin, Cuddalore and Nagapattinam in the Tamil Nadu region.[6]

This rich, centuries-old, maritime tradition of boat building and carrying out trade was skilfully used by Shivaji to build a Maratha Navy. In comparison to indigenous ships, however, the European warships were much superior in sea-keeping as well as in stand-off weapons. As B.K. Apte states, 'Marathas ... admired their huge ships, some of them constructed in the Bombay Docks, moving like leviathans. They were aware that their Ghurabs and Pals were no match for the heavily gunned and scientifically equipped English ships.'[7] Yet, in order to contest Portuguese or British supremacy over sea, the Marathas had no option but to pitch themselves against the two European navies, to the best of their abilities. This they did by making effective use of geographical features in their naval tactics.

The overall development of the Maratha Navy can be divided into two main phases. The first phase was the birth of the navy during the period of Shivaji's rule, and the second period was the growth of the navy under the leadership of his admiral, Kanhoji Angre, when it became much larger and more powerful. While Shivaji preferred smaller ships that could operate well close to the coast, Kanhoji built sturdier and larger ships that could be used on the deep seas. The Maratha ships, as was the trend in that era, were initially merchant ships that carried some armaments to protect themselves against pirates. Progressively, as these ships contested European naval ships with better war-fighting capabilities, they learnt their lesson and improved their own ship construction. In this endeavour they were helped by the following:

(a) The ships captured from foreign navies provided valuable inputs about the newer shipbuilding technologies.
(b) The hiring of experienced European sailors helped in improving weapon firing, cannon casting, modifying ship design, sails and riggings onboard Maratha ships.
(c) Transfer of new European technologies took place through the above means.

It may be important to remember here that in that period only low-caste Hindus were involved in sailing and shipbuilding activities. These people were also generally illiterate and poor. Hence, they put very little effort into learning new scientific technologies or even improving the existing ones. Contrary to this, the Europeans, and to some extent the Arabs, invested great efforts to develop their knowledge of ships and armaments and reaped rich dividends due to such forethought.

The ships of the Maratha Navy can be grouped into three broad categories—warships, merchant ships, and some dual-purpose merchant ships that could be used for either role. Some of these ships were built in Maratha/nearby shipyards, while others were captured and re-flagged as Maratha ships.

⚓ ⚓ ⚓

Maratha Warships

It may be appreciated that all ancient mariners named each type of platform built or used by them, in their own language. Hence the same type of ship was often known by one name in region X, and by another name in region Y. As there was no standardization in the construction or the nomenclature, it was also possible for a newer version of a boat to retain the old name, even though its design characteristics had evolved. Exchanges taking place within the shipping community resulted in one region adopting a vessel design in use in another region along with its name. Hypothetically, for instance, a 'dhow'. After being adopted, the original dhow design would be further refined, based on the adopter's own experience, but it continued to be called a dhow despite its differing characteristics. So, a dhow in two different regions, could mean two different classes of ships. It is also interesting to note that the re-design of these ships evolved very slowly, as the master shipwrights, who built them out of memory, took time to incorporate changes due to lack of proper documentation. Clearly local shipbuilders saw benefits of features from other ships and incorporated it in their own design. Due to these reasons, the distinctions between various classes of Maratha ships are not very clear and precise.

Usually, ships evolved in design and weaponry, as the requirement increased or roles demanded. Thus, the number of types and classes of ships in the Maratha period could be as many as fifty-one![8] Out of these only a few were true warships, most were multipurpose platforms. It may be remembered that there were no fixed criteria for classifying ships by any laid-down parameters. Nonetheless, a few historians like Robert Orme, Manohar Malgonkar and B.K. Apte have attempted to classify them under a few broad categories of ships, viz, the ghurab, galbat, pal, manchwa, shibadi, etc. Charles R. Low has called the 'grabs (ghurab)' and the 'galivats (galbat)' the germ of the Indian Navy.[9] The main classes are described in detail below.

The ghurab: This was mostly a two-masted ship of about 150 to 300 tons. A ghurab carried square sails and included topsails and topgallant sails (Image 1). According to Orme, these had a shallow-draught, wide beam with fine prows and a narrow stern.[10] It had one continuous weather deck and a bulkhead in the forecastle. Due to its peculiar construction, it pitched heavily while heading into the sea. Malgonkar mentions that 'Shivaji's reluctance to undertaking personal command of naval operations was due to his experience in a ghurab in the Karwar expedition, when he is said to have suffered continuously from sea-sickness.'[11]

The ghurab had two cannons on forecastle, which were nine- to twelve-pounders. There were twelve to sixteen other large calibre cannons, fitted in the ship. The cannons on the broadside varied from six- to nine-pounders. Each ghurab carried 150 to 200 combat crew, in addition to the ship's crew. Ghurabs were screened by smaller ships like galbats to protect them, as is done in the modern navies to protect the main body or high-value assets like aircraft carriers.

Image 1. A fully rigged ghurab.[12]

Source: From *A History of the Maratha Navy and Merchantships,* by B.K. Apte

Galbat/gallivat: These were smaller and faster ships with better manoeuvrability, usually of about 70 tons. Like ghurabs, they had very fine prows that gave them a better hydrodynamic shape for faster speed. The ships had two masts with a large triangular main sail, a light mizzen sail as well as oars for rowing (Image 2). The peak of the mainsail, when hoisted, went much higher than the mast itself, thus providing a larger sail area. Some of the later versions also had square topsail and topgallant sails. The galbat/gallivant carried forty to fifty oars that helped it to 'make way' in the becalmed conditions that often existed close to the coast. Normally one crew manned each oar but two could also be employed. The deck was made of split bamboo to reduce the weight. Galbats/gallivats of larger tonnage had a solid deck and carried six to eight two-pounder or four-pounder guns mounted on swivels.[13] Galbats/gallivats were also used to tow ghurabs to the scene of action at sea. Each galbat/gallivat carried about 100 men onboard.

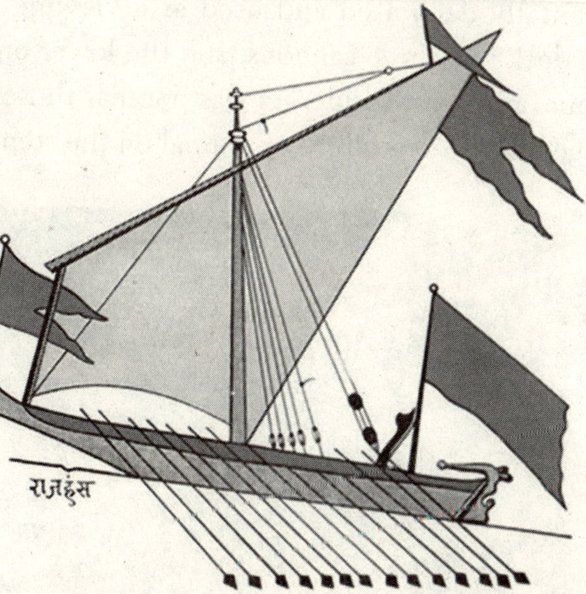

Image 2. The galbat *Rajhans.*[14]

Source: From *A History of the Maratha Navy and Merchantships* by B.K. Apte)

Pal: According to B.K. Apte, the pal was the biggest warship in the Maratha Navy. It had three masts, which were made by joining two wooden poles. It had square sails and European style rigging. Like European ships of that era, it had a decorated square stern. The crew of the ship ranged from 275 to 369, comprising seamen, gunners and soldiers. These ships remained offshore as they could not enter the shallow depth ports/anchorages. They were supplied by smaller boats for transfer of men and materials and for towing them to deeper waters.

As per interpretation of the image of pal *Vijaydurg* (Image 3), the ship had three decks. The uppermost deck was ornamentally decorated and used as a viewing gallery, the middle deck had three cannons, and the lower one was fitted with four on the broadside. As was popular those days, it had an image of a ferocious bird or animal on the stem-head.

Image 3. The pal *Vijaydurg.*[15]

Source: From *A History of the Maratha Navy and Merchantships,* by B.K. Apte

Bomb-Ketch: A bomb-ketch or bomb vessel was one of the smallest warships which carried two guns in the forward part of the ship (Image 4). It had a lateen sail, one square topsail and two jib-sails. The ship carried thirty seamen and forty soldiers.

Image 4. A bomb-sketch.[16]

Source: From *A History of the Maratha Navy and Merchantships*, by B.K. Apte

Captured warships: As practised by several navies of the contemporary period, the ships captured by Marathas were re-purposed for their own use. A painting can be seen below (Image 5) of a European galley flying Maratha flags and being in service of the Maratha Navy. It could have been either built by Marathas as per the European design, or was captured and re-commissioned into Maratha Navy.

Image 5. A galley.[17]

Source: Copied from *A History of the Maratha Navy and Merchantships*, by B.K. Apte

Dual role of Maratha merchant ships: A few merchant ships were also used for dual purpose of war-fighting, in order to economize on the cost of construction of warships. Merchant ships were called 'sahukaritarande', wherein sahukari means merchant and tarande, a vessel. In this category the main classes of merchant ships were machava, batela, hodi, shibadi, padav, phatemar and kotia.[18] These are explained in the subsequent paragraphs.

Batela: This indigenous ship of ancient construction design had a crew of thirty sailors. It had one large lateen sail, like a dhow, and one jib sail. The ship had a large hold to carry cargo and only a part of the upper deck was enclosed (Image 6).

Image 6. A batela.[19]

Source: From *A History of the Maratha Navy and Merchantships*, by B.K. Apte

Machhava: As the name suggests, it was a fishing boat, which could be fitted with six small guns and could carry the associated gunpowder. It carried about fifty men. Its tonnage varied from 2.5 to 3 tons. By the turn of the nineteenth century the machhavas were larger built, with two masts and a tonnage 3 to 4.5 tons. Its overall length was 50 feet, the beam of 14 feet, the length of the keel about 35 feet and the draught of about 7 feet. It had one main mast of 28 feet which was inclined forward by 60 degrees. It carried one lateen sail and a mizzen sail. It also had oars to row the craft. Another version of a similar ship was named balav/balyava. A detailed drawing of a machhava is appended below (Image 7).

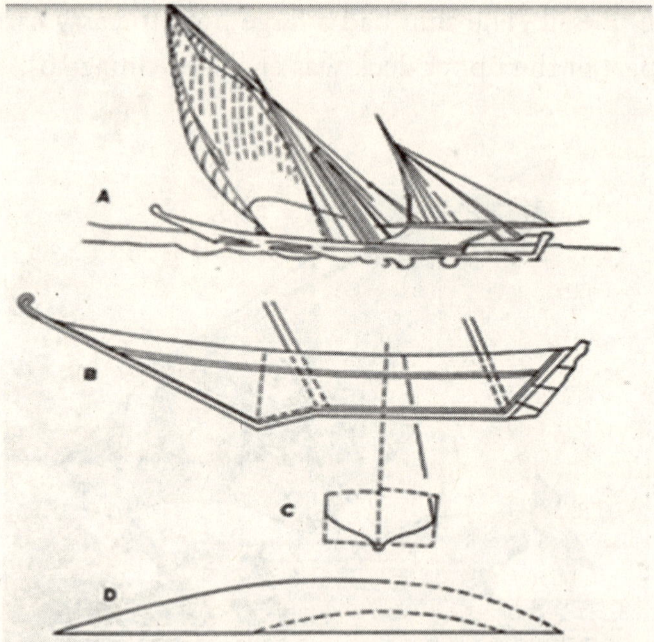

Image 7. A machhawa with details of hull form.[20]

Source: From *A History of the Maratha Navy and Merchantships* by B.K. Apte

Hodi: Essentially a canoe without any sail. It could be dug out of the large trunk of a tree, or made out of a few planks joined together. It was propelled by one or two men rowing it (as shown in mage 8).

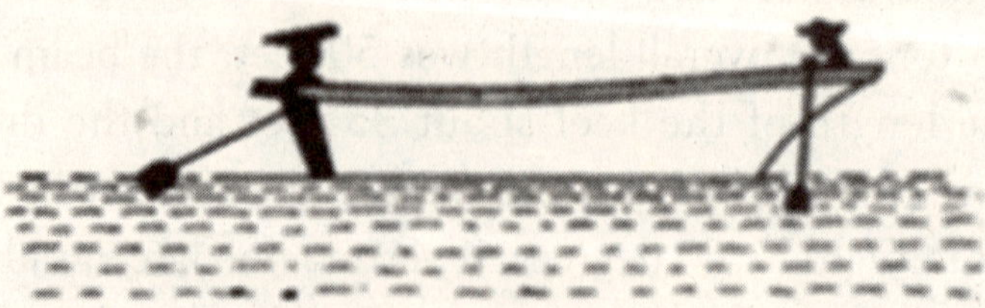

Image 8. A hodi (canoe).[21]

Source: From *A History of the Maratha Navy and Merchantships*, by B.K. Apte

Kotia/kothaya: The kotia was another version of the dhow, albeit with two masts and lateen sails. Its tonnage varied from 100 to 400 khandis (1 khandi = 20 mounds = 746.48 kg). Its overall length was about 60 feet, beam 15 feet, depth of hold about 10 feet and a draught of about 15 feet. It did not have any bow-sprit or jib-boom (Image 9). It had a crew of twelve to sixteen seamen. Kotias were essentially a Kathiawari/Saurashtra cargo ship, owned by Kahchhi merchants and manned by skilled sailors of Kharva or Wagher community from the Salaya region. The details of retrofitted armament are however not known. The manji ships from the Malabar coast were also a similar type of ship and are found to have been in use on the Konkan coast.

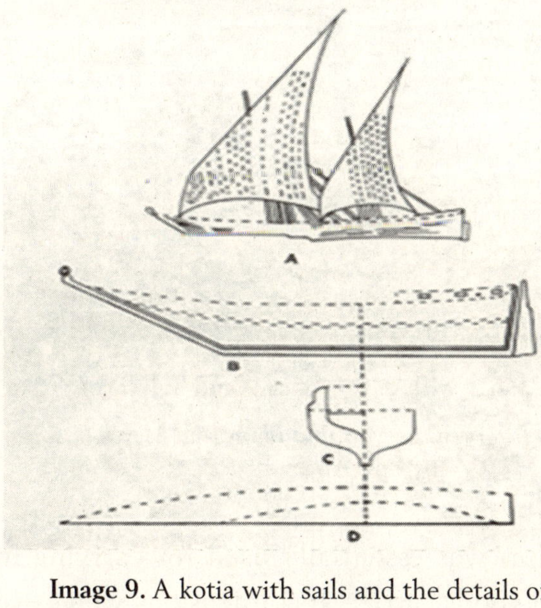

Image 9. A kotia with sails and the details of hull form.[22]

Source: From *A History of the Maratha Navy and Merchantships*, by B.K. Apte

Padav: This ship was a low freeboard, a small ship of about 40 feet length, 14 feet beam and its cargo hold was about 5 feet deep. It was a single mast ship of 25 to 30 feet with a lateen sail (Image 10). Its entire deck was open to the sky and hence not very conducive for crew comfort.

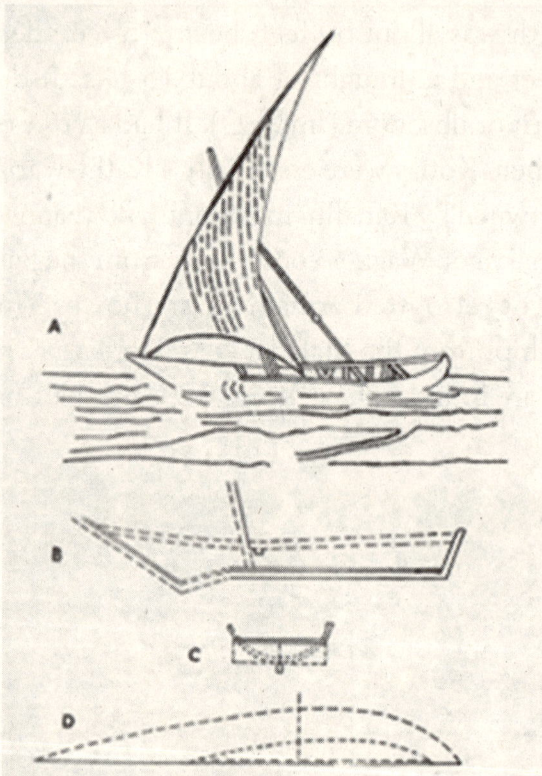

Image 10. A padav with details of sails and hull form.[23]

Source: From *A History of the Maratha Navy and Merchantships*, by B.K. Apte

Phatemar: This ship was essentially used for carrying mail, apart from being a goods carrier. Its dimensions were: overall length 76 feet, beam 21 feet, with a hold of 11-12 feet and 200 tons in weight. It had one or two masts, depending upon its size and the tonnage. Like a dhow, it was propelled by lateen sail(s) (Image 11). It was skilfully navigated by men of the Mopla community and other native Muslims of the Malabar coast.[24] Its deck was made of split bamboo that could be rolled-up to fill-up its hold with cargo. It also had a poop deck to accommodate a wheel-house-cum-crew cabin. The phatemar vessels accompanied the larger warships to the scene of action as support ships.

Image 11. A phatemar.[25]

Source: From *A History of the Maratha Navy and Merchantships*, by B.K. Apte

Sibadi/shibar: This was a broad-bodied vessel that could carry a large quantity of cargo. It accompanied the warships to provide logistic support. It was a single-deck ship usually of about 150 tons with two masts for lateen sails and a triangular one on the jib mast. Its length was about 100 feet, beam 25 feet, length of keel about 60 feet, and the depth of hold about 12 feet. It had a square stern, like the European ships. In a large sibadi the mast could be 60 feet high and the yard-arm could be 80 feet long. Sibadis were built in Jaygad and Vijaydurg. The crew of twenty-five to thirty men normally comprised folk from the Bhandari and Muslim communities of Konkan. The sibadi/ shibar carried light armaments and accompanied the pals and the ghurabs into action.[26]

⚓ ⚓ ⚓

European Warships in the Indian Ocean

It may be interesting to compare Maratha Navy ships with contemporary European ships to understand the similarities and differences. While Dutch East Indiamen, French corvettes and several classes of English ships would have been encountered by the Marathas, Portuguese ships were the first European ships to be engaged by the Maratha Navy. Many of the features of Portuguese ships were incorporated into Maratha ships later.

⚓ ⚓ ⚓

Portuguese Ships

The developments in Portuguese shipbuilding in the fourteenth and fifteenth century resulted in the construction of ships like the naus, gales and caravelas, which in turn resulted in the 'discovery of India'. This development was incremental and progressive. The Portuguese realized that building excessively large ships made them unsuitable for sailing round the Cape of Good Hope and subsequently in the Indian Ocean. They preferred smaller rounded ships of 300 to 500 tons, like the caravelas, to larger ships like the naus and gales that could displace as much as 1000 tons. Later, ships with better manoeuvring qualities, higher speed, and ability to provide better gun-firing capabilities were preferred. These qualities were progressively improved as the Portuguese sailors gained seafaring experience. While about 167 varieties of ships formed a part of Portuguese inventory in the sixteenth to eighteenth century, they were essentially progressive improvements upon some basic classes of the ships.[27] These are discussed below.

Caravela: As the Portuguese started sailing longer voyages in the South Atlantic Ocean, they needed ships of 50 to 100 tons with good speed, manoeuvrability and capacity to carry larger armament. Originating as small fishing boats of 50 to 100 tons in thirteenth century, caravelas became a chosen platform during the Age of Discovery. In the beginning of the sixteenth century, they acquired the characteristics of a warship; wherein their tonnage was kept below 200 tons to help propel them with the use of a triangular sail that made them suitable for long voyages.

The triangular structure of the sail came from the Indian 'pangaios', the ships on which the Muslim merchants carried their goods to the Red Sea.[28] The caravela made better use of the wind and could sail with beam-wind even when it was coming from off the bows.[29] Vasco Da Gama used the caravela *Beira*, for his first voyage to India. Several caravelas took part in various naval operations in the sixteenth and seventeenth centuries—a span of nearly 200 years—before they were replaced with ships of better design. Due to several modifications done on them progressively, their ship design, the number of masts and the types of sails kept getting changed. The sail rigs were also changed to suit the monsoon winds when the caravelas entered the Indian Ocean. Several of them were built in Portuguese shipyards in India during the sixteenth and seventeenth centuries.

Gale: These were the battleships with sails as well as oars for rowing. These ships used lateen (triangular) sails with two or three masts. They had twenty-five to thirty benches, with each bench capable of accommodating five to six rowers, generally rowed by slaves, thus condemned for 'Serving in the Gale'.[30]

Nau: These were some of the largest ships in the Indian Ocean in the late sixteenth century, with the tonnage upto 2,000 tons. The naus had several decks with three masts, carrying six sails of different types. They were often the flagships and carried special marks on the sail to indicate their special status. The nau, *S Gabreil,* was part of the flotilla on the maiden voyage of Vasco Da Gama. The naus were built using thick pinewood, capable of withstanding enemy fire, though this made them slow. A typical nau was about 25 metres long, 8.5 metres wide, carrying a drought of 1.7 metres forward and 2.3 metres in the aft.

Ships of other types: There were several other popular types of Portuguese ships such as the albetoca, barca, pinaca, fusta, etc., but they were used for limited purposes. It is pertinent to mention that several interesting features of Indian/Arabian ships sailing in the Indian Ocean were adopted by the Portuguese and vice versa, to improve their own ship designs. This free flow of adaptation of shipbuilding characteristics was mutually beneficial to all concerned. As mentioned above, this also resulted in frequent and incremental changes in the ship designs, making it difficult to categorize ships of that era into specific type or classes.

⚓ ⚓ ⚓

Dutch Ships

The Dutch, like other navies of that period, initially used merchant ships with large cargo-carrying capacity to maximize the profitability. These East Indiaman were very sturdy ships that could withstand oceanic passage. Their masts were perpendicular to the ship's plane, unlike the Maratha ships which usually had slightly forward-inclined masts in most of. Later, Maratha shipbuilders seem to have adopted this feature in the construction of their own 'pal' ships.

Robert Parthesius has identified eleven categories of Dutch ships in his book *Dutch Ships in Tropical Waters*.[31] These were rated based on their tonnage and the role played by them. 'Rate 0' meant 'undefined ships', and 'Rate 10'meant the 'homeward-bounders' ('retourschip' in Dutch), the largest and the most seaworthy ships the Dutch had. Between these two categories were the yachts, flutes, frigates and big men-o'-war. These are described in the succeeding paragraphs.

Homeward-bounder (*retourschip*) (Rate 10): These were the largest and the best ships that the Dutch East India Company (VOC) built to carry 350 scheepslast, usually called 'last' for short (the term was used by the Dutch to refer to a unit of volume measuring cargo capacity of ships).[32] The Dutch ship *Hollandia* could carry 500 last. These ships were about 160 feet long, with a 20 feet draught and contained multiple decks.

These were the cargo ships that were armed, based on their employment. For example, the ships sent to India and Persia were heavily armed, as they were expected to defeat the main rivals of Dutch in Asia, the Portuguese.

Men-o'-war (oorlogschip) (Rate 9): These were the largest warships built by the Admiralty in the Netherlands and were seconded to the VOC. Like others, these were also dual-purpose ships, albeit with lesser cargo-carrying capacity than the retourschip, even though they were nearly of the same dimensions.

Yachts (jachten) (Rate 1, 3, 5, 7): These were the smaller than ships (Rate 8, tonnage more than 170 last), and further classified based on their cargo-carrying capacities. While the smallest ones were just 20 to 25 last, the larger one built late in the seventeenth century measured 270 to 280 last. All yachts were armed with one cannon in the bow and another firing broadside through gun ports. Big yachts of 170 last and more were graded as Rate 7, medium-sized ones of 70 to 170 last as Rate 5, and those under 70 last were small yachts as Rate 3.[33]

Frigate (Rate 3): Ships of less than 70 last, built in Asia, were listed as frigates. These ships were about 70 feet long with a beam of 15 feet and a crew of thirty men with five cannons as their main weapons. Three of these cannons were fitted in the forward area and two in stern. Some of the smaller frigates carried oars for rowing.

Flutes (fluit) (Rate 4 and 6): These were experimental ships that had a large cargo-carrying capacity but at the same time were easy to sail and could be crewed by a smaller number. With a ratio of one to five/six between the length and beam, these were unusually longships in that era. One such ship was 140 feet long, 24 feet wide with a hold depth of 12 feet.

⚓ ⚓ ⚓

English Ships

Prior to the invention of gunpowder and the cannon firing, English ships were designed for boarding operations, wherein the forecastle was made very strong and high. With the invention of gunfire from stand-off ranges, the ships were designed with multiple decks to fit as many guns as possible, broadside. A few were fitted on the forward area and stern of the ship as well. For battle at sea, ships of both sides would line up in a column and engage each other on the broadside. This resulted in the development of 'ships of the line' that were purely for warfighting and the merchant ships hitherto performing the dual task of warships progressively started reducing.[34]

The history of Bombay Marine: The history of English shipping in the Indian Ocean, during the seventeenth and eighteenth centuries, is the history of Bombay Marine. This begins from 1613, when a squadron was formed in Surat to protect nascent British maritime interests in India. Essentially, the squadron was tasked to protect against the aggressions of the Portuguese and the pirates who infested the Indian seas. Subsequently, this naval establishment attained a respectable strength in the second half of the seventeenth century. Bombay Marine had 'grab' ships (probably similar to ghurab), galleys, frigates, ketchs, cutters, schooners, sloops, snows, shibars, galivats (like the indigenous galbat) and manchua (machhua) class. This listing gives us an indication that the British used indigenously built ships, in addition to those of British origin. A shipbuilding yard was maintained till 1735 in Surat, when most of the work was shifted to Bombay.

This was also the beginning of the glorious shipbuilding tradition of the great Parsee shipbuilder Lowjee Nassaranjee belonging to the Wadia dynasty. Under his supervision (and later that of his descedents) nine ships of the line, seven frigates and six smaller vessels were built in the Bombay yard, besides those for the Bombay Marine, in the latter part of the eighteenth and earlier part of the nineteenth century for the Royal Navy.[35] Those built for the East India Company were prefixed with HCS (Honourable Company Ship) and those for the Royal Navy, with HMS (Her Majesty's Ship). A frigate had forty-four guns, a grab/sketch carried fourteen guns, a frigate about twenty-eight to thirty-two guns and a galivat only six guns.[36]

Four main categories of British ships: In the mid-seventeenth century, during the first Anglo–Dutch War, British ships were divided into four main categories. The main combatants were the ships of the line that carried as many as 100 guns, followed by frigates, then smaller sloops and the corvettes, and finally specialized craft, such as bomb vessels. The ships of the line usually remained close to England for wars in the English Channel, it was the frigates and the smaller ships that were dispatched for the duties in far flung colonies.[37] British frigates like the *Protector* (with forty-four guns), the *Fortune*, *Hunter*, and the *Revenge*, all took part in naval operations during the Maratha period.

⚓ ⚓ ⚓

Shipbuilding Techniques

Construction materials: While the basic materials used in the construction of ships by Europeans and Indians were similar, there were many differences in the structures and sails. One primary difference was the use of iron, wherein the Indian shipbuilders did not use iron in the construction as they suspected that in the presence of a magnetic substance (lodestone) underwater, the ship's planks would fall apart. In addition, iron was expensive and most of it was used for making weapons. However, the Western shipbuilders regularly used iron to bind the wooden planks together. Indian shipbuilders used coir ropes to stitch the planks together. The European ships tended to be stronger, larger but comparatively unwieldy, while Indian boats had pointed ends on both sides.

For shipbuilding, teak was in great demand, and the rain-fed forests of the Sahyadri hills of Thana produced excellent teak wood. Teak neither shrank nor corroded the nails embedded in it. Planks of mango, jack and undalwood were cheaper than teak and therefore went into repair works. The beams and the ribs inside the hull were usually made of these cheaper woods. The punayawood, because of its good length was well suited for mast and yards.[38] The forests of Kolaba and Ratnagiri also produced teak, but of an inferior quality. So, the trees grown on the banks of River Savitri in Bankot were preferred for their durability and hence used for shipbuilding. These bounties of nature, in terms of excellent quality of timber, were exploited by the Maratha shipbuilders.

Shipbuilding centres were scattered along the west coast. The ports of Agashi, Mahim, Sopara, Bessain, Bhivandi, Kalyan, Bombay and Panvel were established as shipbuilding centres under the Gujarat Sultanate. Large ships were being built at Agashi and Bessain as the main constituent, teak wood, was available in the adjoining hinterland. In 1634, the English had four pinnance ships built there for coastal trade. Bassein was another prominent shipbuilding centre under the Portuguese.

The Marathas had their shipbuilding yards at Thana, Kalyan, Bhiwandi, Alibaug, Vijaydurg and Malvan. The Maratha dockyards were located at Alibaug and Vijaydurg. It has been established that having successfully conquered the interiors of Konkan by 1657, sometime before 1659, Shivaji laid the keel of his first ship in the creek of Kalyan.[39] Apart from construction of warships, Shivaji realized the importance of international trade for the development of his empire. In addition to the regular trade in salt with the southern coast of India and the Malabar Coast, he had got large three-masted ships built for trade with Muscat and Mocha.

Construction technologies: Over a period of time the technique and design of Maratha ships witnessed noticeable changes. These changes may be regarded as progressive modifications based on experience or observations. Most of the Maratha warships were built using the clinker method for planking, wherein the planks overlapped each other. For merchant ships, the caraval build was preferred where the planks flushed with each other end-to-end.[40] The clinker build technology was simpler and faster, but made subsequent repairs difficult.

As mentioned earlier, coir and innovative wooden joints, instead of iron nails, were used to join the wooden planks to eliminate the chances of the nails catching rust and the joints becoming loose. It also resulted in the ship keeping well against the stress and strain of the sea waves action (called hogging and sagging in nautical terms), as the coir and innovative wooden joints were able to absorb the shock of wave action better.

The fact that the use of nails was known to Indian shipbuilders but they preferred either using the wooden joints or the wooden plugs, besides using the sewing technology with ropes, indicates their faith in their own technology and their apprehensions about the use of iron nails. In case of accident, the stitches would give way before planks were damaged. However, one major drawback of sewn technology was the seepage of water through the seams, especially if they were worn out, even though caulking the joints was done using a mixture of lime, fish oil and glue from trees. Bitter oil of the undi-nut and fish oil was also used.[41] Sewn planks were a unique feature of shipbuilding in the IOR. This technique continued to remain in use as late as the 1990s, when B. Arunachalam visited Lakshadweep in 1997-98.[42]

Another change in the shipbuilding technique adopted by the Marathas was the European transom method. Using this method Europeans ships were able to make a square cut at the stern, where a few cannons were fitted to engage the enemy. Thanks to this method the recoil of the firing cannons did not swing the ship from one side to the other. The tactical benefit of the transom impressed the Marathas who adopted this design feature (discussed in further detail in the section on Shipbuilding Techniques, below). This was an advance from the traditional use of pointed technology where the ships had narrow bows and a stern to negate the impact of hydrodynamic force.

After learning the use technologies such as the above, the Marathas also started using galbats that had a rudder slung to sternpost, in lieu of a quarter oar, to steer the ship. Progressively, they shifted from pointed ends to rounded stern and later, based on the design of European ships, a square stern was adopted as it was suitable to mount cannons. As far as the sail is concerned, the ships in the Indian Ocean used the triangular (lateen) sail. A sattee sail was a modification of the lateen sail, wherein a small portion of the front was cut-off to give it a quadrilateral shape. These sails required a smaller mast, as compared to a triangular sail. Then, the Portuguese introduced the square rig, which changed the way ships sailed in the Indian Ocean thereafter.[43]

Even though the Maratha Navy did not venture out deep into the sea to execute distant maritime expeditions, the wind patterns did influence the shape of the hull and sails of Maratha ships in the long run. Hence a calm day, with less wind during a naval engagement, resulted in the Marathas having an upper hand over the English or the Portuguese. Another significant aspect of Maratha shipbuilding was that the construction of warships was in consonance with their strategy and tactical requirements. They preferred lighter and easily manoeuvrable warships, which could easily avoid coming to the broadside of the enemy ship during naval combat. Further, such ships aided the Marathas in using the coast to their advantage to break off from a contest or to shake off a chasing enemy.

⚓ ⚓ ⚓

Naval Weaponry

Marathas: The naval weaponry of the Marathas in the initial period was a mere extension of the weapons in use in land warfare. For stand-off weapons, bows and arrows, spears and slingshots with stones were still in use. These weapons could be used up to 100 yards, while guns could be used up to 300 yards with reasonable accuracy.[44] Traditionally, the Maratha method involved boarding the enemy ship, leading to close-quarter combat. Their soldiers fought with the curved Maratha sword and a round shield (dhal). In the absence of firearms and gunpowder, their close-combat weapons constituted their armoury. As the Marathas progressively came in contact with the Portuguese, French, Dutch and English naval forces, it gave them an insight into the many features of armaments, different from the those they had used so far. This did result in improving the Maratha armoury. The Marathas seemed to have learnt the method of mounting artillery onboard their ships from the Muslims, and later improved upon it by imitating their European neighbours, states B.K. Apte.[45]

Apart from weapons, the Marathas borrowed other navigation instruments—such as the compass, the telcscope (nali), and even guns from these European forces—whilst they were in Maratha harbours. They learnt the use of loading/unloading wheeled gear from the British and this helped them to undertake expeditious loading/unloading of cargo on their own ships, while protecting the ship's side from damage due to the cargo loading/unloading operations. The Marathas also hired expert European gunners, mostly renegades, who formed nearly half the fighting strength of a vessel.[46]

Europeans: The Portuguese naus and gales in the fifteenth century were armed with artillery on their stern, upper deck and lower decks (coberta). Small cannons were also placed in the crow's nest, to take advantage of height. Caravelas, being smaller and often used for reconnaissance, carried only light guns. Each gale had large cannon called the coxia, in addition to other smaller cannons. In 1525, Portuguese had about sixty-five ships in Indian waters that carried 1,073 pieces of artillery, of which 667 were made of copper and the rest of iron.[47] The Portuguese policy mandated collection of all firearms from the ship's crew when not in use, as the crew could potentially desert the ship with the weapons. The previous section has already discussed how the VOC and EIC ships were armed, based on their tonnage and purpose.

⚓ ⚓ ⚓

Maratha Crew and Manpower: Some Anthropological Considerations

Recruitment: Under Shivaji, 'all classes of the population, except perhaps the outcastes, had the opportunity of entering and rising in the military service.'[48] The Peshwas themselves were a prime example of this wherein, as Chittapavan Brahmins, they took upon the Kshatriya role of ruling the state. Thus, a Brahmin could become a clerk, a soldier, a banker, a trader, and a farmer who tilled his own farm land.[49] However, there were obvious limitations to joining the navy, as traversing the sea invited the punishment of losing one's caste according to the prevailing taboos in Hindu society. But Shivaji ensured that the coastal communities traditionally used to seafaring activities, viz., the fishermen clans of Konkan were given the opportunity to serve the navy.[50] The Bhandari, Sonkoli, Gabit and Bhoi amongst the Hindus, and the Daldi Kharvi (converted Muslims) were the main seafaring communities from the Konkan. Out of these, the Sonkoli/Koli may be called the true sons of the sea, as their forefathers too sailed the seas on fishing craft—a tradition that continues till today.

Among the indigenous crew, people belonging to the Koli and the Suthar communities played a vital role in the Maratha Navy. These communities are very intimately linked to the sea even today, but their area of operation is limited. They sail close to the coast, even though they are proficient fishermen. The unique Koli culture is representative of many aspects of the sea. Consequently, in Shivaji's navy, they were primarily tasked with manning the ships. In contrast, the Suthar were skilled woodworkers, making them good shipwrights whose traditional expertise was effectively utilized by the Maratha navy. Had caste or religion been the criteria for joining the naval services, the Maratha Navy would never have seen illustrious admirals like Daulat Khan (a Muslim) and Mai Nayak Bhandari (from a 'low' Hindu caste of toddy tappers).[51] This demonstrates that the Maratha Navy also had a secular outlook. It is said that Chhatrapati Sambhaji allied with the Arabs as a countervailing force against Portuguese.

In addition, adventurers and sailors of foreign origin like the Sidi and the European renegades were also employed in the Maratha Navy. The Sidi, also referred to as 'Habshi', were military adventurers of African origin who had distinguished themselves in the military services of the Delhi Sultans.[52] The fact that the Sidi were a great seafaring people, emerges during the period of Shivaji when Janjira was a Sidi stronghold. During the seventeenth century, the Sidi served as admirals of the Nizam Shahi kingdom of Bijapur, and of the Mughals, respectively. Conversely, many Sidis also served the Maratha Navy. For example, during the battle of Janjira in October 1682, a contingent of Sidis, led by Sidi Misry, fought on behalf of the Marathas. Additionally, numerous Europeans were employed by the Marathas as shipwrights, sailors and gunners. Overall, the broad power dynamics showed that the

Marathas were primarily engaged in war against the Sidis, Mughals, Portuguese and English, while receiving support from Dutch and French.[53]

⚓ ⚓ ⚓

Conclusion

For nearly a century, the Maratha Navy was able to hold on its own and challenged the attempts of establishment of supremacy by the foreign naval powers. While making a humble beginning during the reign of Shivaji, it reached its zenith under the able command of the great Maratha admiral, Kanhoji Angre. Building a navy from scratch all the way to a 200-ship-strong fleet in about five decades was indeed a credible feat by the Maratha rulers. The establishment of this endeavour was ably supported by the coastal community of the Konkan who were actively involved in shipbuilding, ship sailing, maritime businesses and such sea-related activities. However, the overall influence of Maratha naval power on the course of India's maritime history during the colonial period was limited. Nevertheless, the successes of the Maratha Navy paved the way for Maratha rulers to open another front against their enemies, and it rekindled maritime awareness amongst the Indian coastal states.

Having evaluated the ships, the crew and the armour of the Maratha Navy, it would be worthwhile to take note of the shiphandling and navigation technique used by Maratha seamen to exploit their ships optimally. These navigational technicalities are discussed in the next chapter.

Notes

1 See p. 28, in Mahan, *The Influence of Sea Power upon History*,1949.

2 The term '*mare liberum*' means '[the] free seas' in Latin. Seas were considered international waters, free for use by all humans; all had equal rights on the seas.

3 The term '*mare clausum*' means '[the] closed sea' in Latin. It meant creation of jurisdiction over the water by one country, which then prevented access to other countries.

4 A 'cartaz' was a security pass issued to a ship for unhindered voyage.

5 See pp.11-12, in Clifford W. Hawkins, The *Dhow: An Illustrated History of the Dhow and Its World*, Nautical Publication Society, 1977.

6 See p. 189, in D.B. Irani, 'Country craft and sailing vessels of India', *The Naval Architect*, September 1980.

7 See p. 62, in Apte, *A History of the Maratha Navy*,1973.

8 See p. 61, in Malgonkar, *Kanhoji Angrey, Maratha Admiral*,1959.

9 See p. 2, Vol. 1, of Low, *The History of The Indian Navy*,1985.

10 See pp. 408-409, in Robert Orme, *History of The Military Transactions of the British Nation in Indostan*, Book V. Luke Hanfard, 1803.

11 See p. 62, in Malgonkar, *Kanhoji Angrey, Maratha Admiral*, 1959; Orme Robert, *A History of the Military Transactions of the British Nation in Indostan*, Book V, pp. 408-409, www.archives.org/details/dli.csl.8483/page/n409/mode/1up?view=theater

12 See p. 134, in Apte, *A History of the Maratha Navy*,1973.

13 Ibid., pp. 120-22.

14 Ibid., p. 126.

15 Ibid., p. 136.

16 Ibid., p. 138.

17 Ibid., p. 140.

18 Ibid., p. 141.

19 Ibid., p. 142.

20 Ibid., p. 145.

21 Ibid., p. 142.

22 Ibid., p. 143.

23 Ibid., p. 149.

24 Ibid., p. 150.

25 Ibid., p. 152.

26 Ibid., p.155.

27 See p. 276, in Mathew, *History of The Portuguese Navigation in India*, 1988.

28 See pp. 150–54, in Gago Coutinho, *A Nauticosdos Descobrimentos*, Vol. 1, Agencia Geraldo Ultamar, 1951.

29 See p. 282, in Mathew, *History of The Portuguese Navigation in India*, 1988.

30 Ibid, pp. 284–85.

31 See pp. 65-95, in Robert Parthesius,'The Development of the VOC Fleet', in *Dutch Ships in Tropical Waters, The Development of the Dutch East India Company (VOC) Shipping Network in Asia 1595-1660*, Amsterdam University Press, 2010; available at http://www.jstor.org/stable/j.ctt45kcpt.8.

32 The term 'Last' was used by the Dutch to refer to a unit of volume measuring cargo capacity of ships. The exact value of a Last could vary based on the nature of cargo and the region where it was being used. For example, a typical Dutch Last would be equivalent of 2,400 litres or 60 barrels of wine. In terms of weight, it could be approximately 2,000 kgs. Robert Parthesius has mentioned that 500 Indian Last is approximately 3,000 pounds of pepper.

33 See p. 73, in Parthesius, 'The Development of the VOC Fleet', 2010.

34 See p. 49, in James L. George, *History of Warships: From Ancient Times to the Twenty First Century*, Naval Institute Press, 1998.

35 See pp. 243-44, in Mookerji, *Indian Shipping*, 1912.

36 See p. 538, in Low, *The History of The Indian Navy*, 1985.

37 See pp. 49-52, in George, *History of Warships*, 1998.

38 See p. 190, in Apte, *A History of the Maratha Navy*, 1973.

39 Ibid., pp. 53-71.

40 See p. 29, in B. Arunachalam, 'Shipbuilding in North Konkan in the Period 1550-1750 A.D.', in *Essays in Maritime Studies* Vol II, Maritime History Society, 2002.

41 See p. 189, in Apte, A History of the Maratha Navy, 1973.

42 See pp. iv and 140, in B. Arunachalam, *Maritime Heritage of Lakshadweep and Minicoy Islands*, Maritime History Society, 2011.

43 See p. 17, in Ruby Maloni, 'Shipbuilding in Western India in Medieval Times', in *Essays in Maritime Studies*, Vol. II, Maritime History Society, 2002.

44 See pp. 61-63, in Malgonkar, *Kanhoji Angrey, Maratha Admiral*, 1959.

45 See p. 88, in Apte, *A History of the Maratha Navy*, 1973.

46 See p. 64, in Malgonkar, *Kanhoji Angrey, Maratha Admiral*, 1959.

47 See pp. 292-96, in Mathew, *History of the Portuguese Navigation in India*, 1988.

48 See p. 73, in Reverend Alexander Kyd Nairne, *History of the Konkan*, Government Central Press, 1894.

49 See p. 64, in Apte, *A History of the Maratha Navy*, 1973.

50 See p. 64, in Malgonkar, *Kanhoji Angrey, Maratha Admiral*, 1959.

51 See p. 73, in Apte, *A History of the Maratha Navy*, 1973.

52 A generic name given to all people from Africa during that era, as they were locally believed to have come from a region named Hubshan in Africa.

53 Indrajeet Bhattacharya, 'Murud Janjira: The Unsung Legacy of Siddis', ResearchGate, March 2016, https://www.researchgate.net/publication/340350102_Murud_Janjira_The_Unsung_Legacy_of_Siddis.

8

Navigational Awareness: Appreciation of Geography

Ankush Banerjee

⚓ ⚓ ⚓

Introduction

That the Marathas had a formidable navy by the early-eighteenth century, jostling their way through the waters of the Konkan coast already crowded with the Dutch, Portuguese, English and Sidis, is now firmly established.[1] It has also been established that the Maratha Navy was a brown-water navy, which implies in simple terms, that it restricted its operations and movements close to the coast, as opposed to the other blue water navies it competed with and fought against, such as the British. The latter, owing to advances in ship-building and design, which were itself a manifestation of the onset of Industrial Revolution in that part of the world, had ships which were bigger, better and fitted with advanced weaponry.

Curiously, the pages of history are littered with narrative accounts veering between surprise and trepidation, hesitance and horror that a lot of adversaries felt after experiencing the

Maratha Navy in action.[2] For instance, in the early 1700s, owing to territorial losses in an ongoing conflict with the Marathas, the Sidi of Janjira abruptly withdrew from battle, leaving his ally—the Portuguese—with their backs to the wall. Later, while the Portuguese negotiated a pointless offensive and defensive alliance with the Raja of Kolhapur against the Maratha sarkhel (admiral), Kanhoji Angre, 'Angria's fleet rode the sea boldly, seizing merchantmen of all nationalities which had omitted to purchase his passports, and the Portuguese found themselves powerless to circumscribe his activities.'[3]

Ironically enough, the formation of the Maratha Navy was founded on the same concerns and aspirations, which had driven its colonial adversaries all the way to the Konkan coast—economic considerations of generating revenue, safeguarding their merchantmen from pirates, protecting their subjects against attacks and raids from rival naval powers, and securing the sovereignty of the sea for their own (nascent Maratha) state. This peculiar phenomenon of a decidedly superior force—in this case the British and the Portuguese—feeling overwhelmed by a supposedly subpar adversary, makes a reader both admire and feel curious about the reasons behind the underdog's persistent tenacity. Scholars over the years have uncovered many aspects, natural and human, overt and covert, which interplayed in the background, contributing to the Maratha Navy pushing the envelope against its many formidable foes. The chapter amplifies on this.

The first section—through a brief comparative analysis of coastal and open sea navigation—argues how the Maratha seamen were adept at coastal navigation, owing to traditional, indigenous knowledge of the coast and its many vagaries. Thereafter, we look at other aspects of the Maratha Navy, such as shipbuilding practices and erection of underwater coastal defences. These further amplify upon, and have roots in, the Maratha seamen's critical appreciation of their geographical context. Lastly, we take a closer look at some Maratha naval tactics and illustrate how their in-depth knowledge of geographical features played a role in formulation of tactics and gaining decisive advantage.

⚓ ⚓ ⚓

Understanding the Epistemic Advantage of Maratha Seamen

The Merriam-Webster dictionary defines the term navigation as, 'the science of getting ships, aircraft, or spacecraft from place to place, especially, the method of determining position, course, and distance travelled.'[4] This definition has implicit in its meaning, an *a priori* knowledge that one has to possess about 'the place', to be able to successfully navigate, i.e., go from 'place to place', as also to determine one's 'position, course, or distance'. Arunachalam has written extensively about the rich corpus of multifarious, indigenous systems of nautical knowledge and practices that existed among northern Indian Ocean seafaring communities, which predates the coming of the Europeans.[5] However, we must be cautious to not conflate navigational practices used by Indian seafaring communities, such as the Gujarati merchants, with those which may have been employed by the Maratha seamen. Seafaring demands usage of, and expertise in, many different types of complex, navigational techniques, such as astral navigation, wind compasses, and dead reckoning.

Shedding light on the traditional Kutchi-Gujarati navigational texts, called 'Pothis', Arunachalam mentions that these were erstwhile versions of the modern navigator's handbook (or almanac), wherein akin to their modern counterparts, the Gujarati-Kutchi seamen/navigators informally and meticulously scribbled notes about trans-sea voyage routes, port locations, navigational hazards, harbour approaches and parallel sailing routes, among other aspects. These were passed from individual to individual within a seafaring community, in addition to transmission of nautical knowledge, and various macro and micro skills, through oral traditions. Here it will be interesting to highlight that macro skills could refer to understanding the approach to a port, seasonal variations and tidal patterns, while micro-skills may refer to handling ropes onboard sailing vessels, undertaking maintenance and cleaning of guns, and rowing well and in unison.

Coming to the Maratha seamen, their knowledge corpus and expertise sheds light not on trans-oceanic routes, but on the length and breadth of the Konkan coast—a narrow strip of land wedged between the Sahayadri mountains running along a north northwest–south southwest orientation on the east and the Arabian Sea on the west. The Sahayadris run parallel to the sea. The peculiarities of this region have been well documented. Between the mountains and the sea, Konkan topography falls into three linear longitudinal physical units, namely, the foothills and the interior lowlands, the coastal lowland plateaus and a very narrow coastal strip, a few kilometres wide.[6] The altitude across these lowland plateaus is variable, sprinkled as it is by hills rising to altitudes of 150 to 300 metres.

As one traverses the length of the Konkan, one comes across rugged landscape, cut by winding creeks, isolated peaks, sandy beaches, coastal sand dunes and alluvial tracts along estuaries.[7] Perhaps the most unusual part of the Konkan is its river system, which consists of many short rivers, most of them emanating from the Sahayadris. In the initial part of their course, these begin by running parallel to the coast, unexpectedly varying in their direction, depth, width and gradient. They traverse mangrove-covered salt marshes and undulating lowlands. At their mouths, they form shallow creeks, unsafe for deep draught vessels.

Speaking of the river Kundalika, B.K. Apte mentions, 'throughout its course, the river has well-wooded hills which rise behind a belt of salt marshes and rice fields. The mouth of the river is picturesque, lined with palm grooves and orchards.'[8] In a similar vein, we are informed of the variations in gradients of Kolaba's two river systems, those flowing northward and others flowing westward. River Amba belongs to the former category. When erstwhile mariners approached from the sea, Amba was navigable at high tides for vessels up to 15 tons, but beyond Dharamtar, navigation was impossible especially at low tides.

Likewise, the geomorphology of the coast, as we traverse from north to south doesn't remain constant, but changes. As Apte has aptly summarized, 'nature divides the whole of littoral Konkan into two parts near the northern-most point of Kolaba.'[9] Such geographical variations have important implications for us to consider. Firstly, navigating through these waters, as the Maratha seamen did, would have required a wholly different set of epistemic systems, when compared to the other Indian seafaring communities. Secondly, such differences would have translated to very different practices, concerns, and tactical objectives.

Hence, as mentioned earlier, while we must be cautious to not conflate navigational practices used by seafaring communities, with those which may have been used by Maratha seamen, it is equally important to take cognisance of the fact that there existed, within their ranks, indigenous systems of nautical knowledge which aided them to skilfully navigate the coast and conduct operations. While such knowledge may have conceptually differed from seagoing navigational practices, such as expertise in astral navigation, the inherent principles and assumptions upon which these were based—i.e., comprehensive understanding of geography (the coast), tidal patterns, coastal navigational marks etc.—were very much part of the Maratha seamen's collective conscience.

For instance, as Arunachalam argues, seamen had developed a nuanced sense of underwater topography, especially at shallow depths, through knowledge of the coastal configuration, and various land/marine features which aided them in close quarter navigation while entering and leaving ports.[10] Grounding in shallow depths may have been a concern, ameliorated via sounding through lead lines at regular intervals. It has also been estimated that much before the Indian coast had been etched and articulated on the British Admiralty's nautical charts, most Indian seamen were using conspicuous landmarks as an aid to navigation, and for identifying different sections of the coast. It will also be instructive here to reflect on whether, and how specific features of the coastal forts built by the Marathas could have aided their seamen to take specific navigational decisions while entering or leaving a port, such as changing course, dropping anchor or increasing speed.

In comparison, the lack of knowledge—or how far behind the Portuguese and English were, in terms of their appreciation of geography—can be ascertained through the fact that the first hydrographic surveys of the west coast were undertaken by English hydrographers, Captain John McCluer aboard the *Endeavour* and Lieutenant Wedge-borough aboard the *Panther*, between 1790-93. McCluer has also been credited with making the earliest plans of the Bombay harbour.[11] Before this, while cartographic developments had occurred owing to English and French efforts, these were quite rudimentary. For instance, the English surveyor, Thornton had published the *English Pilot* in 1745, with 'forty-two charts of bays, sea casts, ports, capes, headlands, straits, shoals, rocks, and dangers for oriental navigation.'[12] However, these charts were essentially small-scale studies of large sketches of coastlines, with few dangers or soundings being marked. A sample of such a chart, perhaps published around 1690, is reproduced (see Image 1).

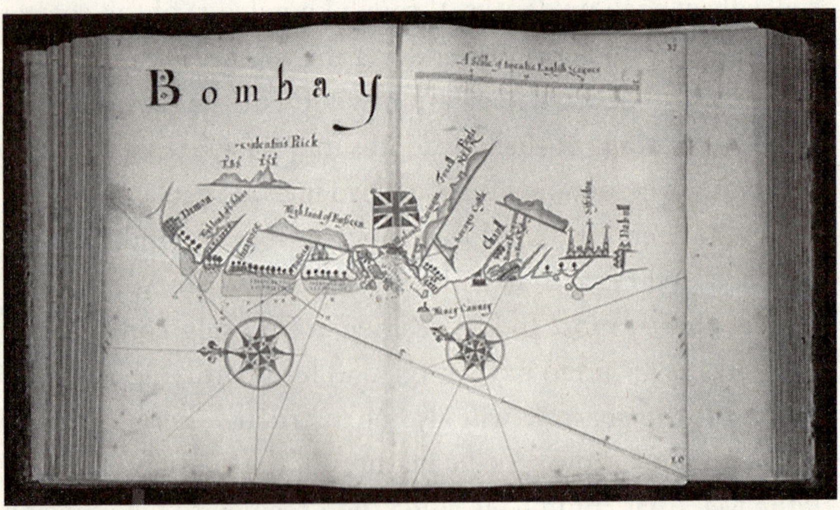

Image 1: William Hacke. Plan of Bombay Harbour, *A Description of the Sea Coasts* (1690), Retrieved from the Library of Congress. www.loc.gov/item/2002626774/, (accessed 10 September 2024)

The scanty knowledge of the coast, as indicated in the above chart, becomes evident when the same is compared with a chart of the Bombay harbour region, surveyed in 1829 by Lieutenant Rob Cogan using the trigonometric survey method (Image 2).

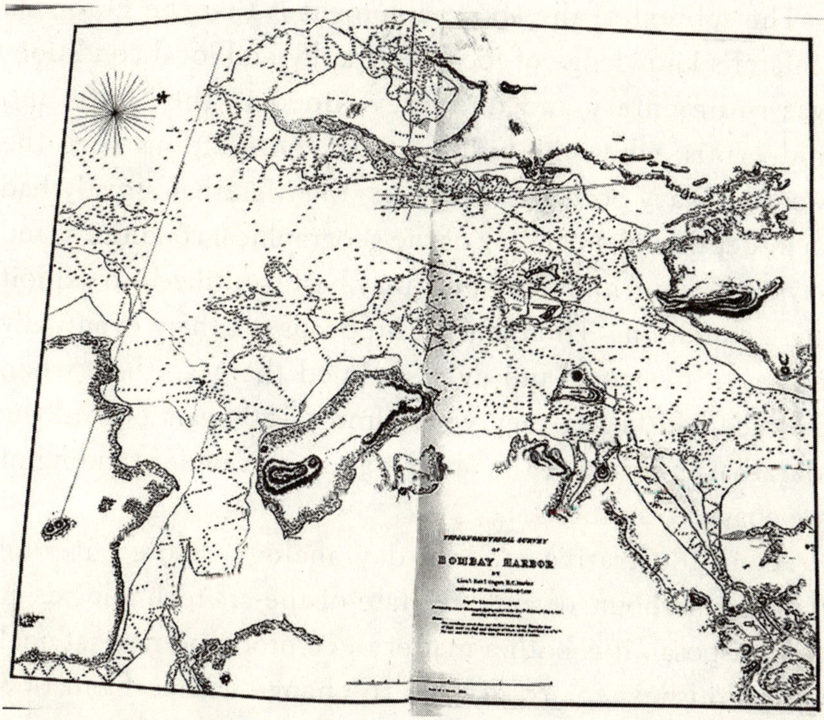

Image 2: Trigonometric Survey of Bombay Harbour undertaken by Lieutenant Rob Cogan, 1829; published May 1833

Source: Bhattacharya, *A History of the Indian Naval Hydrographic Department*, 2004, pp. 64-65

Comparing the two charts raises two important insights. Firstly, the European methods of accruing knowledge were influenced by the undergirding philosophy of Empiricism, which had its roots in the Enlightenment Age in Europe.

This emphasized scientific temper, reason and rationality. Hence, we see better survey and cartographic methods, all based on empirical, scientific principles, slowly maturing as time progressed. Compared to this, indigenous knowledge systems across the coast, relied on oral traditions, passed from generation to generation.

The subtext of the above argument is that the European seafarer's knowledge of local geography and local conditions was rudimentary and underdeveloped in the 1600s and mid-1700s, when the bulk of their contestations with the Maratha Navy occurred. Whereas, the Marathas already had an in-depth understanding of the geographical conditions, and navigational techniques which may best be utilized to exploit these conditions. Though the Europeans got there eventually and even overtook and overwhelmed the Marathas, when the race had begun they were almost 150 years behind the Marathas in terms of the latter's grasp and understanding of the coastal conditions.

As an illustrative modern-day analogy, while entering Mumbai harbour, despite all state-of-the-art technologies at their disposal, it is both a matter of comfort and navigational scrupulousness for navigators to change course from 063 to 029, when the Prongs Reef Lighthouse bears 285 on the compass rose. Hence, one may surmise that the knowledge of familiar coastal landmarks and their sightings were both a source of comfort and guidance to the Maratha seamen, who would have possessed a sound understanding of the coastal features, depths, and tidal and wind patterns, which helped them plan and execute their operations.

⚓ ⚓ ⚓

Curious Case of Underwater Obstructions and Advanced Ship-repair Facilities

The coastal forts built or refurbished by the Marathas need to be carefully considered to shed light on how well Maratha seamen understood various aspects of shipbuilding and ship repair, and how efficiently they capitalized on, or modified surrounding geographical features to achieve their tactical objectives. The Marine Archaeology Centre (MAC) has conducted numerous coastal, sea-bottom surveys since 1983, to investigate the remains of shipwrecks, settlements, marine instruments and other allied aspects of early shipping practices. One such survey which has had significant impact on our understanding of early ship-repair practices of the Marathas was conducted in 1988, when the MAC undertook a marine archaeological survey of areas around the Vijaydurg fort (see Images 3, 4, 5, 6). It must be remembered that the Vijaydurg fort had served as one of the most important forts and naval bases for Shivaji, and later, for Angre.

Diving operations undertaken during the survey revealed many intriguing features. First among these was an underwater stone structure on the western side of the fort, lying along the east-west orientation, before turning towards the north-south direction. It measured 122 metres in length, 7 metres in width, and 3 metres in height, comprising of large, weather-worn stones interlocked by smaller stones (Image 4). The structure may have been built as an underwater obstruction to cause damage and sink English deep draft vessels, as also to 'protect the fort from wave and current action'.[13]

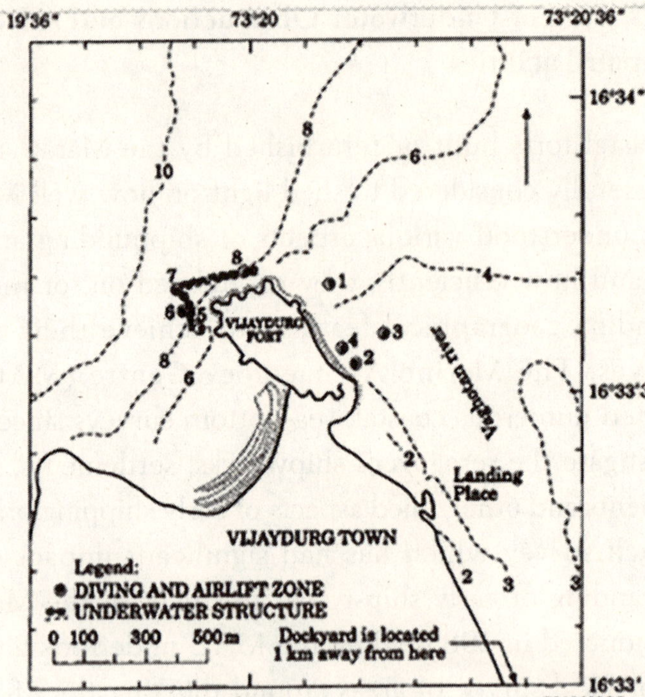

Image 3 (Clockwise from left): Site showing diving and airlift operations and underwater structure.

Image 4: Underwater structures captured by divers.

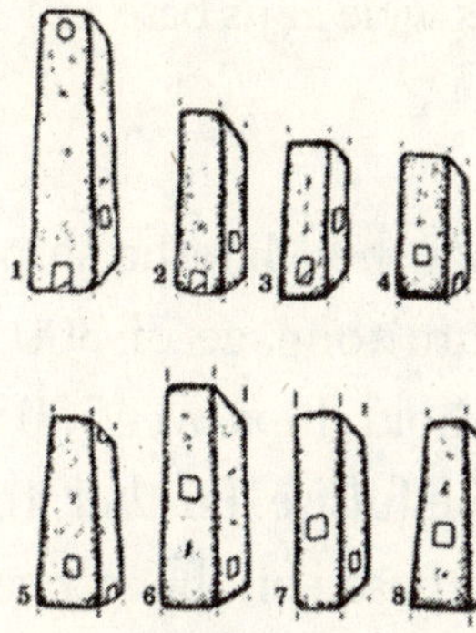

Image 5: Stone anchor of grapnel type found in the adjoining dockyard.

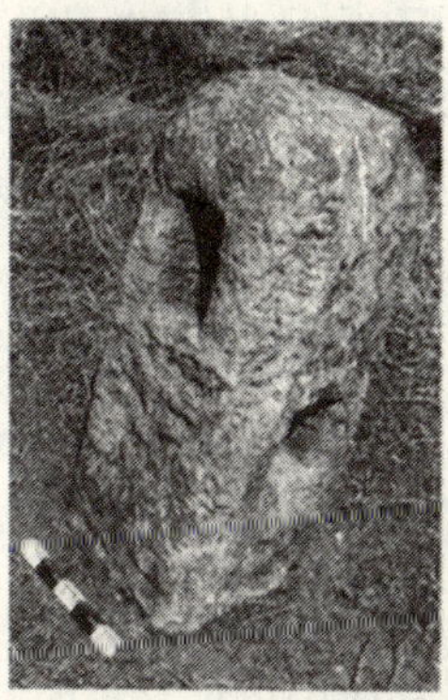

Image 6: Stone anchor used as a mooring bit.

Source: Tripathi, et al.,'Marine archaeological exploration and excavation of Vijaydurg',1998.

At a distance of around 3 kilometres from the fort, along the Vaghotan river, a dockyard was also discovered, which, most likely, was used extensively as a ship-repair yard. As Tripathi et al., have noted:

> The dockyard was built by Maratha Admiral Kanhoji Angre during the 17th century and was remodelled by Anand Rao Dhulup to increase its capacity to hold ships of as much as 500 tons. The length and width of the dock was 110 metres x 75 metres and

> the gateway is 7 metres wide at its base and 11 metres at the top without any gates.[14]

It stands to attention that the Maratha ships, especially the pals, came with the maximum tonnage of 300 to 350 tons. Hence, remodelling the dock to hold ships over 500 tons indicates Angre's foresight and plans for the future. Further, the functioning of such a dock, then as now, was based on the intricate knowledge of tidal patterns and ranges. To illustrate, ships could only enter the dock at high tide, while repair work, both on the ships and of the dock features, could be undertaken at low tide.

Clinching evidence of an advanced ship-repair ecosystem was also discovered in the form of stone anchors of the grapnel type. Some of these were found erected on the wall, while others were embedded into the soil (Image 5 and 6). These must have been used as mooring bits for ships berthed at the dock. Similar stone anchors have also been discovered at Sindhudurg Fort, Malwan, which served a similar function as the Vijaydurg fort.[15] Other objects like pottery, coins and slingshots were also discovered. It maybe deduced from the above discussion that the Marathas had an advanced understanding, not only of the coast and its intricacies (tides, sea-bottom profiles, depths), but also that of associated engineering, and ship-repairing aspects.

⚓ ⚓ ⚓

The Men that Manned these Ships

Another important evidence obliquely testifying to the existence and prolific use of traditional systems of navigational knowledge and expertise comes from the descriptions of the kind of individuals who found employment onboard Shivaji's, and later Angre's ships. The majority of the crew onboard the Maratha ships, unlike the Maratha army, were drawn from different tribes, castes and even nationalities (the Maratha Navy employed European sailors as they had superlative gunnery skills, and were hardy). This is because while anyone could fight on land, fighting at sea (or along the coast), demanded a certain comfort with, and orientation towards, the rigours of sailing onboard a ship. We must remember that Shivaji himself had suffered from persistent seasickness during his one and only Basrur naval expedition to Karwar in 1655.[16]

Apart from the Muslims and Europeans, three of the most ubiquitous castes found onboard Maratha ships were from the Koli, Gabit and Bhandari communities.[17] Mai Nayak, one of Shivaji's admirals belonged to the Bhandari caste. According to the Hindu belief system, one's jaati (caste) was traditionally linked to one's varna (occupation). These castes were traditional fishermen, possessed of deep, intuitive knowledge of the sea, and coastal topography, accumulated over hundreds of years of seagoing practice. For outsiders to navigate these waters was a very tough task. To illustrate, on the morning of 7 November 1718—the third day of the famous Battle of Khanderi—the desperate English company, consisting of ships, *Revenge*, *Victory*, and *Morrice*, decided to launch an amphibious landing operation on Khanderi Fort. This was the second such assault, the first one on 6 November having been convincingly repelled. However, as Manohar Malgonkar writes:

> At the appointed time, after the landing party had been put into their boats, it was 'discovered' that the current was too strong for a landing. The men huddled together in the tossing landing boats had to wait until ten o'clock before the boats could start from shore.[18]

It must be borne in mind that amphibious assaults rely heavily on the element of surprise. However, the boats laden with landing parties were easily spotted from the fort, and were exposed to fire from the fort's guns. We are later told that, 'when the landing boats began to make for the shore, the tide was too strong and capsized some of the boats.'[19] From the perspective of the Marathas manning the fort's guns, the boats laden with hapless soldiers capsizing to currents, would have been a comical site to behold.

From the above discussions, it may be surmised that the Maratha seamen, though having different navigational practices compared to their seafaring Gujarati and Kutchi counterparts, nevertheless possessed both an intricate knowledge of the Konkan coast's many variegated features, and the navigational techniques to exploit these for their own leverage. The fact that Maratha ships were manned by individuals from the Koli, Bhandari and Gapit communities, having rich traditions of indigenous seafaring knowledge, further strengthens this argument.

⚓⚓⚓

A Shoe to Fit the Foot: Considerations of Geography in Ship Design

It has also been estimated that Shivaji's fleet consisted of anywhere between 160 to 200 ships. However, this maybe a misestimate, as argued by S.N. Sen, given that these numbers may also have included non-naval, mercantile vessels, such as the taru, tarandi, pagar, dubare, vabhor, and tirkati.[20] Specific vessels involved in naval engagements included the ghurabs, gallivats (also called galbats), and pals, as well as shibars and manjhuas.[21] Among these the first two were the most widely used. The ghurabs, comparable to British frigates, and ranging from 150-300 tons, were squat (i.e., flat-bottomed), broad-beamed vessels, their prows long and thin, almost touching water. The gallivats were smaller, rowing vessels, weighing not more than 70 tonnes. They were faster, easily manoeuvrable and could operate in shallower depths.

Of their weapon complement, Sen writes, 'the *Ghurabs* carried sixteen guns and 150 men, while the *Gallivats* had six guns and 60 men.'[22] Akin to modern-day fleet formations, which comprise of different types and classes of warships operating together to complement each other's capabilities, these ghurabs and gallivats (and at times, the pals) too operated together. Two or three gallivats always accompanied the larger ghurab, at times towing the ghurab to the designated area of operations. Though the Marathas also had an intricate administration system undergirding their navy's functioning, discussing the same may lie beyond the scope of this chapter.

Scholars have reflected that despite the Marathas employing Europeans in their shipbuilding endeavours, Maratha ships were nowhere close to their European counterparts, in terms of seaworthiness, and the ship's complement of weapons/armaments. One wonders what factors led to these supposedly subpar vessels to triumph over their superior adversaries. It is imperative here to correlate the design of these ships with the geography they were intended to operate in. The Maratha vessels were certainly smaller, both in terms of draft, tonnage and dimensions, from their European counterparts. In addition, they were also flat-bottomed. This specific trait had deleteriously affected their sea-keeping qualities, as these pitched and yawed violently.

However, it must be remembered that they seldom ventured to the high seas. Mostly, their operations were confined to the coast. Hence, within specific coastal settings, these characteristics, i.e., of being decidedly smaller, with lesser tonnage, draft, coupled with the flat-bottomed characteristics granted them tactical advantages not available to larger, heavier British and Portuguese ships. One of these advantages entailed being able to escape into the many shallow creeks or coves after raiding European ships, which the latter had no access to.[23] In this regard, Amarendra Kumar observes:

> Another shortcoming of the Company [British] was the hugeness of the vessels. The big size of the vessels had two obvious disadvantages. One, it could not venture into the shallow waters of the bays and creeks because of its burden [meaning deeper draft], and two, its speed and manoeuvrability was quite slow to have made any impact on the flat-bottomed, light, and fast boats of the Marathas (and other native rulers).[24]

Furthermore, owing to variations in local topographies discussed earlier, wind patterns too varied along the coast, and fluctuated through the day. Hence, the practice of 'gallivats towing the larger ghurabs', which were fitted with bigger guns on their broadside, may have emanated with the objective of offsetting the effects of unpredictable wind patterns.

At the risk of stretching the analogy to its limit, this Maratha practice of a more manoeuvrable/capable vessel towing another vessel with superior weapon capability, foreshadows the Indian Navy's Operations Trident and Python during the 1971 Indo-Pak War, when Indian Naval Ships (INS) *Kiltan* and *Katchall* towed the smaller, Vidyut-class missile boats INS *Nipat*, *Nirghat* and *Veer* all the way to the Pakistani coast and successfully bombarded Karachi. While the objective, scale, and even design of these two operations vastly differed (obviously!), the Marathas' essential principle of combining vessels with different capabilities to achieve an objective, found echoes 350 years later, in 1971 during the Indo–Pak war.

In the case of 1971, tactical and strategic considerations (and limitations) determined the conceptualization of operations; in case of the Marathas—added to their tactical and strategic considerations—was the objective of offsetting untoward dependence on the wind. Here, their geographical knowledge may have been a strong reason for the practice of smaller, manoeuvrable vessels towing larger vessels with bigger guns.

⚓ ⚓ ⚓

Tactics and the Geography Angle

Speaking of the Maratha practice of using rowing boats such as gallivats to tow the larger ghurabs, leads us to an important, and much awaited discussion about other Maratha tactics and how these were informed by, and attuned to, underlying geographical considerations. Sen discusses the general modus operandi employed by Maratha ships:

> … from the few accounts of the naval actions that have come down to us, it appears that they [Maratha ships] generally waited for the calm when they had to fight against a European ship as their oars placed them at an advantage over their adversary, and when discomfited, they readily retired to shallow waters where their heavier rivals could not follow.[25]

Likewise, the description below expands on how the ghurabs and gallivants acted in concert:

> ... on observing a rival vessel from their anchorage in some secure bay, his [Maratha] ships would be put to sea. They would sail if there was a breeze, and if not, the oar-driven *galbats* (*Gallivats*) took the *Ghurabs* in tow. When within firing range, they would quickly gather astern of the target and fire into her rigging, to disable her. They then drew near and attacked from all sides, till she yielded. If she managed to hold out, they closed in on her and the crews armed with swords boarded her, ensuring a quick end to the encounter.[26]

Certain insights about the interplay between tactics and geography can be gleaned from the above two passages. Firstly, that Maratha seamen possessed a sound understanding of wind patterns, as 'calm weather', i.e., lack of wind, would put the heavy European ships at a disadvantage in terms of speed and manoeuvrability since they relied on their sails. Secondly, as mentioned in the second passage, the Maratha ghurabs being towed by gallivats would have offset the dependence on winds. Even if low winds were present and the target vessel was underway, the Marathas would choose to attack and fight from the leeward side, as this would be tactically advantageous.

Thirdly, and most importantly, the zone astern, i.e., behind, a naval vessel is usually considered a shadow zone, as it is neither covered by the firing arcs of its weapons, nor monitored in great detail. For example, if the port (the left) side has broadside gun/cannons, then the starboard area (the right side) falls in its shadow zone. Moreover spotting a small vessel approaching astern is difficult. Such an approach preserves the element of surprise and precludes being detected or being fired upon. Hence the Maratha ships approaching the larger

European ships from astern, and then explicitly targeting its sails could have been a deliberate choice—damaging the sails would have temporarily paralysed the vessel. It would be illuminating to recollect here that even in contemporary times, pirates (for want of a better term), approach merchant vessels from astern (directly from behind) or the quarters (within an arc of 90 degrees directly behind the vessels) in high-powered skiffs, because the same principles, i.e., that of surprise, difficult detection and speed advantage, come into play.[27]

Fourthly, the effectiveness of this practice becomes even more apparent if we realize that such operations were usually undertaken in narrow channels, i.e., estuary mouths, coves, or anchorages; at other times, the Maratha ships—having knowledge of sand bars, submerged rocks, or tidal patterns—would lure European ships to these areas. This would restrict the manoeuvrability of European vessels, severely constricting the choice of responses available to them. Remember, the area astern fell in the shadow arcs of their broadsides. Even in contemporary times, while entering or leaving harbour or when in restricted waters, i.e., close to the coast, warships deploy 'Force Protection Measures'. These measures are carried out by special teams whose sole mandate is to watch out for and neutralize threats such as a fast-moving, suspicious, potentially bomb-laden boat, or individuals armed with projectile weapons such as rocket-propelled grenades, etc., perched on elevated platforms.

Lastly, another way that geography influenced Maratha tactics was in the patterns of quick engagement-disengagement.[28] The Maratha naval vessels did not have the wherewithal to undertake a pitched sea battle with the vastly bigger and well-equipped European ships. Hence, the above two passages depict swift engagement, and later, even quicker disengagement, followed by escape into the numerous shallow-water creeks and coves.

The British ships could not pursue them in view of their larger size, draft and tonnage, as discussed previously.

To summarize, the Maratha seamen's knowledge of geography not only aided them in offsetting their many material limitations, but also had a profound influence on the tactics they deployed.

⚓ ⚓ ⚓

To Conclude

While the Maratha Navy's dominance along the Konkan coast during a particular phase of colonial history has been well established, this chapter has attempted to illuminate the reasons behind this phenomenon; reasons rooted in the knowledge of geography and locally prevailing conditions—knowledge that the Maratha seamen possessed long before the Europeans could arrive at similar levels of understanding. The chapter commenced by undertaking a comparative analysis of seafaring versus coastal navigation practices, to illuminate how techniques for the latter had already been articulated by local Maratha seamen because of their awareness of the coast.

Thereafter we undertook a brief analysis of British charts to illustrate the rudimentary state of British hydrography at this juncture. This was followed by providing an overview of underwater obstructions, and ship-repair facilities which the Marathas had built, thereby testifying to their superlative engineering capabilities. The identity of the ship's crew and their social roots also further our understanding of how the Marathas leveraged indigenous knowledge systems of coastal communities. The last two parts illustrated the correlations between coastal conditions and the design of ships, as also, the tactics employed by the Maratha Navy, and how these were influenced by sound understanding of how to fight in these settings and conditions.

Based on the above discussions, one can surmise that the indigenous knowledge systems pertaining to the Konkan coast played a crucial role in the Maratha Navy's many triumphs against its adversaries.

Bearing these crucial facets of the Maratha Navy in mind, the next Chapter elaborates upon the contestations between the Maratha Navy and its many adversaries i.e. the Sidis of Janjira, Portuguese and British, and illustrate how the Marathas' indigenous knowledge systems played a crucial role in gaining decisive tactical superiority.

Notes

1 A detailed study of the Maratha naval establishment can be found in the following works. Sen, *The Military System of the Marathas*, 1979; Amarendra Kumar, 'Maratha Navy: An Enquiry into its Limitations and Contemporary Challenges', PhD Thesis submitted to Pune University, 2009; Sachin Pendse, *Maritime Heritage of the Konkan*, Maritime History Society, 2011.

2 Clement Downing, an Englishman and sailor, was part of the squadron employed by the East India Company to attack the Maratha admiral, Kanhoji Angre. A close reading of Downing's account provides a gist of how the British viewed Angre. In one of his accounts, Downing writes:

> ...from this time, Angria grew very insolent again, and took several Ships belonging to the Country Merchants, whereby he strengthened his own Fleet. He afterwards ingaged [sic] the *Arabella*, Capt. *Read*, a small Ship belonging to the Company, the *Blenheim*, Capt. *Parrot* and the *Godolphin*, Capt. Ingram Commander, who all made gallant Defences. Whereupon the President and Council finding that hardly any Shipping could pass or re-pass; they for the Company's Interest in the way of Trade, thought proper to make Peace with him [Angria].

See pp. 14-15, in Downing, *A History of Indian Wars*, 2024.

3 See pp. 177-78, in Sen, *The Military System of the Marathas*, 1979.

4 See https://www.merriam-webster.com/dictionary/navigation (accessed 30 August 2024).

5 See pp. 23-25, in B. Arunachalam, *Heritage of Indian Sea Navigation*, Maritime History Society, 2002.

6 See pp. 17-20, in Pendse, *Maritime Heritage of the Konkan*, 2011.

7 See p. 313, in Kumar, 'Maratha Navy: An Enquiry into its Limitations and Contemporary Challenges', 2009.

8 See p. 12, in Apte, *A History of the Maratha Navy*, 1973.

9 Ibid., p. 8.

10 See pp. 88-92, in Arunachalam, *Heritage of Indian Sea Navigation*, 2002.

11 See pp. 36-37, in Manoshi Bhattacharya, *A History of the Indian Naval Hydrographic Department*, National Hydrographic Office, 2004.

12 Ibid., pp. 37-38.

13 See pp. 51-63, in S. Tripathi, et al., 'Marine archaeological exploration and excavation of Vijaydurg', 1998.

14 Ibid., pp. 56-57.

15 Ibid., pp. 28-41.

16 See p. 65, in Manohar Malgonkar, *The Sea Hawk: Life and Battles of Kanhoji Angrey*, Mehta Publishing House, 1984.

17 See p. 116, in Kumar, 'Maratha Navy', 2009.

18 See pp. 232-33, in Malgaonkar, *The Sea Hawk*, 1984.

19 Ibid., p. 233.

20 See p. 158, in Sen, *The Military System of the Marathas*, 1979.

21 Ibid., pp. 160-62.

22 Ibid., p. 160.

23 See p. 313, in Kumar, 'Maratha Navy', 2009.

24 Ibid., p. 138.

25 See p. 159, in Sen, *The Military System of the Marathas*, 1979.

26 See pp. 37-38, in Naval Study Group, 'Maratha Naval Resistance to European Powers on the Konkan Coast', in *Essays in Maritime Studies*, ed., B. Arunachalam, Vol.1, Maritime History Society, 1998.

27 Indrajit Roy, 'Effects, Consequences and Remedial Actions against Somali Pirates', *Journal of the United Services Institution of India*, Vol CXLI, No. 588, April-June 2012, https://www.usiofindia.org/publication-journal/effects-consequences-and-remedial-action-against-somali-piracy.html (accessed 4 September 2024).

28 See p. 318, in Kumar, Maratha Navy, 2009.

9

Naval Contestations for Control of the Sea

Amarendra Kumar

⚓ ⚓ ⚓

Introduction

The causes of Maratha naval contests and their nature can be better understood within the context of the political landscape of the time and the factors influencing naval power. The Maratha naval fleet was essential for demonstrating and exerting state power and sovereignty in the coastal surroundings. Maratha ships were purpose-built in various sizes and designs to suit specific operational needs. These vessels were not only designed for defence but also equipped to carry out offensives and inflict damage on enemy ships during conflicts. What were the causes of contestations? Did the naval conflict arise because the Maratha Navy was used as an instrument of violence to establish economic, political and sovereign authority? Alternatively, did the contest primarily stem from the need to defend coastal territories and territorial waters from incursions by enemies of the Maratha Swarajya? To what extent was the power projection of the Marathas, and their denial of European claims—to sovereignty over the sea, the control of sea lanes and the desire to establish overseas colonies—instrumental in provoking these naval contestations? Otherwise, were the naval conflicts more closely related to the Maratha state-building efforts, similar to those of the Mughals?

A close examination of the activities of the Maratha Navy, from its inception to its decline, reveals that the Marathas were not focused on establishing a maritime empire like the Europeans. However, it cannot be denied that they were intent on using their navy to thwart such attempts within their territory. The geographical surroundings along the west coast—particularly the steep gradients that rendered the Konkan Rivers un-navigable upstream—limited the Marathas' ability to use naval vessels for territorial expansions inland. In contrast, the Mughals could easily navigate their vessels through the subcontinent's navigable rivers year-round, reaching far-off corners with ease.

The Maratha Navy was indeed designed and organized to project power offshore, but it did so in a different manner. Similar to the Cholas, who traversed the Bay of Bengal and brought the Southeast Asian powers within their ambit and promoted trade and commerce, the Maratha trading vessels also frequented the West Asian ports like Mocha, without any impediments from the European opponents. The primary purpose was not to control the high-sea maritime lanes; rather, coastal defense was essential, much like it was for the Cholas. Therefore, the Maratha Navy was essentially conceived as a brown-water or coastal navy. Its primary function was to protect the interests of the Maratha Empire in the northern Arabian Sea, especially the Konkan littoral.

The Marathas deployed their navy strategically, because of economic and security concerns. A string of coastal forts provided logistics to the naval ships engaged in coastal patrolling. The collection of taxes from merchants and trade in merchandise brought wealth to the state. As a matter of policy, the Marathas encouraged foreign merchants to settle near the ports while also regulating the movements of foreign trading vessels.[1] They issued navigational passes for that purpose. In addition to regulating trade and navigation, the state also generated revenue by directly participating in overseas trade. The importance and lucrative economic prospects of Shivaji's salt fleet, along with the state's monopoly over salt trade should not be underestimated.[2] The deployment of Maratha naval vessels to escort the mercantile fleet and safeguard it from piracy, was an essential service rendered by the state.

The Maratha Navy was equipped to resist and retaliate when challenged within its sphere of influence. Contestations occurred often, and frequently they were in a violent manner. However, what is particularly noteworthy in these conflicts is how Shivaji strategically employed his navy as both a diplomatic tool and a bargaining chip with the Europeans. Shivaji understood that only the Europeans could meaningfully contribute to the strength of the Maratha Navy. Therefore, Jadunath Sarkar's assertion that Shivaji's Navy was weak and never sought pitched battle at sea with the Europeans, should be approached with caution, as it does not accurately reflect the ground reality.[3] Perhaps the fact that it was not large, coupled with the inadequate artillery onboard Maratha ships, led Sarkar to make this comment. The Marathas preferred smaller fighting vessels due to geographical considerations, which they effectively exploited in their naval contests. Additionally, their tactical acumen allowed them to operate without actually depending upon a single pivotal weapon. This chapter takes note of these aspects of Maratha naval warfare while analysing their engagements with various enemies.

⚓ ⚓ ⚓

Maratha Sidi/Mughal Contestations

The prime motive of the Maratha Navy under Shivaji, according to the *Sabhasad Bakhar*, was to fight the Sidi of Janjira.[4] The Konkan coast frequently experienced raids by the Sidi forces, which stealthily landed to plunder Maratha territories in search of food, provisions and slaves. The coastal pocket designated as the Sidi's Jagir, struggled to meet the needs of his people and the garrison stationed at Danda-Rajpuri and Janjira. During the Maratha–Sidi war, the Maratha Army successfully drove away the Sidis from the coast, capturing the coastal fort of Danda-Rajpuri under Shivaji's leadership. Afterwards, Shivaji applied pressure from the seaside, nearly confining the Sidi in the island fortress of Janjira. Under intense pressure, the Sidi reportedly sought help from the Portuguese, who came to his aid with a timely supply of rice and other provisions in 1667.[5]

This indirect involvement of the Portuguese in the Sidi–Maratha naval contestation prevented Shivaji from achieving a decisive victory over his most formidable adversary. The Marathas were unable to defeat or destroy the Sidi's fleet. In due course, the Sidi wrested back control of his lost possessions on the coast and retook the Danda-Rajpuri fort. Determined to assert dominance over Konkan littoral, Shivaji intensified his campaign against the Sidi. He made several attempts to capture Janjira from the Sidi. The Sidi port was routinely blockaded and Maratha ships relentlessly bombarded Janjira fort, placing its garrison under constant threat of starvation.

The Sidi's master, the sultan of Bijapur, often failed to provide timely relief, further compromising his position. Meanwhile, the Sidi took a realistic view of the situation weighing the pros and cons of his position. The most prudent solution that appeared to him, was 'to join his enemy's enemy'. As Khafi Khan noted, the Sidi felt so fed up with the continued deprivation that he decided to surrender and cede the fort to the Maratha Chhatrapati. However, a faction within the Sidi garrison opposed capitulation and sought refuge with the Mughal emperor, Aurangzeb. Seizing this opportunity, Aurangzeb sent assurances to the dissenting leader. Following this, there was a coup in the fort in which the dissidents prevailed. Sidi Sambal, the leader of the dissidents was crowned the Mughal admiral on the west coast and given a fixed annual salary.[6]

It is important to note that the Mughals had a capable flotilla, originally commissioned by Emperor Akbar. Abul Fazl, the official historian of Akbar's reign, detailed the specifics of the Mughal Navy in his work, the *Akbarnama*.[7] Though the Mughal–Sidi alliance was opportunistic, the incorporation of the Sidi into the Mughal establishment influenced the military dynamics of the Konkan littoral, directly affecting the Marathas' naval prospects. The Mughal–Sidi alliance forced Shivaji into a war of survival against the resourceful Mughals, making his ability to counter their land offensives crucial for Maratha political survival.

The Sidi naval challenge off the Konkan coast opened another front in the Anglo-Maratha war, which kept Shivaji preoccupied. For the Marathas the contest was a struggle for survival, while from the Mughal perspective, the Sidi naval campaign represented a state-building exercise, akin to Aurangzeb's Assam campaign under Mir Jumla.[8] The Maratha–Sidi naval conflicts soon escalated to a terminal stage, marked by extreme violence. Shivaji needed to keep the coastal waters clear of Sidi control, as escape by sea provided the most viable alternative in case the Marathas failed to offset the Mughal pressure on land.

So long as Shivaji was alive, he dedicated himself not only to keeping the Sidi of Janjira in check, but also to capturing Janjira fort itself. However, the fort's formidable walls and ramparts resisted any breach or demolition by Maratha shelling. After repeated failures to take Janjira from the Sidi, Shivaji resolved to establish a similar stronghold for his Swarajya. The construction of the offshore marine fort at Malvan can be understood in this context. Named Sindhudurg, meaning the 'Ocean Fortress', it quickly became the Maratha Naval headquarters. Shivaji aimed to establish his own offshore naval base, providing him with strategic advantages that the Sidi had over his adversaries.

Chhatrapati Sambhaji, Shivaji's son and successor, maintained naval pressure on Janjira and devised innovative and equally lofty plans to capture it. He wanted to 'fill the sea channel' between the coast of Danda-Rajapuri and Janjira with rock, rubble and other materials.[9] By doing so, Sambhaji planned to create a causeway from the coast so that he could march his army till the gate of the island fort and take it by dual action involving his navy. The young Chhatrapati had almost accomplished his objective when the Mughal military suddenly appeared on the scene and threatened the Swarajya's boundaries. Aurangzeb's Deccan campaign saw the rampaging Mughal troops advance rapidly, inaugurating a war of political survival for the Deccani powers. The Maratha Swarajya was no exception, as Sambhaji had to wind up the Janjira campaign midway to counter the Mughals on land.[10]

While he tried his best to negate the Mughal military challenge, the idea of keeping the seaboard and adjoining waters free from the Sidi's control never skipped Sambhaji's attention. The Maratha Navy fought relentlessly against the

Sidi in the Konkan surroundings. Sambhaji's eagerness to subdue the Sidi can be guessed from the fact that in 1684, he reached an understanding with Captain Richard Keigwin, the then EEIC Governor of Bombay, to weaken the position of the Sidi in the Konkan Sea.[11] As the Mughal admiral on the west coast of India, the Sidi received preferential treatment from the EEIC. In particular, his fleet was permitted to winter at the EEIC port of Bombay. Ironically, the Sidi misused the privilege by using Bombay as a springboard for depredation of the adjoining Maratha coast. Sambhaji, however, did not live long enough to make further attempts to capture Janjira. After his death, the Mughal overran Maratha territory and transferred control of the coastal area to the Sidi.

In the first half of the eighteenth century, the Maratha–Sidi naval conflicts reignited with renewed vigour thanks to the redoubtable Maratha admiral, Kanhoji Angre, and his successors. At the same time, the EEIC, viewing Kanhoji Angre as a pirate, was firmly determined to eradicate the Maratha Navy. To achieve this, the EEIC used diplomacy to rally support from detractors of the Maratha Navy. The Sidi of Janjira was one such detractor who was approached by the EEIC Governor of Bombay in 1720, with a proposal for a joint action on the Marathas.[12] But, Kanhoji Angre remained undefeated during his lifetime.

After his death in 1729, his son and successor, Sekhoji Angre launched a huge naval offensive against the Sidi, receiving strong support from the Maratha Peshwa on land.[13] Soon, the Sidi was cornered by the Marathas. Sambhaji Angre, another son of Kanhoji Angre, besieged Underi, the Sidi's offshore base near the channel leading to Bombay, which raised an alarm within the EEIC establishment at Bombay.

At that time, the Maratha naval outpost of Khanderi was already established in the area. In the eventuality of Underi's capitulation, the navigation and safety of Bombay would have been further compromised. Consequently, the EEIC sprung into action, approaching the Sidi to negotiate an 'offensive-defensive alliance' against the Marathas. Following this, a naval expedition was launched by the EEIC to 'defend' the Sidi's Underi fort.[14] Thus, European intervention once again saved the Sidi of Janjira from imminent extinction.

⚓ ⚓ ⚓

Euro–Maratha Contestations

Portuguese control over the western coast was yet to wane when Chhatrapati Shivaji conceived of the Maratha Navy. After conquering the tidal creeks of Kalyan-Bhiwandi from Mughals in 1657, he commenced shipbuilding activities there. The first two Maratha warships were launched at Sangameri near Durgadi fort. Initially, shipwrights of Portuguese origin assisted the Marathas in designing and constructing nearly twenty Maratha warships. To launch these vessels, Shivaji obtained Portuguese 'passes' by persuading them that the Maratha warships would be deployed against his rival—the Sidi of Janjira.

However, as the Maratha warships began patrolling the Konkan waters, the prospect of a native power becoming a naval force made the Portuguese uneasy. This concern is evident in a letter they sent, which ordered the destruction of some of the newly constructed Maratha warships docked at Nagaon Creek.[15] However, the Portuguese were clever not to reveal their apprehensions to the Marathas. They adapted their strategies according to circumstances, shifting between alliances, rivalries and neutrality with the Marathas. Their involvement and sponsored support for the Sidi during the Sidi–Maratha conflicts contributed significantly to the naval clashes between the Portuguese and the Marathas. However, these conflicts were generally low-intensity, involving actions such as reprisals and capture of ships and crew.

Shivaji employed a similar strategy with all the European powers along the west coast. He was careful to prevent Euro–Maratha naval contestations from escalating beyond a certain point, as such conflicts could negatively impact the Maratha prospects. To ensure this, Shivaji's port officials were strictly warned not to steal any goods from the European vessels until proper restitution was secured from the concerned party to which the ship belonged. The impounded ship, along with its crew and cargo, was restored after successful restitution. This approach suggests that the Maratha naval actions against the Europeans, especially during the time of Shivaji, should not be viewed as mere commerce raiding. Rather, the confinement of vessels was a well-considered policy that Shivaji used to advance the political and economic interests of the Maratha Swarajya.

The seized vessels, along with their goods and crew, were used as valuable bargaining chips. There are references indicating that Europeans occasionally retaliated by seizing local Maratha vessels. However, after negotiations, the vessels, goods and the crew were typically restored to their respective parties. This process allowed for specific demands—such as money, arms, trading concessions—to be negotiated. While these exchanges could involve elements of coercion, both negotiating sides were often accustomed to such interactions due to the underlying political and economic necessities.

Although Shivaji outwardly maintained amicable relations with the European powers, he seized every opportunity to assert his sovereignty and maritime rights along the Konkan coast. For instance, in 1665 the Maratha Navy launched a naval expedition from Sindhudurg to the southern port town of Basrur, primarily to demonstrate its strength. The nascent Maratha fleet, with Shivaji onboard, passed through Goa—the headquarters of the Portuguese *Estado da India*—unopposed.[16]

As mentioned earlier, Shivaji was unable to achieve a decisive naval success against the Sidi of Janjira. Recognizing the importance of offshore naval bases, he built forts like Sindhudurg, Padamdurg, Kolaba, etc. In 1679, Shivaji decided to fortify the barren rocky projection known as 'Henry-Kennery', situated near the sea channel leading to the EEIC's Bombay harbour. Caught off guard, the EEIC declared a naval war on the Marathas to assert its claim over 'Henry-Kennery'.[17] However, the deep-hulled, well-equipped ships of the Company's Marine could not approach the site to destroy it through bombardment or land lascars to physically occupy it. There were two main reasons for this. First, the marine charts of the area had not been completed, and the water depth around the circumference of the rocky outcrop was uncharted. Second, the Maratha guns were positioned on the wall facing the landing site, delivering a constant barrage of grapeshot that prevented the EEIC vessels from approaching near the fortification.

The coastal defenses helped Shivaji to keep the EEIC ships at bay. In response, the EEIC resorted to the time-tested strategy of enforcing a naval blockade. This aimed to prevent food, construction materials, ammunition, etc. from reaching the fort. However, the EEIC struggled to enforce the blockade effectively. The EEIC records noted that under the cover of the night, smaller Maratha vessels, laden with provisions and munitions, could easily slip past the blockade and reach the fort.

The Marathas frequently exerted military pressure on European coastal and inland settlements, besieging and threatening them from land. In 1684, for example, Chhatrapati Sambhaji launched a direct attack on the headquarters of the Portuguese *Estado-da-India*.[18] Success, however, eluded the Marathas by a narrow margin, as rising sea tides came to the Portuguese rescue. Like his father Shivaji, Sambhaji also sought alliances with the Arabs—the dreaded enemies of the Portuguese—to maintain constant pressure on them.[19] In the early eighteenth century, Kanhoji Angre's fleet boldly cruised along the Konkan coast. The Maratha flotilla defiantly rejected European claims to control the sea. While his merchant ships traded with Bombay, they refused to buy the EEIC's navigational passes or pay harbour dues.[20] Furthermore, Kanhoji sought to assert his sovereign authority over the Konkan Sea by mandating that all vessels obtain 'dastaks', the Maratha navigational passes.

The claims and counterclaims among the Marathas, Sidis and Europeans over control of navigation, and the validity of honouring navigational passes, significantly escalated naval conflicts. The Maratha Admiral was ruthless, showing no discrimination between indigenous and foreign powers; anyone who challenged his authority along the Konkan coast was at risk of attack. Kanhoji Angre knew that a more robust flotilla, with a steady supply of crew and fighters was needed to enforce his authority over the sea in an effective manner. He appeared to be following a carefully planned strategy to assert Maratha sovereign control over the coastal surroundings, evidenced by his extensive teak plantation efforts along a large stretch of coast. The Portuguese well comprehended the importance of teak as a 'wood not subject to decay' during the sixteenth century, too.[21] At the same time, Kanhoji Angre's naval operations benefitted from the military labour market, as it employed Portuguese shipwrights to enhance the compatibility of the Maratha ships with European designs. Manual Moraes de Caravello is mentioned as an advisor for Maratha ship-designing and construction. Further, European military adventurers were employed as gunsmiths and gunners in Kanhoji Angre's Navy.[22] The presence of Daud Khan, a Muslim who served as a commander of his naval unit in 1724, indicates that Kanhoji Angre looked beyond narrow sectarian interests in building his naval force.[23] These choices reflect a broader vision for strengthening his naval establishment.

In the interregnum between Chhatrapati Shivaji's death and the rise of Kanhoji Angre, the EEIC had shifted its headquarters in India from Surat to Bombay. Its marine force, renamed the Bombay Marine, was strengthened to eliminate the threat of 'pirates' along the west coast and the Arabian Sea. Charles Boone, the then Governor of Bombay, decided to confront the Maratha Admiral head on. During Boone's tenure, the EEIC fitted out three major naval expeditions between 1717 and 1722. Of these, two, in 1718 and 1720, were directed against Vijaydurg (formerly known as Gheria) the headquarters of the Maratha admiral, whereas one was planned against Kolaba in 1720-21. The EEIC began with an expedition against Khanderi and Vijaydurg without success. Thereafter, it allied with the

Portuguese to launch a joint attack on Kolaba. On the other hand, in a second expedition against Vijaydurg, the EEIC courted assistance from the other enemies of Kanhoji, like the Sawant of Wadi and the Sidi of Janjira.[24]

The nature of these conflicts was in sharp contrast to the Euro-Maratha contestations during the time of Shivaji. By the time of Kanhoji Angre and his successors, the Anglo–Maratha naval confrontations had reached a critical point. The EEIC seemed increasingly focused on eliminating Maratha naval power entirely. For instance, the first action against Vijaydurg was planned late in the season when the monsoon rains were to commence. At that time, the Maratha vessels at Vijaydurg had been overhauled for necessary repairs. The EEIC's strategy was to destroy the Maratha fleet by causing fires. But Kanhoji Angre's monsoon preparedness was masterfully executed, allowing him to perfectly outmanoeuvre the EEIC's cunning plan.

He had constructed a boom at the entrance of the channel leading to the dockyard, where the Maratha ships were lined up for overhaul. This strategic barrier prevented the EEIC vessels from advancing and executing their plan. This incident serves as a great example of effectively assimilating geographical features into naval strategy. In the case of the Kolaba expedition, the Anglo–Portuguese strategy aimed to corner the Maratha Admiral by simultaneously engaging him on two war fronts: land and sea.[25] However, Kanhoji Angre, skillfully employed diplomacy to isolate the Portuguese from the EEIC, undermining their plan. The Maratha Peshwa also came to the rescue of the Maratha Admiral during this conflict.[26]

Later, when the EEIC launched a second offensive against Vijaydurg, their approach was to besiege the fort. They deployed specially designed boats and even constructed a so-called 'floating castle' named *Phram* to cannonade and breach the fort's walls. Despite these efforts, they failed miserably—their troops could not even land on the coast for a direct assault.[27] Ultimately, Boone had no choice but to call off the mission. The most significant aspect of this phase of the Euro–Maratha naval engagements was that the Europeans faced the same lessons as during the Anglo–Maratha naval contest for Khanderi rock. Geographically, it highlighted the effectiveness of smaller boats for defense and logistics. Surprisingly, before relinquishing his charge, Boone admitted in his dispatch to London that pursuing the 'lighter' and 'speedier' Maratha boats during naval engagements was quite challenging. He wrote that this factor that denied the EEIC success against an 'inferior' and 'ill-equipped Maratha fleet'. Boone further recommended that the Bombay Marine include more 'smaller' ships. It is said that the Dutch also attacked Vijaydurg shortly afterward, intending to storm the fort by landing their troops. However, due to the fort's strong defenses, they quickly retreated as well.[28]

Under these circumstances, Kanhoji Angre decided that diplomacy was a better approach, to avoid confrontations for the time being. He was also aware that until teak plantations bore fruit and timber became readily available, or until large-calibre guns could be fitted on the Maratha vessels to match the European men-o'-war, he would need to rely on traditional tactics and forego the use of pivot weapons and advanced technology in Euro–Maratha conflicts. Kanhoji Angre breathed his last in 1729, and was succeeded by his son Sekhoji Angre, who was equally competent and daring. Without the Maratha pass, Sekhoji would not let the Sidi or Europeans vessels navigate in the Konkan waters.

During this period, the Bombay Marine and the Maratha Navy fiercely contested sovereignty over the west coast.[29] In 1735, the EEIC hired Lovji Nusserwanjee Wadia, the first Parsi master-builder of the Bombay Government Dockyard, to build teakwood ships. In due course of time, the Wadia master-builders constructed over 170 war vessels and other craft for the Company, 34 warships for the Royal Navy, 87 merchant vessels for private firms, and 3 ships for the Imam of Muscat. One of them, *The Bombay*, built for the Bombay Marine in 1739, was described as a 'staunch and stout vessel'.[30] Therefore, it can be inferred that the indigenous features were likely adopted and integrated into the European ships to navigate the geographical conditions.

⚓⚓⚓

Strategy and Tactics

In the Maratha naval engagements, marine forts played a crucial role. In the previous chapter we took note of the Maratha policy regarding marine forts. Thanks to the naval forts, coastal policing was carried out effectively. The Maratha vessels operated under the protection of the cannons mounted over the parapets, deterring the enemy ships from venturing too close to the coast. The fort guns also protected the coast from amphibious assaults of the enemy. It should be remembered that Shivaji and Sambhaji were unable to capture the Janjira island fort from the Sidi due to its formidable defenses and the cannons positioned there. Despite the brave efforts of the Maratha soldiers who attempted to scale the fort's wall with ladders, they were thwarted by the enemy. The Maratha strategy of cannonading and blockading Janjira had not yielded results. Consequently, Sambhaji decided to build a causeway to reach the fort. However, the arrival of the Mughal troops in the Deccan, cut short his ambitious plan to subdue Janjira as he had to rush to save his territory from being occupied by the 'bigger' enemy.

Kanhoji Angre strategically utilized his marine forts to outmanoeuvre his enemies in naval conflicts. The Battle of Kolaba is a prime example of his tactical brilliance. Later, when Vijaydurg—the then headquarters of the Maratha Navy—faced a serious threat from the EEIC, Kanhoji Angre showcased his tactical brilliance yet again.

Clement Downing, who participated in the naval actions supporting the EEIC efforts against Kanhoji Angre, wrote an account that offers valuable insight into Maratha naval strategies and tactics employed during this critical engagement. Coastal forts also acted as bases for ships and its crew. The annual overhauling of the ships was done under the protection of the fort so that their safety would not be compromised.[31] The navies dreaded the destruction of their fleet during the monsoon season, when the inclement weather did not permit sailing. During this time, the ships were typically laid up ashore for maintenance and repairs, making them vulnerable to sabotage. A spark could quickly engulf the entire fleet in flames within no time.

It should be noted that the EEIC attack on Vijaydurg fort was undertaken quite late in the monsoon season, when Maratha ships were removed from the sea to prevent against any damage from the very heavy rain and to carry out necessary repair works. The Bombay Marine aimed to destroy Maratha ships by causing a fire. Anticipating their intentions, Kanhoji Angre erected a boom (to act as a blockade) at the mouth of the channel leading to the dockyard where the Maratha ships were lined up for overhaul. Additionally, the fort's guns kept a close vigil of the site and its surroundings. Not expecting this level of preparedness from the Marathas, the English plan failed miserably. They again tried to land, reach the fort walls and attack. But the continuous barrage of fire from the fort's cannons and guns forced them to flee for safety. The Maratha admiral had again won the day.

Maratha forts represented more than just a garrison and an impenetrable defence, they were symbols of resilience and ingenuity. Vijaydurg, for instance, included a well-planned dry dockyard that could accommodate larger ships of up to 500 tons displacement.[32] Underwater security architecture was also in place, to prevent enemy ships from approaching too close to the fort.[33] Kolaba fort was designed such that the tides regulated entry and exit to the fort from the sea. In addition to the marine forts, various types and sizes of fighting ships played a crucial role in naval battles. Most Maratha vessels were small, flat-bottomed rowing boats, while larger sailing ships known as the galbat and the ghurab had one or two masts. By the eighteenth century, the Marathas deployed even larger ships called pals which featured three masts. The iconographic representations of Konkan ships on stone panels during the medieval period inform us of the coexistence of the oar and the sail. According to Jean Deloche, rowing was preferred for quick and easy maneouvres. Hence, the sails were not shown in stone panels despite the depiction of ship masts. At the same time, when the wind was fair, a single sail would provide rest to the rowers. However, during naval combat, the sail was always lowered and stowed away to ensure that great handiness given by the oars.[34]

As a part of their strategy, the Marathas achieved numerical superiority over the enemy by concentrating their smaller, faster vessels in their preferred area of engagement. Benjamin Hall, an English naval official whose ship was captured by small Maratha vessels led by Admiral Sambhaji Angre, gives a glimpse of their daring tactics:

> Their Grabbs and Gallivats, being there never so many in number, always keep astern of our ships, or any other they may engage, and so close, that there is no danger of missing you when they fire their prow guns, which were six pounders. They tack and give you a broadside, and shear off and load again.[35]

The smaller Maratha vessels, typically carrying around a dozen or more soldiers, were designed to accommodate small artillery pieces at the front. They approached the enemy ship from the rear and their artillery fire targeted its main mast. Once the enemy ship was dismasted, Maratha soldiers swiftly boarded from all sides and overpowered the crew. Maratha strategy included a combination of firepower and boarding action. Secondly, fighting in coastal waters was convenient to them. The near absence of wind denied sail propulsion to European ships; the presence of submerged rocks and sandbars, shallow creeks and pattern of tidal occurrences, etc.—all of which the Marathas were familiar with—gave them the advantage over the enemy. The flat-bottomed Maratha rowing boats were best suited to exploit coastal conditions to their advantage.[36]

Once the enemy was lured to the killing ground, or waters, the Marathas chose the right moment to disengage and escape to the many creeks and coves along the tidal coast, leaving the enemy to languish in a difficult position. Their use of guerrilla tactics minimized their losses in terms of men and materials. Furthermore, the loss of a smaller vessel (which the Marathas had in plenty), was insignificant compared to the loss of bigger ships such as those that the Europeans had. Building medium to large ships required enormous resources and time—luxuries that Shivaji never had. The loss of a bigger ship could be devastating to his plans. On the other hand, constructing smaller ships required comparatively less time and was economically viable. Kanhoji Angre's thrust for extensive teak plantation can be understood in this context. He aimed to strengthen his naval defences and deploy more fighting vessels, comprehending the nature and severity of European challenges in the struggle for maritime sovereignty.

The Maratha Navy showcased remarkable ingenuity, allowing it to carve out a distinct niche in the early modern period. Its naval traditions and lessons continue to resonate within the Indian Navy well into the 21st century. The next chapter seeks to draw parallels between the two navies in order to emphasize this point.

Notes

1 See p. 31, in Amatya, *Shivarajniti*, 1928.

2 See pp. 188-90, in A.R. Kulkarni, 'Protection to Salt Industry by Shivaji', *Proceedings of the Indian History Congress*, Vol. 24, 1961.

3 See p. 252, Sarkar, *Shivaji and HIs Times*, 1973.

4 See pp. 84-86, in Sabhasad, *Sabhasad Bakhar*, 2000.

5 See p. 41, in Pissurlencar, *Portuguese Marathe Sambandha*, 1967.

6 See p. 76, in H.M. Elliot, 'Muntakhabu-l-Lubab by Muhammad Hashim Khafi Khan', in *The History of India as Told by its Own Historians (The Muhammadan Period): The Posthumous Papers of the Late Sir H.M. Elliot*, ed., John Dowson, Susil Gupta (India) Ltd., second edition, 1952. See pp. 261-62, in Sarkar, *Shivaji and His Times*, 1973.

Also see Vol. 1, No. 171, in Paranjape, *English Records on Shivaji*, 1931.

7 See pp. 289-92, in Allami, *Ain-i-Akbari*, 1927.

8 See pp. 41-54, in P. Konwar, 'Mir Jumla's Invasion of Assam (1662–63), War Experience of a Dutch Sailor Heiden and Translator Glanius', *Indian Historical Review*, Vol. 46, No. 1; also see pp. 368-74, in I.S. Mumtaza, 'Mir Jumla's Assam Invasion as Depicted by the Ahom Buranji: A Study In Historical Geography', *Proceedings of the Indian History Congress*, Vol. 55, 1994.

9 See pp. 75-76, in Robert Orme, *Historical Fragments of the Mogul Empire, of the Morattoes, and of the English Concerns in Indostan from the year MDCLIX*, ed. and Introduction by J.P. Guha, Associated Publishing House, reprint,1974; see also pp. 82-84, in Kamal Gokhale, *Chhatrapati Sambhaji*, Navkamal Prakashan, 1978.

10 See pp. 303-13, in George Moraes, 'A Portuguese Embassy to Sambhaji – 1684', PIHC, Vol. 22, 1959.

11 See pp. 320-24, in Kumar, 'Keigwin's Bombay (1683-84) and the Maratha-Siddi Naval Conflict', 2014.

12 See pp. 17-18 in Vol II, of Forrest, ed., *Selections from the Letters, Dispatches and other State Papers*,1887.

13 G.S. Sardesai, ed., *Selections from the Peshwa Daftar*, Vol. III: '*Janjirachya Siddiwar Shahuchi Muhim* (*Shahu's Campaign against the Sidis of Janjira*), *1733-1736*'; and Vol. XXXIII: '*Janjiryachi Muhim–Puravani* (*Shahu's Campaign against the Sidis of Janjira – Supplementary*), (Marathi and English), Government Central Press, Bombay, 1930-33.

14 See pp. 54-55, 57, in Vol. II of Forrest, ed. *Selections from the Letters, Dispatches and other State Papers*,1887; also see Nos. 34, 42, etc., in Vol. XXXIII, of Sardesai, ed., *Selections from the Peshwa Daftar*, 1930-33.

15 See Vol. I, No. 235 and No. 242, in Paranjape, *English Records on Shivaji*, 1931.

16 See pp. 135-46, in Shejwalker, 'Shivaji's Raid on Basrur',1942.

17 See pp. 32-40, in Amarendra Kumar, 'The Khanderi Rock: A Note on its Strategic Importance During the 17th Century', in *Indian Cartographer*, Vol. 42, No. 1, 2022; see pp. 81-90, in B.K. Apte, 'Capture of Kennery or Khanderi Island by Shivaji', in *Bulletin of Deccan College Research Institute*, Vol. 4, no. 1, 1942; See pp. 180-86, in D.A. Dalvi, 'The Khanderi Affairs and Shivaji's Relations with

English Factors at Bombay', *Proceedings of the Indian History Congress*, Vol. 28, 1966.

18 The contemporary Venetian, Manucci, also makes a mention of Sambhaji's invasion of Goa. See p. 262 in Vol. II, of Niccolao Manucci, *Storia da Mogoror Mogul India, 1653-1708*, tr., with Introduction and Notes by William Irvine, Vol. I-IV, Atlantic Publishers, reprint, 2022. See also, R.V. Oturkar, 'Sambhaji's Relations with the Sea Powers in the Konkan', in *Proceedings of the Indian History Congress*, Vol. 15, 1952.

19 See pp. 245-52, in M.R. Kantak, 'Shivaji-Arab Relations vis-a-vis Portuguese', in *Bulletin of the Deccan College Post-Graduate Research Institute*, Golden Jubilee Vol. 50, 1990; see pp. 254-58, in Oturkar, 'Sambhaji's Relations with the Sea Powers,' 1952.

20 See p. 99, in Biddulph, *The Pirates of Malabar and an Englishwoman in India'*, 1992.

21 See pp. 257-60, in S.M. Edwardes, 'A Note on the Durability of Indian Teak', in *Empire Forestry Journal*, Vol. 1, No. 2, 1922.

22 See p. 143, Pissurlencar, *Portuguese Marathe Sambandha*, 1967.

23 See p. 12, in B.K. Shrivastavya, *The Angreys of Kolaba in British Records (1719-1884)*, 1950.

24 Ibid., pp. 3-4.

25 Seep. 64, in Biddulph, *The Pirates of Malabar: And an Englishwoman in India*, 1992. It was agreed upon in the Anglo-Portuguese alliance that after their victory over the Marathas, Kolaba would be given to the Portuguese, whereas the EEIC will occupy Vijaydurg (Gheria).

26 See pp. 250-51, in Malgaonkar, *Kanhoji Angrey, Maratha Admiral*, 1959.

27 See p. 48, in Clement Downing, *A compendious history of the Indian wars with an account of the rise, progress, strength, and forces of Angria the Pyrate*, T. Cooper, 1737; The concept of a floating fortress was not new in India. The Mughals reportedly used this method and formation during their naval actions on the enemy vessels and forts along the banks of rivers. This was particularly applied during the Bengal and Assam campaign of Aurangzeb. For more information refer to Chapter 3, in Atul Chandra Roy, *A History of the Mughal Navy and Naval Warfare*, World Press, 1972. Also see pp. 143-44, in Jadunath Sarkar, *Studies in Aurangzib's Reign*, Sangam Publication, reprint, 1989.

28 See pp. 271-72, Malgaonkar, *Kanhoji Angrey, Maratha Admiral*, 1959.

29 See pp. 546-51, in Ruby Maloni, 'The Angres and the English: Contenders for Power on the West Coast', *Proceedings of the Indian History Congress*, Vol. 66, 2005-2006.

30 See pp. 257-60, in Edwardes, 'A Note on the Durability of Indian Teak', 1922. For more information on the construction of EEIC ships in India see, Ardeshir Ruttonji Wadia, *The Bombay Dockyard and the Wadia Master Builders*, R.A. Wadia, 1957.

31 See p. 51, in Amatya, *Shivrajniti*, 1928.

32 See p. 111, in MacDougall, *Naval Resistance to Britain's Growing Power in India*, 2016.

33 See pp. 51-63, in Tripathi et al., 'Marine archaeological exploration and excavation of Vijaydurg', 1998.

34 See pp. 165-84, in Jean Deloche, 'Etudes La Circulation En Inde: VII, Konkan Warships of the XIth-XVth Centuries as Represented on Memorial Stones', in *Bulletin de l'Ecole francase d'Extreme-Orient*, 76, 1987.

35 See p. 103, in MacDougall, *Naval Resistance to Britain's Growing Power in India*, 2014.

36 See pp. 157-88, in Kumar, 'The Idea of Navy and Naval Warfare under Shivaji', 2011.

10

From Sails to Stealth: A Comparative Study of the Maratha Navy and the Indian Navy

Janhavi Lokegaonkar

⚓ ⚓ ⚓

'Jalameva Yasya, Balameva Tasya'
He who rules over the seas is all-powerful.

Introduction

Maritime Visionary of India—this facet of Chhatrapati Shivaji Maharaj needs wider appreciation. Well-renowned for his military prowess and able statesmanship, his genius at administration was unparalleled amongst his contemporaries as he effectively adapted to new challenges. A factor seldom appreciated or generally overlooked is his strategic vision regarding the sea and the use of sea power. This chapter highlights the key aspects of Chhatrapati Shivaji Maharaj's Maratha Navy and its parallels with the modern navies of our times also looks at the lessons and inspirations that can be gleaned for modern naval forces today. Under the able leadership of Chhatrapati Shivaji Maharaj, the Maratha Navy played a crucial role in securing maritime dominance along the western coast of India. Realizing the importance of maritime power and adhering to the principle of *Jalameva Yasya, Balameva Tasya,* Chhatrapati Shivaji Maharaj established a formidable naval force to protect the Maratha territories along the Arabian Sea.

This chapter provides a comparative analysis of two distinct yet interconnected naval forces, separated by centuries—the Maratha Navy and the Indian Navy—exploring the tactical, organizational, and strategic differences between them. By examining the Maratha Navy's guerrilla tactics and coastal defence strategies, and juxtaposing them with the technological advancements, institutional frameworks and blue-water ambitions of the modern Indian Navy, this chapter seeks to draw lessons from history. These lessons—ranging from innovative coastal defence techniques to maintaining maritime control—offer valuable insights for modern navies worldwide. Understanding how past naval practices can inform present strategies underscores the enduring relevance of historical maritime traditions in shaping the future of global naval operations.

⚓⚓⚓

Maratha Navy: An Instrument of the State

Establishing a navy, was a symbol of political sovereignty and independence for the Maratha State. It allowed Chhatrapati Shivaji Maharaj to exert control over his maritime domain without relying on external naval powers, as was usually the case in those times. His pioneering efforts in building the Maratha naval fleet laid the foundation for modern maritime power in the Indian subcontinent. The naval flotilla—the Maratha 'Armaar' as it was known—successfully challenged the maritime dominance of European and inimical native powers in the Arabian Sea, and ensured the security of the coastal regions of the Maratha state.[1] Shivaji Maharaj recognized the strategic importance of controlling the Konkan coastline and its key ports. By establishing a strong navy, he ensured the safety of maritime trade routes and protected them from pirates and rival powers, particularly the Sidis, the Portuguese and the English. This helped in boosting regional and intercontinental trade.

The Maratha Navy was one of the first organized and hierarchical navies in the history of India.[2] The Sabhasad Bakhar, one of the most reliable primary sources of information on the Maratha period, provides a rough estimate of the Maratha Navy.[3] It discloses details regarding the different types of vessels and warships of the Maratha fleet; the fleet that summarizes the spirit of the Maratha naval enterprise under the Chhatrapati.[4] The documentation available, sheds light on topics of complex naval administration such as the construction of docks and ships, recruitment of crew purely based on merit and credibility, lists of equipment of the navy, relations with friendly states, non-discrimination and inclusivity in the forces, permits, religious beliefs of seafaring communities etc., that show in detail the Maratha naval organization.

Recruitment from local seafaring communities ensured that the crew had 'sea legs' and an understanding and appreciation of the topographical features of the coast in addition to the indigenous navigational knowledge, wisdom and expertise.

The establishment of a powerful Maratha Navy encouraged local and foreign merchants to engage in maritime trade with confidence of security. As a result, trade and commerce in the Maratha Swarajya prospered. The revenue generated from maritime trade, customs duties, dastaks and other economic activities associated with ports and coastal regions, significantly contributed to the Maratha treasury. This revenue helped finance the expansion of the Maratha empire. The vision and policy of the Maratha state focused on geoeconomics while maritime governance was one of the key principles of the Maratha Swarajya—which Chhatrapati Shivaji Maharaj referred to as the 'Hindavi Swarajya'. The same remains a key takeaway for our national policy planners with regard to inclusion of matters maritime and promoting consciousness of the same in the national discourse.

In terms of its location, the Maratha Swarajya can also be categorized as a 'Maritime state', i.e., a territory that has access to sea and is also connected by land. Chhatrapati Shivaji, deployed naval forces not merely for defense purposes, but also for maritime commerce. The Maratha Navy stands as a testament to the significance of indigenous maritime power in safeguarding national interests. Many lessons learned from the naval strategies of the Marathas continue to be relevant for modern navies today. By combining historical wisdom with modern technological advancements, modern navies can navigate the complex maritime challenges of the twenty-first century and maintain a position of strength in the global seascape.

The Maratha Navy and the Indian Navy, as we see it today, represent distinct and unique phases in India's maritime history. The Maratha Navy was a dominant force in the Arabian Sea during the eighteenth century, often employing innovative tactics of maritime guerrilla warfare to combat indigenous contestations and technologically superior European naval forces. In contrast, the modern Indian Navy operates in a complex global environment, balancing power projection with diplomatic engagement. It is important to underscore the historical continuity in naval strategy and examine how modern naval doctrines across the world continue to evolve in the context of modern threats and maritime challenges.

⚓ ⚓ ⚓

Shipbuilding Technology and Foreign Collaboration: A Step Towards Atmanirbharta

Nations with a robust shipbuilding and shipping industry have historically prospered well. The Maratha shipbuilding industry commenced building vessels for the Maratha Armaar after the areas of Kalyan and Bhiwandi were captured around 1657.[5] The hinterland of the port site of the Kalyan area, with its ready availability of timber, made it an ideal venue for building ships. A Portuguese letter dated 28 November 1659 confirms that Kalyan-Bhiwandi were under the control of Chhatrapati Shivaji Maharaj.[6] Having local indigenous shipbuilding processes and imbibing technology through foreign collaborations, the Marathas were practically self-reliant in terms of building, manning and maintenance of vessels—both for trade and military. These seeds, of Atmanirbharta, sown have rejuvenated and continue to offer rich dividends.

In his book *New History of Marathas*, noted historian G.S. Sardesai writes that Chhatrapati Shivaji Maharaj borrowed the services of and consulted a few naval and artillery experts from Goa (which was then under Portuguese rule) and enhanced the Maratha shipbuilding yards and arsenals.[7] This shows that the Maratha naval fleet also encouraged foreign alliances, so as to keep up with the development of technology and designs effectively. It is stated that two Portuguese artisans, Roe Leitao Viegas and his brother Fernao Leitao Viegas, supervised some 340 workmen—Portuguese and others—and helped develop the Maratha fleet.[8] On 5 December 1664, Chhatrapati Shivaji laid the foundation stone of the island sea-fortress Sindhudurg at Malvan and eventually also took possession of many other coastal forts and re-strengthened them.[9,10] It is possible that the Chhatrapati anticipated a naval action of such a magnitude from his adversaries with sea-going capabilities; hence he wanted to secure the outlook towards the sea. A contemporary Marathi source *Ajnapatra* of Ramchandra Pant Amatya outlines: 'Those merchants who reside in the foreign countries should be persuaded to come and settle ... by sending an assurance of safety to seafaring merchants at various ports, they should be given the freedom of intercourse in trade.'[11]

Chhatrapati Shivaji's desire to accommodate the Europeans in trade and other commercial activities has been well reflected in the travel accounts of contemporary travellers.[12] The nature of hospitality extended to the Europeans testifies to the desire of the great Maratha ruler to promote the commerce of his realm and ensure that the Maratha Swarajya prospered. At the same time, however, there was a certain element of caution and anxiety as regards the Maratha policy towards the Europeans. The *Ajnapatra* continues:

> Their [the European traders'] intercourse should be restricted to the extent of only their coming and going [for trade] ... therefore, if any place is at all given to them, it should be

> given in the midst of two or four famous great towns distant about eight to 16 miles from the mouth of the sea ... thus by fixing their place of habitation factories should be permitted to be built.[13]

Chhatrapati Shivaji Maharaj's emphasis on a well-equipped and strategically positioned navy serves as an inspiration for the modern navies to maintain a forward-looking vision. This involves staying abreast of technological advancements and adapting strategies to emerging challenges in the maritime domain. His willingness to incorporate advanced European naval technologies into his fleet emphasizes the importance of technological innovation. This is a lesson for modern navies to draw inspiration from, this approach to continually modernize their fleet and stay ahead of the threat curve. This is a cornerstone of the Indian Navy that has set the nation on the path of Atmanirbhar Bharat.

⚓ ⚓ ⚓

Doctrine, Strategy and Tactics

Naval forces have played a critical role in shaping India's maritime history, whether in the pre-colonial period under the Marathas or in modern times in the Indian Republic. The Maratha Navy demonstrated significant naval prowess during the seventeenth and eighteenth centuries. In contrast, the modern Indian Navy, established post-1947, has evolved into one of the most formidable naval forces in the Indo-Pacific region. While the geopolitical contexts differ, there are insightful parallels and distinctions in their maritime policies, infrastructure, economic contributions, and strategic doctrines. The Indian Maritime Doctrine propounded by the Indian Navy in 2009, has enunciated certain principles of war that include 'Selection and Maintenance of Aim, Offensive Action, Concentration of Force, Economy of Effort, Surprise, Cooperation and Synergy, Logistics, Morale, Security, Intelligence and Flexibility and Management of Change.'[14] While these principles of war are reviewed to include and adapt to the modern environment which is dynamic in nature, conceptually these tenets were also put into practice by the Maratha Navy in varying degrees. The similarities in the core concept of war and the art of military operations and naval combat make it universal and a lesson of relevance for modern navies even to this day.

The theory of sea power—as articulated by classical thinkers like Alfred Thayer Mahan and modern theorists like Geoffrey Till and John Hattendorf—emphasizes the strategic, economic and political importance of naval dominance. Mahan, in particular, identified six key factors that contribute to the strength of a nation's sea power: geographic position, physical confirmation, extent of territory, population, national character and the character of government.[15] These characteristics of Mahan's sea-power theory align closely with the Maratha Navy, which stresses the importance of command over the seas for national prosperity and security. The Marathas leveraged sea power to maintain autonomy in an age of expanding European colonialism, despite their relatively limited naval technology compared to European powers but enhanced tactics.

Sea Lines of Communication (SLOC) protection and interdiction as concepts, did not exist in the eighteenth century. Yet, the Maratha Navy's actions, aimed at safeguarding the movement of ships through key maritime routes, mirror modern SLOC protection objectives. The Maratha Navy sought to assert its dominance over the western Indian coast by levying taxes on passing ships, establishing a form of localized control over navigational freedom in the Arabian Sea. The Maratha naval forces disrupted the trading activities of the English East India Company and other European powers by demanding tribute, effectively controlling sea lanes and defending Maratha maritime interests. By analysing the modern concepts of maritime power, it can be inferred that the Maratha Navy excelled in sea control and sea denial strategies as well. By leveraging coastal fortifications, hit-and-run attacks, blockading enemy ports, intercepting merchant vessels, and knowledge of local geography, the primary objective of sea control by the quaint Maratha Navy was established, and it was that which deterred the hostile European powers, particularly the Portuguese, English and Dutch, from establishing uncontested dominance over the western Indian coast.

In modern naval warfare strategy, sea denial refers to preventing an adversary from using specific sea areas without necessarily establishing control over them.[16] The Indian Navy's sea denial strategy is aimed at deterring potential adversaries from accessing critical maritime zones in the Indian Ocean Region, with a host of frameworks that are outlined for operational preparedness.[17] Key elements of this strategy include the deployment of submarines, land-based missile systems, defensive mining and network-centric warfare. By focusing on nine vital chokepoints in the IOR, the Indian Navy ensures that sea lanes remain secure from adversarial encroachment. On similar principles, the Maratha naval forces targeted both military and commercial vessels, weakening European influence and protecting Maratha interests in regional waters.

The Maratha Navy excelled in guerrilla tactics at sea, leveraging speed and surprise to disrupt enemy fleets and secure strategic advantages. Their small, fast ships were adept at coastal raids, and their knowledge of local geography allowed them to outmanoeuvre larger European ships. Forts along the coast served as defensive strongholds and supply bases. The time and place of the naval battles and skirmishes, were many times orchestrated by the Marathas which played to their advantage. Lacking the large ships and firepower of their European adversaries, the Marathas relied on swift, agile vessels and intimate knowledge of the coastal waters to outmanoeuvre enemy fleet. The *Ajnapatra* outlines some of these tactics in detail. Hit-and-run tactics, surprise raids on enemy ships, and the use of fortified coastal strongholds made the Maratha Navy formidable despite its comparatively smaller size and capabilities. It also mentions that they would lure the enemy ships, which were larger in size and firepower, up creeks during high tide which restricted their manoeuvrability and eventually ran them aground as the tide changed.[18] Such tactics allowed the Marathas to inflict significant damage on more powerful naval forces while maintaining mobility and evasion.

While the Indian Navy today operates more conventionally as a blue-water navy, elements of asymmetric warfare are embedded in its naval doctrine. During the 1971 India-Pakistan War, the Indian Navy used guerrilla-style tactics—'shoot and scoot' to great effect—such as the daring bombardment of Karachi harbour. The Indian Navy's missile boats launched surprise attacks, destroying Pakistani naval assets cutting off their vital supply chains that crippled the nation.[19] Today, trained Marine Commandos (MARCOS), stealthy submarines, and unmanned systems—both underwater and aerial, and such —are part of clandestine operations as part of conventional and non-conventional warfare. The Indian Navy operates under a broad strategic doctrine, which emphasizes sea control and power projection. Its tactics involve carrier-based air power, submarine warfare, and multi-domain operations, leveraging technological superiority to protect national interests. The Indian Navy has developed strategies to deal with both symmetric and emerging asymmetric threats, conducting operations across blue-water and littoral zones. The Navy also focuses on maritime diplomacy, conducting joint exercises with various navies and contributing to regional security frameworks.

Many scholars have brought to the fore the fact that diplomacy and intelligence gathering were given equal importance by the Marathas in the state administrative affairs. They established diplomatic relations with the emissaries to keep a check on the adversaries—both native (Sidis, Mughals, Deccan sultanates, etc.) as well as the European—on their socio-economic and political intent, improvement in technology and a general overview. Even today, diplomacy is considered the first line of defence. Be it gunboat diplomacy or soft power projection at a global level, modern navies are adept at maintaining rule-based order.

In times of yore, piracy played a central role in the maritime domain, as the line between piracy and legitimate naval engagement was often blurred. The Marathas targeted European naval and merchant vessels to disrupt colonial trade routes and monopolies. The Maratha Navy's actions reflected their claim to sovereign rights over the west coast of India. Like other European and native powers, the Marathas also issued passes (dastaks) for safe navigation in the Konkan waters. Most contestations, therefore, were over the honouring of these passes and politico-economic concerns. Maratha naval actions aimed to weaken the pecuniary foothold of colonial powers in India, and served as a means of defending Maratha sovereignty while asserting control over the coastal regions. Thus, they cannot be termed piratical acts.

Today, the term piracy itself has assumed wider attention and detail due to the nature of the activity. The Indian Navy is a key player in international anti-piracy operations, especially off the coast of Somalia in the Gulf of Aden. India's involvement in counter-piracy patrols is driven by the need to protect global trade routes, many of which pass through the Indian Ocean. The Indian Navy collaborates with international forces, deploying its assets to deter and neutralize pirate threats. The Indian Navy as an instrument of the Government of India's maritime policy has been undertaking anti-piracy patrols in the Gulf of Aden region since 2008, and has been highly successful in containing the High Risk Area (HRA).[20] These operations not only protect Indian commercial interests but also demonstrate India's commitment to maritime security in the IOR, thereby, providing safety and succour to global maritime trade in the region—'Anytime, Anyhow, Anywhere.'[21]

⚓⚓⚓

Maritime Vision and Policies for Governance

For any nation, policies are integral to the functioning of the state and its instruments. A national or grand strategy has the tenets of Diplomacy, Information, Military, and Economics at its core. While political scientists, theorists and policymakers have undertaken systematic study and analysis of the same, these principles in crude form were applied by many principalities and states from the ancient to modern times including the Marathas.

The Maratha Navy's primary focus lay in securing coastal waters and ensuring control over maritime trade routes in the Arabian Sea. The state developed policies that emphasized safeguarding economic interests, challenging native and European powers (especially the English and Portuguese), and asserting sovereignty over coastal territories. The Marathas—seeing the sea as an extension of their military and commercial power—implemented policies for coastal defence and fortification, attacking hostile ships to ensure dominance and power projection. The maritime policies of the Indian Navy, on the other hand, have been far more focused on national defence, regional security, and contributing to global maritime peace. Shivaji's idea of protecting coastal territories from the marauders, by strengthening the coastal fortifications and his defensive fleet of warships, is similar to the Indian Navy's Local Naval Defence (LND) operations consisting of shore-based missile systems, minor war vessels, and shallow water defence systems for protecting offshore and onshore maritime assets.

While both navies prioritized securing maritime routes and coastal defence, the Maratha Navy's policies were more aggressive, focusing on regional dominance and economic control. The Indian Navy's maritime policy has a broader, defence-centric approach with an emphasis on cooperation, diplomacy, and multilateralism in the IOR and beyond. The Maratha Navy's successful alliances with various regional powers and sometimes factional foreign powers, highlight the importance of diplomatic and strategic collaborations. In the contemporary context, the Indian Navy can benefit from fostering partnerships with like-minded nations to enhance collective maritime security. The SAGAR (Security and Growth for All in the Region) policy articulated by Hon'ble Prime Minister Shri Narendra Modi in the year 2015, reiterates this approach, as a result of which the Indian Navy is a preferred partner in the region today.[22] About '90% of the country's trade by volume and 77% by value' is moved through maritime transport. So, it is good prudence to draw parallels from the Maratha Navy to apply in the present.[23] While technology may have far advanced since the time of the Marathas, the coastal geography and the principles of war have remained more or less the same for the Navy. Some lessons from Chhatrapati Shivaji Maharaj's Maratha Navy that remain germane are discussed below.

The Maratha Navy was known for its adaptability. The naval flotilla had the ghurabs, galbats and pals as the major warships, and a host of other crafts as merchant vessels.[24] In times of conflict, these merchant vessels were converted into auxiliary warships and used in battle.[25] Such was their prowess to adapt to situations. The emphasis was on the use of traditional ship designs, while incorporating modern European naval tactics. This flexibility allowed the Maratha Navy to effectively counter the advanced naval technologies of the Portuguese and the English.

The Maratha Navy employed asymmetric warfare techniques, such as waterborne guerrilla tactics, to challenge the powerful European naval forces. The ships and tactics of the Maratha Navy were primitive when compared to the European naval fleet. Nonetheless, the Marathas were able to defend and also launch destructive offensive attacks against the adversaries since the lay of the land was well known to the Maratha Navy. Maratha naval vessels, being smaller and suitable for shallow-water operations, were effective in attacking the large blue-water vessels of the Europeans due to their easy manoeuvrability. This approach can be relevant in today's naval operations and war strategies, especially in dealing with unconventional threats and asymmetric conflicts. The smaller vessels operated in large groups confusing the 'OODA loop'[26] of the European cannonades and first-rate ships, possibly the earliest and simpler but effective form of swarm warfare.

⚓⚓⚓

Operations

According to Milan Vego, the success of major naval operations depends on how quickly and covertly their forces are concentrated (or built up) in the sector of main and secondary efforts. The concentration of one's naval forces participating in a major naval operation should ensure the accomplishment of the assigned operational objective.[27] This has remained true in yesteryears as well as in the modern day and age.

In order to operationalize the grand strategy at the national level, as discussed earlier, it is important to ensure that certain prerequisites are fulfilled and are constantly upscaled and maintained. These include, but are not limited to, infrastructure, capital assets like ships, submarines, aircraft, logistical support and sustenance is rendered, optimal use of human resources with their upskilling is given an impetus along with perspective planning, training, ordnance and maintenance of hard and soft assets.

The infrastructure supporting the Maratha Navy was relatively rudimentary but effective for its time. Coastal and off-shore forts such as Sindhudurg and Vijaydurg, built and repaired respectively, under Chhatrapati Shivaji's reign and further enhanced by Sarkhel Angre and other admirals of the Maratha Navy, acted as naval bases and fortified havens for Maratha fleets. The Marathas maintained a robust shipbuilding industry, particularly along the Konkan coast which was an integral part of the state. The Maratha Navy's guerrilla tactics reflected the limitations of its resources but also showcased its ingenuity in asymmetrical naval warfare. In contrast, the Indian Navy operates with a much larger and more technologically advanced fleet, allowing for comprehensive strategies that include power projection, sea control and international cooperation.

While the Maratha Navy's strategies were primarily focused on regional conflicts, the Indian Navy's strategies reflect global maritime interests and defence against both conventional and emerging threats. Under the Marathas, the shipyards and ports of coastal Maharashtra became centres of naval activity, with the local population trained in maritime skills. In contrast, the infrastructure supporting the Indian Navy is highly sophisticated, with modern naval bases, shipyards and extensive dry docks. India has invested heavily in state-of-the-art shipbuilding facilities, with major shipyards in Mumbai, Goa, Visakhapatnam, Kochi and Kolkata today, producing advanced warships, aircraft carriers, and submarines underlining the Indian Navy's focus on technological advancement and self-reliance (Atmanirbhar Bharat).

While both navies contributed to economic stability, the Maratha Navy's direct involvement in controlling trade and trade routes was a core economic strategy. The Indian Navy's contribution is more indirect and focused on ensuring the security of trade and energy routes in a globalized economy.

However, the Indian Navy's role in regional security also promotes economic stability at a macro level.

⚓⚓⚓

Conclusion

The Maratha Navy and the modern Indian Navy have both demonstrated innovative approaches to naval warfare, adapted to their respective contexts and challenges. While the Marathas relied on guerrilla tactics and sea denial to protect their coasts and disrupt European powers, the Indian Navy employs modern naval strategies, mission-based deployments, and joint deployments with sister services to safeguard its maritime interests. Despite the technological advancements and doctrinal shifts, the underlying principles of maritime security, regional dominance, and the protection of trade and trade routes have remained central to India's naval legacy from the Marathas to the present day. The Maratha Navy and the Indian Navy, though separated by centuries, demonstrate significant similarities in their commitment to securing the maritime interests of the state. However, the differences in their infrastructure, economic roles and strategic approaches, reflect the evolution of maritime power in India. The Maratha Navy, driven by regional dominance and economic control, laid the foundation for India's naval tradition. The Indian Navy, with its modern technological capabilities and global reach, continues to carry forward this legacy, adapting to the complex geopolitical realities of the twenty-first century.

The Maratha Navy, despite its relatively limited scope compared to modern global navies, exemplified core principles of sea-power theory long before they were formalized by thinkers and theorists today. Its ability to control local waters, disrupt enemy trade and use maritime tactics to assert regional influence is a testament to the timeless relevance of sea power. Comparing the Maratha Navy with the modern Indian Navy illustrates how sea-power theory evolves but retains its fundamental principles. While the Marathas focused primarily on coastal defence, the Indian Navy today operates as a key player in regional and global maritime security. Drawing from the classical theories of Alfred Thayer Mahan and the modern interpretations of Geoffrey Till in his book *Seapower* amongst others, India's maritime and naval journey reflects the continuous interplay between geography, strategy and the pursuit of power at sea.[28]

Learning lessons from our history, it is important to examine the maritime policies, infrastructure, economic significance and strategic approaches to understand how significant naval powers navigated geopolitical waters and developed naval capabilities and further apply them to contemporary times with a futuristic extrapolation. It also highlights how maritime strategies have evolved from pre-colonial to post-colonial periods, reflecting broader changes in global and regional politics, economic imperatives and technological advancements. Resonant to the ongoing national endeavour to move away from the colonial past, the Indian Naval Ensign was amended to a new design that draws inspiration from our history and the great Maratha legacy.

The Indian Navy adopted a new Naval Ensign on 2 September 2022.[29] The octagon shape draws inspiration from Shivaji Maharaj's 'Rajmudra' or the 'Royal Seal', and represents the eight directions (four cardinal and four intercardinal), symbolizing the Indian Navy's maritime outreach. The new design of the ensign highlights India's glorious maritime heritage and also symbolizes a powerful, courageous, confident and proud Indian Navy.[30]

In conclusion, the history of the Maratha Navy and the role of Chhatrapati Shivaji Maharaj are important in the modern context of understanding India's maritime heritage, while also underscoring concepts of maritime defence. Both navies emphasize sea control, sea denial, indigenous shipbuilding, administration and best practices, power projection, constabulary role and many such overlapping principles of a full-fledged navy. Chhatrapati Shivaji's contributions to the development of the Maratha Navy and his understanding of naval warfare form an integral part of India's maritime heritage, which also includes other dynastic warfighting navies such as the Mauryas, Satvahanas, Kadambas, the Pallavas, the Cholas and Marakkars amongst many others.

Notes

1 See p. 48, in Sachin Pendse, *Maratha Armaar: Ek Anokhe Parva*, Merven Technologies, 2017.

2 See pp. 173-75, in Apte, *A History of the Maratha Navy*, 1973.

3 See Sabhasad, *Sabhasad...Bakhar*,2000.

4 See pp. 93-94, in Sen, *Siva Chhatrapati*, 1920.

5 See p. 67, in Purandare, *Shivaji: India's Great Warrior King*, 2023.

6 See p. 41, in Pissurlencar, *Portuguese Mahratta Relations*, 1983.

7 See p. 219, in Vol. I, of Sardesai, *New History of Marathas*, 1986.

8 pp. 41-42, in Pissurlencar, *Portuguese Mahratta Relations*,1983.

9 Ibid., p. 44.

10 See p. 137, Vol. 1, in Duff, *History of the Mahrattas*, where Duff writes, 'He (Shivaji) built Sindeedroog or Malwan ... He rebuilt and strengthened Kolabah; repaired Severndroog and Viziadroog and

prepared vessel at all these places.' [Quoted from: p. 183, in Kumar, 'The Politics of Control in the West-Coast', 2014.]

11 See Vol. 8, p. 31, in Amatya, *Shivrajniti*, 1928.

12 See pp. 184-84, in Kumar, 'The Politics of Control in the West-Coast', 2014.

13 See Vol. 8, p. 32, in Puntambekar, 'The Ajnapatra or Royal Edict', 1929.

14 See p. 35, in *Indian Maritime Doctrine 2009*, Indian Navy, Integrated Headquarters, Ministry of Defence (Navy), New Delhi, 2015.

15 See pp. 28-29, in Mahan, *The Influence of Sea Power Upon History*, 2003.

16 See pp. 18-19, in Milan Vego, *Maritime Strategy and Sea Denial: Theory and Practice*, Naval Policy and History, Routledge, 2019.

17 See p. 78, in *Indian Maritime Doctrine 2009*, 2015.

18 See p. 175, Apte, *A History of the Maratha Navy*,1973.

19 See pp. 9-11, in Cmde Vijay Jerath (Retd), *25 Missile Boat Squadron: An Untold Story*, Prakash Books, 2013; See also, G.M. Hiranandani, *Transition to Triumph: History of the Indian Navy – 1965–1975*, Lancer Publishers, 2000.

20 Harsh V. Pant and Kartik Bommakanti, 'Dynamic Shift: Indian Navy in the Red Sea', Observer Research Foundation. 2024. (Accessed and retrieved on 5 October 2024) https://www.orfonline.org/research/dynamic-shift-indian-navy-in-the-red-sea

21 The phrase 'Anytime, Anyhow, Anywhere' is taken from the Inaugural Address delivered by Admiral D.K. Tripathi, Chief of the Naval Staff, Indian Navy, on his maiden address to the officers at the Naval Headquarters at New Delhi on 22 May 2024. (Accessed and retrieved on 30 August 2024) https://www.aninews.in/news/national/general-news/anytime-anywhere-anyhow-protect-nations-maritime-interests-navy-chief-tells-officers20240522105631/

22 Press Information Bureau, Prime Minister's Office, Government of India dated 12 March 2015. (Accessed and retrieved on 1 September 2024) https://pib.gov.in/newsite/printrelease.aspx?relid=116881

23 See p. 4, in N. Chandrasekaran and S. Mohan Kumar, *Seaport: Challenges and Issues in India*, CII Institute of Logistics, Chennai, Undated. (Accessed and retrieved on 8 October 2024) https://sourcing.essar.com/GS/Portals/0/Download/India_Seaport_Issues_and_Challenges.pdf

24 See p. 93 in Vol. 1, of Sen, *Siva Chhatrapati*, 1920.

25 See p. 120, Apte, *A History of the Maratha Navy*. 1973.

26 OODA Loop is anacronym for Observe – Orient – Decide – Act Loop which is a four step process for decision making which was developed by Colonel John Boyd, United States Air Force which supports the quick, effective decision-making that is necessary during military operations. (Accessed and retrieved on 4 September 2024)https://thestrategybridge.org/the-bridge/2020/3/17/the-ooda-loop-and-the-half-beat

27 See p. 175, in Milan Vego, *Operational Warfare at Sea: Theory and Practice*, Routledge, New York, 2009.

28 Noted theorist and retired naval personnel Geoffrey Till, in his book, focuses on five fundamental characteristics that modern naval professionals need to understand when thinking about strategy and establishing good order at sea. These are: the sea as a resource; the sea as a medium for transportation and exchange; the sea as a medium of information and the exchange of ideas; the sea as a medium for dominion; and the sea as an area of sovereignty. See pp. 287-305, in Geoffrey Till, *Seapower: A Guide for the Twenty-First Century*, Routledge, 2004.

29 Press Information Bureau, dated 2 September 2022. (Accessed and retrieved on 22 September 2024) https://pib.gov.in/PressReleaseIframePage.aspx?PRID=1880977

30 Ibid.

Summing Up

⚓ ⚓ ⚓

The use of the sea for livelihood and trade is the most common maritime activity people have engaged in, since time immemorial. In due course, states developed specialized naval forces for the promotion and security of trade and other interests. This resulted in the advancement of nautical technologies, including shipbuilding, which subsequently shaped marine identities worldwide. The marine identity of a country is reflected through its historical, cultural, economic and technological facets, highlighting the enduring connections between people and the sea.

India boasts a vibrant maritime tradition that dates back to the Harappan Civilization, which flourished along the river valleys and sea coast about 5,000 years ago. The Maratha Navy also forms a glorious chapter of our nation's illustrious naval traditions and reflects our marine identity. Under the stewardship of Chhatrapati Shivaji Maharaj, the modest beginnings of the Maratha Navy were made in the mid-seventeenth century. By the first half of the eighteenth century, under the Admiralty of Kanhoji Angre, the Maratha Navy had emerged as the top contender for the control of the sea along India's west coast. It fiercely competed with European powers, notably the English, effectively delaying their colonial expansion plans in India. The era of the English conquest of India began at Panipat in 1757, following their decisive naval victory over the Marathas in the battle of Vijaydurg in 1756. Robert Clive, who later became Lord Clive, was the key figure representing the English in both battles.

This volume has closely examined how Shivaji's orientation towards the sea in the early stage of his military career proved to be a master strategy facilitating the Maratha state-building process. He organized a navy and deployed it along his Swarajya's coast. Under his leadership, the Maratha Navy fought naval wars and projected state power in its coastal vicinity. It accomplished military objectives by securing the Maratha coastline. At the same time, in concert with the ancillary establishments like the forts and naval bases on and off the coast, the Maratha navy achieved geographical objectives.

While Shivaji declared that the Maratha Navy was created and organized to fight the Sidi of Janjira along the west coast, he skillfully used his navy as a tool of diplomacy in his dealings with contemporary European powers. He was in the process of carving out an independent empire in the heyday of Mughal imperialism and was on the opposite side of the mighty Mughals. By integrating the Sidi of Janjira into the Mughal military structure, Aurangzeb heightened the challenges that Shivaji faced in the Mughal–Maratha wars. But the nascent Maratha Swarajya—even if deficient in resources—was always high in spirit under Shivaji's energetic leadership.

The people of the 'Maratha race' were united by a shared aspiration for the Swarajya and were determined to go to great lengths to attain liberation from foreign rule. Still, sustaining war efforts required vast amount of money and materials. The Marathas needed money for state-building and consolidation of their conquests. Through the various ports under its control, the Maratha State facilitated coastal and overseas trade. The foreign merchants were given assurances of protection and other facilities to bring more trade, thereby contributing to the prosperity of the Maratha state. At the same time, the state also engaged in overseas trade as its ships traded with the ports of the Red Sea.

The strength of the Maratha Navy enabled them to introduce their navigational passes, such as the dastak and caul, akin to the European passes in prevalence within their coastal territory. The Maratha Navy played a vital economic role and contributed significantly to the state's success. As per an estimate, in the 1720s, Kanhoji Angre annually earned about Rs 7 lakh through the sale of dastaks. Additionally, port taxes and monopoly over commodities like salt also contributed handsomely to the treasury. Much of the revenue earned in this manner was invested in strengthening the Maratha naval establishment. Kanhoji Angre forcefully asserted his legitimate rights over the sea and its sovereignty along the west coast, identifying himself as the admiral of the house of Shivaji, who was the sovereign of the Deccan. This assertion inaugurated an era of competing sovereignties in the Arabian Sea off the coast of Konkan, leading to fierce naval contestations involving the Angres, the European powers and the Sidi of Janjira. As the Europeans struggled to compete with Kanhoji Angre and his successors, they framed the character and accomplishments of the Angres within a narrative of piracy—a construct of their own making. It is ironic that the same Europeans—the English and the Portuguese—who labeled the Angres as pirates, also engaged in negotiations with them over maritime and other issues during the eighteenth century.

While discussing the success of the Maratha Navy in challenging circumstances, such as resource crunch, technological limitations—particularly related to shipbuilding and artillery onboard—and the presence of more vigorous European opponents, this volume has argued in favour of the crucial role of traditional knowledge the Maratha seamen possessed. How the knowledge of the seabed translated into Maratha success, while ignorance of the same proved detrimental to the Europeans, was demonstrated when the Marathas succeeded in occupying and fortifying the uninhabited island of Khanderi, situated at some distance from the mouth of the Bombay harbour, in 1679. The Bombay Marine—the naval arm of the EEIC—despite blockading Khanderi from all sides, could not prevent Maratha supply boats laden with provisions, munitions and other essential supplies, from reaching the island and strengthening its fortifications. Bombay Marine failed to demolish Maratha fortifications at Khanderi through bombardment and were unable to take the island through direct action by landing troops because of their unfamiliarity with the seabed. This was because marine charts had not yet been prepared to serve as reference guides for navigation in the coastal regions. The underlying implication is that the European seafarer's knowledge of geography and local conditions was rudimentary and underdeveloped in the 1600s and mid-1700s, when the bulk of their contestations with the Maratha Navy occurred. In-depth understanding of the geographical conditions and navigational techniques helped the Marathas effectively leverage prevailing conditions.

Maratha marine forts were classified according to their location: coastal, promontory and offshore. To explain the success of the Portuguese in the Indian Ocean Region, M.N. Pearson notes that the Portuguese built a series of forts, positioned at strategic maritime locations. The forts functioned as 'choke points,' effectively controlling vital shipping lanes. In India, at Vasai (Bassein), the Portuguese experimented with a new defensive feature in their fort construction: 'trace Italienne', to enhance defences against local threats. Similarly, the Marathas also built several marine forts with specific needs in mind, including water-resistant construction that would prevent the extremely corrosive seawater from destroying material stored in the fort. Artillery pieces were mounted on these forts to deter enemy ships from venturing closer to the fort walls and put the fort's security at risk. Gunpowder magazines required for effective artillery would have to be specially secured against humidity and salt water, for which adequate measures were taken. Further, mounting guns atop the fort's ramparts aligned with Mahanian principles, which advised weaker navies to seek shelter under the artillery of the coastal fortifications.

This volume has demonstrated how the architecture of Maratha marine forts incorporated elements specifically suited to maritime defence. High walls resistant to cannon fire, strategic placement of artillery and intricate systems for storing fresh water were some standard features in these forts. In other words, if Maratha warships lacked artillery penetration for a vigorous offensive, this was compensated for by the strong defences of the forts. Additionally, adequate precautions were taken for the safety of the sheltered ships in forts that had docking facilities. Many docks were situated on the landward side, out of sight of larger enemy vessels. In some cases, like Sindhudurg, these docks were intentionally concealed for added protection.

Maritime interactions also resulted in exchange of ideas, culture, mannerisms, technology, etc. Exchanges in shipbuilding technology could also be seen in the period of our study. The application and usage of technology is always influenced by practical realities and actual needs. The Indian shipbuilding industry was quite advanced on the eve of the arrival of Europeans in India. Subsequently, the demands of naval warfare necessitated changes in Indian ship design, as earlier ships were not known to have mounted guns or cannons onboard. Since the Maratha naval challenge to the European powers in the Indian surroundings persisted for nearly a century, some changes, especially in rigging, sails, decks structure and gun ports of the Maratha ships are noticed during this period. However, such exchanges and changes were not one-sided. European shipping also underwent a systematic transformation by adopting native designs and utilizing local materials and artisans for shipbuilding. In the *History of the Indian Navy 1600-1863*, (1985), Charles Rathbone Low highlights how frequently the EEIC's Indian Marine and later the Bombay Marine, incorporated smaller ships into their fleets to compete with native forces during naval conflicts with them in the coastal vicinity. This trend became particularly evident in the first half of the eighteenth century, when the EEIC hired Wadia master builders to construct ships for the Bombay Marine.

Shipbuilding techniques mostly concurred with the climate of navigational surroundings, whether coastal or open sea.

The Maratha Navy remained a coastal or brown-water navy throughout, because of strategic considerations and tactical requirements. It consisted of a mix of vessels of different sizes and designs, but most were comparatively smaller than the ships built in Europe. This was despite the Marathas employing Europeans in their shipbuilding enterprise. Since Maratha naval operations were confined to the coast where the seabed was mostly uneven or rocky, most Maratha ships were flat-bottomed rowing boats. These boats were easy to manoeuvre as they were less affected by the vagaries of wind, the pattern and velocity of which fluctuated near the coast.

Furthermore, the Marathas carefully considered their geographical surroundings when formulating strategic imperatives and tactical nuances. For example, their ships were manned by the people of coastal communities from traditional seafaring classes, who possessed a thorough knowledge of the coastal features. Secondly, the Marathas were adept in choosing when and where to engage in battle at sea, and, perhaps more importantly, when to disengage and wait for a more favourable opportunity to re-engage. After disengaging, their flat-bottomed boats rowed to safe shelter in nearby shallow creeks or coves beyond the enemy's reach. By employing these tactics, the Marathas avoided incurring unnecessary losses under demanding circumstances. Hence, their knowledge of their surroundings gave them a more decisive advantage in naval battles. The flag of the Maratha Navy remained flying high for almost a century, till its final defeat in 1756 by the combined forces of the British Royal Navy and the EEIC's Bombay Marine.

The history of the Maratha rule and its achievements have inspired successive generations and will continue to inspire future generations as well. The main objective of this volume has been to offer a fresh perspective of Maratha achievements by exploring a lesser-known aspect of their 'triumph over the sea'. In doing so the diverse essays of this volume have underscored the importance of the history of the Maratha Navy, contextualizing its accomplishments within the prevailing circumstances and needs of the time.

The relevance of the study of the Maratha Navy doesn't lie in its connection to our proud maritime heritage, but in helping us form an idea of how the theory of sea power has evolved while still adhering to the fundamental principles that guided many aspects of the Maratha Navy. Consider the Maratha practice of combining vessels with different capabilities—like galbats (rowing boats) and ghurabs (sailing vessels)—to achieve their objectives. This approach mirrors the operational success of the Indian Navy's Operations *Trident* and *Python* during the Indo–Pak War of 1971. Just as the Marathas effectively utilized diverse vessels, the Indian Navy demonstrated how a strategic blend of capabilities can lead to mission success. To execute the offensives against the Pakistani coast, INS *Kiltan* and *Katchall* towed the smaller Vidyut-class missile boats—INS *Nipat*, *Nirghat* and *Veer*—right up to Karachi for bombardment and accomplished the mission objectives. The Indian Navy's ensign, inspired by the octagonal Royal Seal of Chhatrapati Shivaji Maharaj, embodies a proud nation's dedication to one of the most significant chapters of its maritime legacy. I am confident the new ensign will continue to infuse the Indian Navy with indomitable spirit, enabling them to adapt and thrive amid the complex geopolitical realities of the twenty-first century.

Acknowledgements

⚓ ⚓ ⚓

I want to express my sincere appreciation to the Maritime History Society (MHS), Mumbai, and the Indian Navy for the wonderful opportunity they have given me to get this book published. Commodore Aasheesh Khanna, director, MHS, has been instrumental in planning this volume since its inception. Throughout the compilation of this volume, he had been more than generous in every way. This book owes a great deal to the contributors—each an expert in their respective domains—who enthusiastically agreed to write for this project the moment I shared my plans with them. Though I have known most of them for a long time, I must admit that I have been extremely fortunate to have collaborated professionally with all of them for this project. We worked on a very tight schedule, and I am happy that their articles were placed in a meaningful sequence.

Many friends, colleagues at Visva-Bharati—where I teach—and other well-wishers have sincerely and whole-heartedly prayed for the success of my academic endeavours. Some have provided me with the luxury of an ambience where I can work uninterruptedly. It isn't easy to name all of them here, but I want to acknowledge the selfless affection I have always received—a big THANK YOU to them. I would be failing in my duty if I didn't mention the highly professional work of the editorial team of HarperCollins *Publishers* India, who made this book possible in this fantastic format in a very short time. Thanks especially to Commodore M. Doraibabu, NM, Additional Director, MHS, for his liaisoning skills, as he would regularly ask how long it would take to revise and complete the manuscript.

I am ever grateful to my parents, who have always been my continual sources of inspiration and encouragement. My father always wanted to see my name on the cover of a book. Though he is no longer here to witness that moment, I know my mother would share in his joy.

Seeing that the book is published when our country is celebrating the 350th anniversary of the coronation of Chhatrapati Shivaji Maharaj gives me great satisfaction.

Amarendra Kumar

Bibliography

⚓ ⚓ ⚓

Alavi, Seema. *The Eighteenth Century in India*. Oxford University Press. 2000.

Allami, Abul Fazl. *Ain-i-Akbari*, translated by H. Blochmann and edited by D.C. Phillot. Vol. I-III, second edition. The Asiatic Society of Bengal. 1927.

Alpers, Edward A. *The Indian Ocean in World History*. Oxford University Press. 2014.

Amatya, Ramchandra Pant. *Shivrajniti, A Royal Edict on the Principles of State Policy Organisation*, translated by S.V. Puntambekar. Diocesan Press. 1928.

Anselm, Abraham. *A Faithful Narrative of the Capture of the Ship DERBY by Angria the Pirate, on the Coast of Malabar, December 26. 1735*. S. Osborn. 1738.

Anonymous. 'An Authentick and *Faithful History* of That Arch-Pyrate Tulagee *Angria*'. *In The Scots Magazine. Edinburgh*. 1756.

Apte, B.K. 'Capture of Kennery or Khanderi Island by Shivaji'. In *Bulletin of Deccan College Research Institute*. Vol. 4, No. 1. 1942.

Apte, B.K. 'Sovereignty of the Sea as Practiced in the Maratha Period'. In *Proceedings of the Indian History Congress*. Vol. 29, No. 1. 1967.

Apte, B.K. *A History of the Maratha Navy and Merchantships*. State Board for Literature and Culture, Bombay (Mumbai). 1973.

Apte, D.V. 'When Did Shivaji Start His Career of Independence?' In *The Indian Historical Records Commission* (Proceedings of Meeting), XVII Session, Baroda. 1940.

Arunachalam, B. 'Naval Expeditions of Rajendra Chola: A Nautical Enquiry'. In *Journal of Indian Ocean Studies*. Vol. 10, No. 3. 2002.

Arunachalam, B. 'Shipbuilding in North Konkan in the Period 1550-1750 A.D.' In *Essays in Maritime Studies*. Vol II. Maritime History Society, 2002.

Arunachalam, B. *Heritage of Indian Sea Navigation*. Maritime History Society, 2002.

Arunachalam, B. *Maritime Heritage of Lakshadweep and Minicoy Islands*. Maritime History Society. 2011.

Athavale, B.V. *Swami Daryache*. Rajhans Prakashan. 1997.

Ayyar, K.V.K. *The Zamorins of Calicut (From the Earliest Times down to A.D. 1806)*. University of Calicut. 1938.

Bal Krishna. *Shivaji The Great*. Vol. I-IV, D.B. Taraporewala Sons & Co. 1938.

Ballard, G.A. *Rulers of the Indian Ocean*. Neeraj Publishing House. Reprint. 1984, 1998, cited in this book. Originally printed in 1927.

Balsari-Shah, Shefali and Sunita Nair, eds. *Gateways to the Sea: Historic Ports and Docks of Mumbai Region*. Publications Division, Ministry of Information and Broadcasting. Government of India. 2024.

Bhattacharya, Manoshi. *A History of the Indian Naval Hydrographic Department*. National Hydrographic Office. 2004.

Bhattacharya, Indrajeet. 'Murud Janjira: The Unsung Legacy of Siddis'. ResearchGate. March 2016. https://www.researchgate.net/publication/340350102_Murud_Janjira_The_Unsung_Legacy_of_Siddis

Beveridge, H., ed. *Tuzuk-i-Jahangiri or the Memoir of Jahangir*, translated by A. Rogers. Oriental Translation Fund. 1909.

Biddulph, John. *The Pirates of Malabar: And an Englishwoman in India Two Hundred Years Ago*. Lancer International. Reprint. 1992. Originally published by Smith, Elder and Company in 1907.

BISM Quarterly. Vol. XX, No. III. Bharat Itihas Sanshodhak Mandal, n.d.

Bhaware, N.G. 'Castes, Favours, Patronage and Privileges under Shivaji's Rule'. In *Studies in Shivaji and His Times*, edited by B.R. Kamble. Shivaji University. 1982.

Bouchon, Genevieve. *Regent of the Sea: Cannanore's Response to Portuguese Expansion, 1507-1528*, translated by Louise Shackley. Oxford University Press. 1998.

Boxer, C.R. *The Portuguese Sea-Borne Empire 1415-1825*. Alfred A. Knopf. 1969.

Carre, Abbe. *The Travels of the Abbe Carre in India and the Near East 1672 to 1674*. Asian Educational Services. Reprint. 1990.

Chandrasekaran N. and S. Mohan Kumar. *Seaport: Challenges and Issues in India.* CII Institute of Logistics, Chennai, Undated.

Chauhan, R.R.S. 'Kunjali's Naval Challenge to the Portuguese'. In *Essays in Goan History*, edited by Teotino R. De Souza. Concept Publishing Company. 1989.

Coutinho, Gago. *A Nauticos dos Descobrimentos.* Vol. 1. Agencia Geraldo Ultamar. 1951.

Danvers, Frederick Charles. The *Portuguese in India being a History of the Rise and Decline of Their Eastern Empire.* W.H. Allen & Co. 1894.

Dalvi, D.A. 'The Khanderi Affairs and Shivaji's Relations with English Factors at Bombay'. In *Proceedings of the Indian History Congress.* Vol. 28. 1966.

Das Gupta, Ashin. *Malabar in Asian Trade, 1740-1800.* Cambridge South Asian Studies. Cambridge University Press. 1967.

Das Gupta, Ashin. *Indian Merchants and the Decline of Surat c. 1700-1750.* Manohar. Reprint with a new Preface. 1994.

da Cunha, Joseph Gerson. *Notes on the History and Antiquities of Chaul and Bassein.* Thacker, Vining & Co. 1876.

De Romanis, Federico. 'Patchworking the west coast of India: Notes on the Periplus of the Erythraean Sea'. In *The Indian Ocean Trade in Antiquity.* Routledge. 2018.

Deloche, Jean. 'Etudes La Circulation En Inde: VII, Konkan Warships of the XIth-XVth Centuries as Represented on Memorial Stones'. In *Bulletin de l'Ecole francaise d'Extreme-Orient* 76. 1987.

Desai, W.S. *Bombay and the Marathas up to 1774*. Munshiram Manoharlal. 1970.

Deshpande, Anirudh. 'The Bombay Marine: Aspects of Maritime History'. In *Studies in History*, Vol. 11, No. 2. 1995.

Deshpande, Anirudh and Muphid Mujawar. *The Rise and Fall of a Brown Water Navy: Sarkhel Kanhoji Angre and the Maratha Seapower on the Arabian Sea in the 17th and 18th Centuries*. Aakar Books. 2021.

Deshpande, P.L., *Kanhoji Angre*, Mehta Publishing House, 1986.

Dhabu, D.G. *Kulabkar Angre Sarkhel (Angre Gharanachya Itihas)*. Alibaug. 1959. Originally published in 1939.

Dikshitar, V.R. Ramachandra. *War in Ancient India*. Motilal Banarasidass. 1987.

Douglas, James. *Bombay and Western India*. Vol. I. K.K. Book Distributors. Reprint. 1995.

Downing, Clement. *A History of Indian Wars*. Oxford University Press. Reprint. 1924. Also cited in the present book is a 2024 copy by Lifespan Publishers. The work was originally printed in 1737 (see below).

Downing, Clement. *A compendious history of the Indian wars with an account of the rise, progress, strength, and forces of Angria the Pyrate*. T. Cooper. 1737.

Duff, James Grant. *History of the Mahrattas*. Vol. I-III, R. Cambray & Co. 1918. Also cited in present book is a 1986 reprint by Avishkar Publishers. The work was originally published in 1826.

Edwardes, S.M. 'A Note on the Durability of Indian Teak'. In *Empire Forestry Journal*. Vol. 1, No. 2. 1922.

Elliot, Derek L. 'Pirates, Polities and Companies: Global Politics on the Konkan Littoral, c.1690–1756'. Working Papers No. 136/10. Department of Economic History, London School of Economics. 2010.

Elliot, H.M. *The History of India as Told by Its Own Historians* (The Muhammadan Period): *The Posthumous Papers of the Late Sir H.M. Elliot,* edited by John Dowson.Vol. I-VIII. D.K. Publishers. Reprint. 1996.

Elliot, H.M. '*Muntakhabu-l-Lubab* by Muhammad Hashim Khafi Khan'. In *The History of India as Told by its Own Historians (The Muhammadan Period): The Posthumous Papers of the Late Sir H.M. Elliot,* edited by John Dowson. Susil Gupta (India) Ltd. Second edition. 1952.

Forrest. G.W., ed. *Selections from the Letters, Dispatches and other State Papers preserved in the Bombay Secretariat,* (*Home Series*). Vol. I-II. Bombay Central Press; Government Central Press. 1885, 1887.

Foster, William, ed. *The English Factories in India, 1618-1621: A Calendar of Documents in the India Office, British Museum and Public Record Office*. Clarendon Press. 1906.

Fryer, John. *A New Account of East India and Persia: Being Nine Years' Travels, 1672-1681*, edited, with notes and an Introduction by William Crooke. Vol. I-III. Kraus Reprint. 1967.

Gazetteer of the Bombay Presidency: Ratnagiri and Savantvadi. Vol. X. Government Central Press. 1880.

Gazetteer of the Bombay Presidency: Kolaba and Janjira. Vol. XI. Government Central Press. 1883.

Gazetteer of the Bombay Presidency: Thana – Places of Interest. Vol. XIV. Government Central Press, 1882.

George, James L. *History of Warships: From Ancient Times to the Twenty First Century*. Naval Institute Press. 1998.

Glete, Jan. *Warfare at Sea, 1500-1650: Maritime Conflicts and the Transformation of Europe*. Routledge. 2001.

Gokhale, Kamal. *Chhatrapati Sambhaji*. Navkamal Prakashan. 1978.

Gordon, Stewart. *The Marathas: 1600-1818*. The New Cambridge History of India series. Cambridge University Press. 1993, 2008.

Gordon, Edward. 'Grotius and the freedom of the seas in the seventeenth century'. In *Williamette Journal of International law and dispute resolution*. Vol.16, No.2. 2008.

Harding, Richard. *Amphibious Warfare in the Eighteenth Century, The British Expedition to the West Indies 1740–1742*. Royal Historical Society Studies in History, 62. Royal Historical Society. 1991.

Hawkins, Clifford W. *The Dhow: An Illustrated History of the Dhow and Its World*. Nautical Publication Society. 1977.

Hiranandani, G.M. *Transition to Triumph: History of the Indian Navy, 1965–1975*. Lancer Publishers. 2000.

Indian Maritime Doctrine 2009. Indian Navy. Integrated Headquarters, Ministry of Defence (Navy). Government of India. 2015.

Indra. *Ideologies of War and Peace in Ancient India*. Vishveshwaranand Vedic Research Institute. 1957.

Irani, D.B. 'Country craft and sailing vessels of India'. *The Naval Architect*. September 1980.

Jain, Kirti. 'Boat Building and the Son Kolis of the Raigad District, Maharastra'. *Marine Archaeology*. Vol. 4. 1993.

Jerath, (Retd) Cmde Vijay, *25 Missile Boat Squadron: An Untold Story*, Prakash Books. 2013.

Joshi, S.N., ed. *Shiva Kalin Patra-Saar Samgraha*. Vol. I-III. Shiv Charitra Karyalaya. 1930-37.

Kamble, B.R., ed. *Studies in Shivaji and His Times*. Shivaji University. 1982.

Kangle, R.P., ed. *The Kautilya Arthashastra*. Vol. I-III. Motilal Banarasidass. 1997.

Kantak, M.R. 'Shivaji-Arab Relations vis-a-vis Portuguese'. In *Bulletin of the Deccan College Post-Graduate Research Institute*. Golden Jubilee Vol. 50. 1990.

Kelkar, N.C. and D.V. Apte, eds. *Shivkalin Patra Saar Sangraha*. Vol. 1. Shiva Charitra Karyalaya. 1930.

Ketkar, D.R. *Sarkhel Kahoji Angre*. Mrunmayi Rugvedi Prakashan. 1997.

Khare, Soniya and Dr Jayashree Sathe, transl. *Shivabharata: Shree Shivabharata by Kavi Parmananda, The Only Contemporary Biography of Chhatrapati Shivaji Maharaj*. Murkumbi Itihas Upakram. 2024.

Konwar, P. 'Mir Jumla's Invasion of Assam (1662–63), War Experience of a Dutch Sailor Heiden and Translator Glanius'. In *Indian Historical Review*. Vol. 46, No. 1. 2019.

Kulkarni, A.R., ed. *Jedhe Shakavali-Kareena*. Diamond Publications. 2007.

Kulkarni, A.R. 'Protection to Salt Industry by Shivaji'. *Proceedings of the Indian History Congress*. Vol. 24. 1961.

Kulkarni, A.R. *Maharashtra in the Age of Shivaji (A Study in Economic History)*. Diamond Publications. Reprint. 2008.

Kulke, Herman, K. Kesavapany and Vijay Sekhuja, eds. *Nagapattinam to Suvarnadwipa: Reflections on the Chola Naval Expeditions to Southeast Asia*. Manohar. 2010.

Kumar, Amarendra. 'Maratha Navy: An Enquiry into its Limitations and Contemporary Challenges'. PhD Thesis submitted to Pune University. 2009.

Kumar, Amarendra. 'The Idea of Navy and Naval Warfare under Shivaji'. In *Warfare and Politics in South Asia from Ancient to Modern Times*, edited by Kaushik Roy. Manohar. 2011.

Kumar, Amarendra. 'Keigwin's Bombay (1683-84) and The Maratha-Siddi Naval Conflict'. In *Proceedings of the Indian History Congress.*Vol. 75. Platinum Jubilee. 2014.

Kumar, Amarendra. 'The Politics of Military Control in the West Coast: Marathas, Mughals, and the Europeans, 1650-1730'. In *Chinese and Indian Warfare: From the Classical Age to 1870*, edited by Kaushik Roy and Peter Lorge. Routledge. 2015.

Kumar, Amarendra. 'The Khanderi Rock: A Note on its Strategic Importance During the 17th Century'. In *Indian Cartographer*. Vol. 42, No. 1. 2022.

Lahori, Abdul Hamid. *Badshah Nama,* edited by Maulvi Kabiruddin Ahmad and Maulvi Abd-ur-Rahim. (Persian). Vol. I. Part I. Asiatic Society, Bengal. 1867.

Low, Charles Rathbone. *History of The Indian Navy (1613-1863).* Vol. I. Manas Publications. Reprint. 1985.

Lynn, John A. 'The Trace Italienne and the Growth of Armies: The French Case'. In *The Journal of Military History,* Vol. 55, No. 3. 1991.

MacDougall, Philip. *Naval resistance to Britain's growing power in India, 1600-1800: The Saffron Banner and the Tiger of Mysore.* The Boydell Press. 2014.

Mahan, Alfred Thayer. *The Influence of Sea Power upon History 1660-1783.* Little Brown and Company. 1949. A 2007 Project Gutenberg eBook copy, and a 2023 reprint by Natraj Publishers have also been cited in the present book.

Malekandathil, Pius. 'From merchant capitalists to corsairs, the response of the Muslim merchants of Malabar to the Portuguese commercial expansion (1498-1600)'. *Proceedings of the Indian History Congress,* Vol. 64. 2003.

Malekandathil, Pius and Jamal Mohammed, eds. *The Portuguese, Indian Ocean and European Bridgeaheds, 1500-1800.* Festschrift in Honour of Prof. K.S. Mathew. Institute for Research in Social Sciences and Humanities, MESHAR. 2001.

Malgonkar, Manohar. *Kanhoji Angrey, Maratha Admiral: An Account of His Life and His Battles with the English*. Asia Publishing House. 1959.

Malgaonkar, Manohar. *The Sea Hawk: Life and Battles of Kanhoji Angrey*. Mehta Publishing House, 1984.

Maloni, Ruby. 'Shipbuilding in Western India in Medieval Times'. In *Essays in Maritime Studies*. Vol. II. Maritime History Society. 2002.

Maloni, Ruby. 'The Angres and the English: Contenders for Power on the West Coast'. In *Proceedings of the Indian History Congress*. Vol. 66. 2005-06.

Manucci, Niccolao. *Storia da Mogoror Mogul India, 1653-1708*, translated, with Introduction and Notes, by William Irvine. Vol. I-IV. Atlantic Publishers. Reprint. 2022.

Marathyanchya Itihasachi Sadhane: Portuguese Dapter Khand 3: Asia Vibhag (Bhag 1-5) (1663-1739). Translated into Marathi by S.S. Desai. Maharashtra Rajya Sahitya Va Sanskruti Mandal, 1968. The original work was in Portuguese and was edited by A.B. de Bargança Pereira.

Markham, Clements R. *A Memoir on the Indian Surveys*. W.H. Allen and Company.1871.

Marshall, P.J. *The Eighteenth Century in India: Evolution or Revolution?* Oxford University Press. 2002.

Mathew, K.M. *History of the Portuguese navigation in India 1497-1600*. Mittal Publications. 1988.

Matthew, K.S. 'Portuguese Trade with India and Theory of Royal Monopoly in the Sixteenth Century'. In *Essays in*

Medieval Indian Economic History, edited by Satish Chandra. Indian History Congress. Golden Jubilee Year Publication, Vol. III. Munshiram Manoharlal Publishers. 1987.

Mathew, K.S. 'Taxation in the Coastal Towns of Western India and the Portuguese in the Sixteenth Century'. In *Mariners, Merchants and Oceans: Studies in Maritime History*, edited by K.S. Mathew. Manohar. 2015.

Mathew, K.S. *Shipbuilding, Navigation and the Portuguese in Pre-modern India*. Manohar. 2017.

Mehendale, Gajanan Bhaskar. *Shri Raja Shiv Chhatrapati*, (Marathi). Vol. 1. Diamond Publications. 2008.

Mhamai, S.K. *The Sawants of Wadi and the Portuguese*. Concept Publishing House. 2018.

Monteiro, Luis Nuno Sardinha. 'Fernando Oliveira's *Art of War at Sea* (1555): A Pioneering Treatise on Naval Strategy'. *Naval War College Review*. Vol. 68, No. 4. 2015.

Mookerji, R.K. *Indian Shipping (A History of the Sea-Borne Trade and Maritime Activity of the Indians from the Earliest Times*). Orient Longmans. Reprint. 1957. Also cited in the present book is a 1999 copy, republished by Munshiram Manoharlal Publishers; as also a citation from the original 1912 edition published by Longman, Greens.

Moraes, George. 'A Portuguese Embassy to Sambhaji – 1684'. In *Proceedings of the Indian History Congress*. Vol. 22. 1959.

Mumtaza, I.S. 'Mir Jumla's Assam Invasion as Depicted by the Ahom Buranji: A Study in Historical Geography'. In *Proceedings of the Indian History Congress*, Vol. 55. 1994.

Nairne, A.K. *History of the Konkan*. Asian Education Services. Reprint, 1988.

Naravane, M.S. *The Maritime and Coastal Forts of India*. APH Publishing Corporation. 2002.

Naravane, M.S. *Forts of Maharashtra*. APH Publishing Corporation. 1995.

Nath, Pratyay. 'Battles, Boats, and Bridges, Mughal Amphibious Warfare, 1571-1612'. In *Chinese and Indian Warfare: From the Classical Age to 1870*, edited by Kaushik Roy and Peter Lorge. Routledge. 2015.

Nathan, Mirza. *Baharistan-i-Ghaybi: A History of Mughal Wars in Assam, Cooch Behar, Bengal, Bihar and Orissa during the reign of Jahangir and Shahjahan*, translated by M.I. Borah. Vol. I-II, Government Press, Assam 1936.

Naval Study Group. 'Maratha Naval Resistance to European Powers on the Konkan Coast'. In *Essays in Maritime Studies*, edited by B. Arunachalam. Vol. 1. Maritime History Society. 1998.

Newaskar, Kavindra Paramananda Govind. *Shri Shivabharata*. Translated from Sanskrit to Marathi by S.M. Divekar. Bharat Itihas Sanshodhak Mandal. 1927.

Nikitin, Afanasy. *Afanasy Nikitin's Voyage Beyond the Three Seas, 1466-1472*. Raduga Publishers. 1995.

Orme, Robert. *History of The Military Transactions of the British Nation in Indostan*. Luke Hanfard. Book V. 1803.

Orme, Robert. *History of The Military Transactions of the British Nation in Indostan From the Year MDCCXLV: to which is prefixed a dissertation on the establishments made by*

Mohomedan conquerors in Indostan, Vol.I. Printed for John Nourse, bookseller in ordinary to His Majesty. 1803.

Orme, Robert. *Historical Fragments of the Mogul Empire, of the Morattoes, and of the English Concerns in Indostan from the year MDCLIX*, edited, and with an Introduction by J.P. Guha. Associated Publishing House. Reprint. 1974.

Oturkar, R.V. 'Sambhaji's Relations with the Sea Powers in the Konkan'. In *Proceedings of the Indian History Congress*. Vol. 15. 1952.

Pagadi, Setumadhavrao. *Chhatrapati Shivaji*. Continental Prakashan. 2017.

Panikkar, K.M. *Geographical Factors in Indian History*. Bharatiya Vidya Bhavan. 1955.

Pant, Harsh V. and Kartik Bommakanti. 'Dynamic Shift: Indian Navy in the Red Sea'. Observer Research Foundation. 2024.

Paranjape, B.G., ed. *English Records on Shivaji (1659-1682)*. Vol. I-II. Shiv Charitra Karyalaya. 1931.

Parthesius, Robert. 'The Development of the VOC Fleet'. In *Dutch Ships in Tropical Waters, The Development of the Dutch East India Company (VOC) Shipping Network in Asia 1595-1660*. Amsterdam University Press, 2010. Available at http://www.jstor.org/stable/j.ctt45kcpt.8.

Pearson, M.N. *The Portuguese in India*. The New Cambridge History of India. Cambridge University Press. Editions cited in present book: 1987, 2008.

Pearson, M.N. *Merchants and Rulers in Gujarat: The response to the Portuguese in the sixteenth century*. University of California Press. 2020.

Pendse, Sachin. *Maritime Heritage of the Konkan*. Maritime History Society. 2011.

Pendse, Sachin. *Maratha Armaar: Ek Anokhe Parva*, Merven Technologies. 2017.

Pissurlencar, P.S. *Portuguese Marathe Sambandha, (arthat Portugezanchya Daftaratil Marathayancha Itihash)*, (Marathi). Pune University Press. 1967.

Pissurlencar, P.S. *Portuguese–Mahratta Relations*, translated by T.V. Parvate. Maharashtra State Board for Literature and Culture. 1983.

Portuguese Documents on Malacca, collected, translated and annotated by M.J. Pintado.Vol. I: 1509-1511. National Archives of Malaysia. 1993.

Pour, Ali Bahrani. 'The Trade in Horses between Khorasan and India in the 13th–17th centuries'. In *The Silk Road*.Vol. 11. Silk Road Foundation. 2013.

Prakash, Om. *European Commercial Enterprise in Pre-Colonial India*. The New Cambridge History of India series. Cambridge University Press. 1998.

Prange, Sebastian. 'The Contested sea Regimes of violence in the Pre-Modern Indian Ocean'. *Journal of Early Modern History*. Vol. 17, No. 1. 2013.

Puntambekar, S.V. 'The Ajnapatra or Royal Edict, Relating to the principles of Maratha State polity'. In *Journal of Indian History*. Vol. 8. 1929.

Purandare, Vaibhav. *Shivaji: India's Great Warrior King*. Juggernaut Publications. 2022. Also cited in present book is the 2023 edition.

Purohit, Dolly. 'Relation between Marathas and the Siddis of Janjira in the seventeenth century.' *Journal of Research in Humanities and Social Sciences*. Vol. 9, No. 7. 2021.

Ray, H.P. 'Shipping in the Indian Ocean'. In *Ships and Development in Maritime Technology on the Indian Ocean*, edited by David Parkin and Ruth Barnes. Routledge. 2002.

Razzak, Abdul. 'Narrative of the Voyage of Abd-Er-Razzak, Ambassador from Shar Rukh – a.h. 845, 1442 a.d'. In *India in the Fifteenth Century: Being a Collection of Narratives of Voyages to India, in the Century Preceding the Portuguese Discovery of the Cape of Good Hope; From Latin, Persian, Russian and Italian Sources*, translated and edited by R.H. Major. The Hakluyt Society. 1857.

Rodger, N.A.M. *The Command of the Ocean: A Naval History of Britain, 1649-1815*. W.W. Norton. 2005.

Roy, Atul Chandra. *A History of the Mughal Navy and Naval Warfare*. World Press. 1972.

Rose, Susan. *Medieval Naval Warfare: 1000-1500*. Routledge. 2001.

Rothermund, Dietmar. *Violent Traders: Europeans in Asia in the Age of Mercantilism*. Manohar. 2014.

Roy, Indrajit. 'Effects, Consequences and Remedial Actions against Somali Pirates'. *Journal of the United Services Institution of India*. Vol. CXLI, No. 588. April-June 2012. (Accessed 4 September 2024) https://www.usiofindia.org/publication-journal/effects-consequences-and-remedial-action-against-somali-piracy.html.

Russel-Wood, A.J.R. *A World on the Move: The Portuguese in Africa, Asia and America, 1415-1808*. Palgrave MacMillan. 1993.

Sabhasad, Krishnaji Anant. *Sabhasad Virachit Chhatrapati Shivaji Raje Yanchi Bakhar*, edited by U.M. Pathan. (Marathi). Snehvardhan Publishing House. 2000.

Sardesai, G.S., ed. *Selections from the Peshwa Daftar.*Vol. III: '*Janjirachya Siddiwar Shahuchi Muhim* (*Shahu's Campaign against the Sidis of Janjira*), *1733-1736*'. (Marathi and English). Government Central Press. 1930-33.

Sardesai, G.S., ed. *Selections from the Peshwa Daftar*, Vol. XXXIII: '*Janjiryachi Muhim – Puravani* (*Shahu's Campaign against the Sidis of Janjira – Supplementary*). (Marathi and English). Government Central Press. 1930-33.

Sardesai, G.S. *New History of The Marathas*. Vol. I-III. Munshiram Manoharlal Publishers Pvt. Ltd. 1986.

Sarkar, Jadunath. *History of Aurangzib*. Vol. I. M.C. Sarkar & Sons. 1912.

Sarkar, Jadunath. *House of Shivaji*. M.C. Sarkar & Sons. 1948.

Sarkar, Jagadish Narayan. 'New Light on Mughal-Portuguese Relations, 1665-67 (Based on Portuguese Sources)'. In *Proceedings of the Indian History Congress*. Vol. 31. 1969.

Sarkar, Jadunath. *Studies in Aurangzib's Reign*. Sangam Publication. Reprint. 1989.

Sarkar, Jadunath. *Shivaji and His Times*. Longmans, Green and Co. 1920. Also cited in present book: Orient Longman, reprint, 1973; and Orient BlackSwan, 2010.

Sen, Surendra Nath. *Life of Siva Chhatrapati: Being a Translation of the Sabhasad Bakhar, Extracts and Documents Relating to Maratha History*. Vol. 1. University of Calcutta. 1920.

Sen, S.N. *Early Career of Kanhoji Angria and Other Papers*. Calcutta University. 1941.

Sen, S.N. *Foreign Biographies of Shivaji*. K.P. Bagchi. 1977.

Sen, S.N. *The Military System of the Marathas*. K.P. Bagchi. Reprint. 1979. Originally published in 1928.

Shejwalker, T.S. 'Shivaji's Raid on Basrur'. In *Bulletin of Deccan College Research Institute*. Vol. 4, No. 2. 1942.

Shivde, Sadashiv. *Dayraraj Kanhoji Angre*. Utkarsh Prakashan. 2006.

Shrivastavya, B.K. *The Angreys of Kolaba in British Records (1719-1884)*. 1950.

Singh, R.L. *India: A Regional Geography*. The Geographical Society of India. 1971.

Sohoni, Pushkar. 'From Defended Settlements to Fortified Strongholds: Responses to Gunpowder in the Early Modern Deccan'. In *South Asian Studies*. Vol. 31, No. 1. British Association of South Asian Studies. January 2015.

Sohoni, Pushkar. 'The Fort of Janjira'. In *African Rulers and Generals in India*. Afro-South Asia in the Global African Diaspora, Vol. 1. University of North Carolina, Ethiopian and East African Studies Project; Ahmedabad Sidi Heritage and Educational Center. 2020.

Sohoni, Pushkar. 'Janjira Fort and Rajapuri Port: Connected Histories in a Coastal Complex'. In *Gateways to the Sea:*

Historic Ports and Docks of Mumbai Region, edited by Shefali Balsari-Shah and Sunita Nair. Publications Division, Ministry of Information and Broadcasting. 2024.

Spate, O.H.K., and A.T.A. Learmonth. *India and Pakistan: A General and Regional Geography*. Third revised edition. Methuen & Co. Ltd. 1967.

Subramanian, Lakshmi. *The Sovereign and the Pirate: Ordering Maritime Subjects in India's Western Littoral*. Oxford University Press. 2016.

Subrahmanyam, Sanjay. 'The Portuguese, the port of Basrur, and the rice trade, 1600-50'. In *The Indian Economic and Social History Review*, Vol. 21, No. 4. 1984.

Subrahmanyam, Sanjay. 'Iranians Abroad: Intra-Asian Elite Migration and Early Modern State Formation'. In *The Journal of Asian Studies*, Vol. 51, No. 2. May 1992.

Tamaskar, B.G. 'Ports and Harbours of Shivaji's Kingdom'. In *Proceedings of the Indian History Congress*. Vol. 40. 1979.

Tazzara, Corey. *Ports and free ports in the Old World: Political economy in the Mediterranean and the Indian Ocean (1500–1750)*. Routledge. 2024.

Thomaz, Luis Filipe F.R. 'Precedents and Parallels of the Portuguese Cartaz System'. In *The Portuguese, Indian Ocean and European Bridgeaheds, 1500-1800*, edited by Pius Malekandathil and Jamal Mohammed. Festschrift in Honour of Prof. K.S. Mathew. Institute for Research in Social Sciences and Humanities, MESHAR. 2001.

Till, Geoffrey. *Seapower: A Guide for the Twenty-First Century*. Routledge. 2004.

Trim, D.J.B. and Mark Charles Fissel, eds. *Amphibious Warfare 1000-1700: Commerce, State Formation and European Expansion*, Brill. 2006.

Tripathi, S., et al. 'Marine archaeological exploration and excavation of Vijaydurg: a naval base of the Maratha Period, Maharashtra, on the west coast of India'. In *The International Journal of Nautical Archaeology*. Vol. 21, No. 1. 1998.

Unger, Richard W. 'Warships and Cargo Ships in Medieval Europe'. In *Technology and Culture*, 22(2). 1981.

Varma, Pavan K. *The Great Hindu Civilisation: Achievement, Neglect, Bias and the Way Forward*. Westland. 2021.

Vego, Milan. *Maritime Strategy and Sea Denial: Theory and Practice*, Naval Policy and History. Routledge. 2019.

Vego, Milan. *Operational Warfare at Sea: Theory and Practice*. Routledge. 2009.

Wade, Geoff. 'Zheng He and Ming China's Voyages in the Early 15th Century'. In *Oxford Research Encyclopedias*, Asian History. 2020. Published online: https://doi.org/10.1093/acrefore/9780190277727.013.235; accessed 16 September 2023.

Wadia, Ardeshir Ruttonji. *The Bombay Dockyard and the Wadia Master Builders*. R.A. Wadia. 1957.

Warner, Oliver. *The Navy*. Penguin Books Ltd. 1968.

Wills Jr., John E. 'Maritime Asia 1500-1800: The Interactive Emergence of European Domination'. Review Article. *The American Historical Review*, Vol. 98, No. 1. 1993.

Zaynuddin, Shaykh. *Tuḥfatu'l-Mujāhidīn*, translated by M.J. Rowlandson as *Tohfut-ul-mujahideen*. London, 1833.

Index